International Nietzsche Studies
Richard Schacht, series editor

A list of books in the series appears at the end of this book.

International
Nietzsche Studies

Nietzsche has emerged as a thinker of extraordinary importance, not only in the history of philosophy but in many fields of contemporary inquiry. Nietzsche studies are maturing and flourishing in many parts of the world. This internationalization of inquiry with respect to Nietzsche's thought and significance may be expected to continue.

International Nietzsche Studies is conceived as a series of monographs and essay collections that will reflect and contribute to these developments. The series presents studies in which responsible scholarship is joined to the analysis, interpretation, and assessment of the many aspects of Nietzsche's thought that bear significantly upon matters of moment today. In many respects Nietzsche is our contemporary, with whom we do well to reckon, even when we find ourselves at odds with him. The series is intended to promote this reckoning, embracing diverse interpretive perspectives, philosophical orientations, and critical assessments.

The series is also intended to contribute to the ongoing reconsideration of the character, agenda, and prospects of philosophy itself. Nietzsche was much concerned with philosophy's past, present, and future. He sought to affect not only its understanding but also its practice. The future of philosophy is an open question today, thanks at least in part to Nietzsche's challenge to the philosophical traditions of which he was so critical. It remains to be seen—and determined—whether philosophy's future will turn out to resemble the "philosophy of the future" to which he proffered a prelude and of which he provided a preview, by both precept and practice. But this is a possibility we do well to take seriously. International Nietzsche Studies attempts to do so, while contributing to the understanding of Nietzsche's philosophical thinking and its bearing upon contemporary inquiry.

—Richard Schacht

Making Sense of Nietzsche

Making Sense of
NIETZSCHE

Reflections Timely and Untimely

Richard Schacht

University of Illinois Press
URBANA AND CHICAGO

© 1995 by the Board of Trustees of the University of Illinois
Manufactured in the United States of America
1 2 3 4 5 C P 5 4 3 2 1

This book is printed on acid-free paper.

Library of Congress Cataloging-in-Publication Data

Schacht, Richard, 1941–
   Making sense of Nietzsche : reflections timely and untimely /
Richard Schacht.
      p.   cm. — (International Nietzsche studies)
   Includes bibliographical references and index.
   ISBN 0-252-02125-8 (cloth: alk. paper). — ISBN 0-252-06412-7
(paper: alk. paper)
   Nietzsche, Friedrich Wilhelm, 1844–1900. I. Title.
II. Series.
B3317.S359 1995
193 — dc20   94-1914
                                              CIP

To Eric

Contents

Preface

Making sense of Nietzsche is something I have been attempting to do ever since I first became aware of him as an undergraduate in the early 1960s, when he was deemed either a proto-Nazi or a proto-existentialist. I am still at it today because I continue to find it challenging and rewarding, and because it still needs doing. Nietzsche is no longer taboo in philosophical circles, and studies of his thought are no longer few and far between. For many who have become curious about him or interested in him, however, he remains a perplexing problem. The difficulty is not (as in the case of Kant or Hegel or Heidegger) that he is so hard to read. On the contrary: unlike them he reads easily. But that only makes it all too easy to read him superficially, and to (mis)understand him in ways that make nonsense — or silly or insidious sense — of what he is saying.

Most of the essays in the first part of this volume were occasioned by what I take to be misguided interpretations of a philosophically more sophisticated nature. Superficial caricatures of Nietzsche may be given short shrift, even if they cannot be entirely ignored; but more sophisticated interpretations that go astray must be taken more seriously, and countered more carefully. For if left unchallenged, they are all too likely to give many in and beyond the philosophical community all the excuse they need to continue to decline to take Nietzsche seriously. The essays in the second part assume that such obstacles have been (or can be) removed. They experiment with various ways of approaching Nietzsche, both textually and methodologically.

Many of these essays have been published previously, mostly in the decade following the appearance of my *Nietzsche* (published in 1983 by Routledge & Kegan Paul). Together here they serve as a defence and advocacy of the general way in which I deal with Nietzsche there, and also as an introduction to his philosophical thinking that stands on its own. It is with the latter aim in mind that I include versions of two previously published essays that were incorporated into the last chapter of that book. These two discussions of Nietzsche's early and later thinking about art and life function in a very different way here, nicely framing the other essays that make up the central part of the present volume. While some readers will already know them (as some will already know others of these essays), many will not; and it seems to me that the picture of Nietzsche offered here is the better for their inclusion.

The first part of this volume is intended to set the stage for the rest of it by situating my way of interpreting and reckoning with Nietzsche in relation to various others that have emerged during the past few decades. These essays are some of my contributions to what might be called "the Nietzsche wars." Several of these other ways of dealing with him have attracted considerable attention—in some cases owing at least in part to the ways in which they have managed to appeal to certain rather wide-spread anxieties (in some cases) and enthusiasms (in others). (This sort of thing amused Nietzsche no end on some days, and deeply depressed him on others—for good reason in both cases.) They cannot be ignored, and deserve to be taken seriously. I have attempted to do that—and also to move beyond them.

In the second part I offer what are actually a variety of related approaches of my own to the understanding of what Nietzsche was up to, by way of a series of considerations of a number of his writings I believe to be of particular interest and importance in this connection. If my readings of these writings rings true to them, then my way of dealing with him—as a thinker with recognizably philosophical concerns, and with constructive as well as deconstructive things to say about a good many recognizably philosophical issues—must at least be on one right track.

I have found that Nietzsche wears amazingly well. Decades after I first made his acquaintance, he continues to draw my attention, and to reward it in terms of what I get philosophically out of thinking about questions relating to aspects of his thought. As long as that is so, I shall no doubt keep on returning to the well. I know no more stimulating and rewarding philosophical company, dead or alive, than Nietzsche. I can think of no higher tribute to pay to a philosopher than that.

Acknowledgments

I would like to express my gratitude to all of those who had so much to do with the various pieces of this volume; to the students, audiences, and readers whose enthusiasm for Nietzsche has helped to sustain mine; to the colleagues whose interest, encouragement, and challenges have contributed so much both to my motivation and to my thinking; to NEH seminar participants, North American Nietzsche Society members, and others in the growing community of friends of Nietzsche whose involvement in Nietzsche studies has been inspirational to me; to the conference organizers and editors of various projects whose invitations have been the occasion of so much of what I have written here and elsewhere on Nietzsche; to two superb research assistants, James Janowski and Alexandra Bradner; to two excellent secretaries, Cheri Beck and Glenna Cilento; to the University of Illinois Research Board for its support; and to Richard Martin and the University of Illinois Press for their interest in my work and willingness to enter into the publication of Nietzsche studies in a serious way. I also am grateful to the editors and publishers of the original versions of the pieces listed below, for their permission to use them here.

"A Way with Nietzsche," originally published in *International Studies in Philosophy*, vol. XV, no. 2 (Summer 1983), pp. 79–85. Reprinted with the permission of Leon J. Goldstein, editor, *International Studies in Philosophy*. (This essay has been incorporated into the Introduction.)

"Nietzsche Introduced," originally published as "Nietzsche, Friedrich Wilhelm" in the *Oxford Companion to Philosophy*, ed. Ted Honderich (New York: Oxford University Press, 1994). Reprinted (in modified form) with the permission of Auriol Milford, copyright manager, Oxford University Press. (This essay has been incorporated into the Introduction.)

"Nietzsche and Nihilism," originally published in *Journal of the History of Philosophy*, vol. IX, no. 1 (Jan. 1973), pp. 65–90. Reprinted with the permission of Rudolph Makkreal, editor, *Journal of the History of Philosophy*.

"Beyond Nihilism: Nietzsche on Philosophy, Interpretation, and Truth," originally published as "Nietzsche on Philosophy, Interpretation and Truth" in *Nietzsche as Affirmative Thinker*, ed. Y. Yovel (Dordrecht: Martinus Nijhoff, 1986), pp. 1–19. Copyright © 1986 by Martinus Nijhoff Publishers, Dordrecht. Reprinted with the permission of Kluwer Academic Publishers.

"Beyond Deconstruction: Nietzsche's Kind of Philosophy," originally written for and to be published in the forthcoming *Cambridge Companion to Nietzsche,* ed. Bernd Magnus (New York: Cambridge University Press), as "Nietzsche's Kind of Philosophy." Preprinted with the permission of M. P. Anderson, rights and permissions manager, Cambridge University Press.

"Beyond Aestheticism: Nietzsche, Nehamas's Nietzsche, and Self-Becoming," originally published in *Nietzsche-Studien*, vol. 21 (1992), pp. 266–80, as "On Self-Becoming: Nietzsche and Nehamas's Nietzsche." Reprinted with the permission of Wolfgang Mueller-Lauter, editor, *Nietzsche-Studien.*

"Beyond Scholasticism: On Dealing with Nietzsche and his *Nachlaß*," originally published in *International Studies in Philosophy*, vol. XXII, no. 2 (Summer 1990), pp. 59–66, as "Nietzsche as Colleague." Reprinted with the permission of Leo J. Goldstein, editor, *International Studies in Philosophy.*

"Making Life Worth Living: Nietzsche on Art in *The Birth of Tragedy*," originally published in *Art and Aesthetics: Theories and Critiques*, ed. R. J. Sclafani and G. Dickie (New York: St. Martin's, 1977), pp. 369–412. Reprinted (in modified form) from the revised version published in *Aesthetics: A Critical Anthology,* second edition, ed. Sclafani, Dickie, and R. Roblin (1989), pp. 489–512, with the permission of St. Martin's Press Incorporated. Copyright © 1989 St. Martin's Press, Inc.

"Nietzsche's First Manifesto: On *Schopenhauer as Educator*," originally published in Friedrich Nietzsche, *Unmodern Observations*, ed. W. Arrowsmith (New Haven: Yale University Press, 1990), pp. 149–61, as the "Introduction" to *Schopenhauer as Educator.* Reprinted with the permission of Elaine Maisner, permissions manager, Yale University Press.

"The Nietzsche-Spinoza Problem: Spinoza as Precursor?" originally written for and to be published in *Desire and Affect: Spinoza as Psychologist* (*Spinoza by 2000,* vol. 3), ed. Y. Yovel (London: E. J. Brill), under the title "The Spinoza-Nietzsche Problem." Preprinted with the permission of M. Kniper, for E. J. Brill.

"How to Naturalize Cheerfully: Nietzsche's *Fröhliche Wissenschaft*," originally published as "Nietzsche's *Gay Science*, Or, How to Naturalize Cheerfully" in *Reading Nietzsche*, ed. Robert C. Solomon and Kathleen

M. Higgins. Copyright © 1989 Oxford University Press. Reprinted by permission.

"Of Morals and *Menschen:* Nietzsche's *Genealogy* and Anthropology," originally published in *Nietzsche, Genealogy, Morality: Essays on Nietzsche's* On the Genealogy of Morals, ed. R. Schacht (Berkeley: University of California Press, 1994). Reprinted (in modified form) with the permission of the University of California Press.

"How to Revalue a Value: Art and Life Reconsidered," originally published as "Nietzsche's Second Thoughts about Art" in *The Monist,* vol. 64, no. 2 (April 1981), pp. 231–46. Reprinted with the permission of Sherwood B. Snyder, managing editor, *The Monist.*

"On *The Case of Wagner,*" originally published as "*The Case of Wagner* by Friedrich Nietzsche" in *The Opera Quarterly,* vol. 1, no. 3 (Autumn 1983), pp. 210–12. Copyright © Duke University Press. Reprinted (as a postscript to "How to Revalue a Value: Art and Life Reconsidered") with the permission of the publisher (Duke University Press).

Reference Key

		Published	KGW Vol.[1]
BT	= The Birth of Tragedy (*Die Geburt der Tragödie*)	1872	III:1
TL	= On Truth and Lies in an Extra-Moral Sense (*Über Wahrheit und Lüge im aussermoralischen Sinn*)[2]	—	III:2
PTA	= Philosophy in the Tragic Age of the Greeks (*Die Philosophie im tragischen Zeitalter der Greichen*)[2]	—	III:2
UDH	= On the Uses and Disadvantages of History for Life (*Vom Nutzen und Nachteil der Historie für das Leben*)[3]	1874	III:1
SE	= Schopenhauer as Educator (*Schopenhauer als Erzieher*)[3]	1874	III:1
UM	= Untimely Meditations (*Unzeitgemässe Betrachtungen*)[4]	1874–76	III:1,2
HH	= Human, All Too Human (*Menschliches, Allzumenschliches*)		
	Volume I	1878	IV:2
	Volume II, Part I[5]	1879	IV:3
WS	= The Wanderer and his Shadow (*Der Wanderer und sein Schatten*)[6]	1880	IV:3
D	= Daybreak (*Morgenröthe*)	1881	V:1
GS	= The Gay Science (*Die fröhliche Wissenschaft*)		
	Books I–IV	1882	V:2
	Book V	1887	

		Published	KGW Vol.[1]
Z	= Thus Spoke Zarathustra (*Also Sprach Zarathustra*)		
	Parts I–II	1883	VI:1
	Part III	1884	
	Part IV	1885	
BGE	= Beyond Good and Evil (*Jenseits von Gut und Böse*)	1886	VI:2
GM	= On the Genealogy of Morals (*Zur Genealogie der Moral*)	1887	VI:2
CW	= The Case of Wagner (*Der Fall Wagner*)	1888	VI:3
TI	= Twilight of the Idols (*Die Götzen-Dämmerung*)[7]	1889	VI:3
A	= The Antichrist (*Der Antichrist*)[7]	1895	VI:3
NCW	= Nietzsche contra Wagner (*Nietzsche contra Wagner*)[7]	1895	VI:3
EH	= Ecce Homo (*Ecce Homo*)[7]	1908	VI:3
WP	= The Will to Power (*Der Wille zur Macht*)[8]	—	—

Notes

1. Volume number in the *Kritische Gesamtausgabe: Werke,* ed. Colli and Montinari (Berlin: de Gruyter, 1967–78).

2. Essays written in the early 1870s, which Nietzsche left unfinished and unpublished.

3. Subsequently published as part of *Untimely Meditations.*

4. A collection of four essays, consisting of UDH, SE, and two others on David Strauss and Richard Wagner.

5. First published as a supplement to HH under the title *Vermischte Meinungen und Sprüche.*

6. Subsequently published as the second part of volume II of HH.

7. Works completed by Nietzsche in 1888 but published after his collapse.

8. Compiled after Nietzsche's death from material in his notebooks of 1883–88 (KGW volumes VII:1,2,3 and VIII:1,2,3).

Making Sense of Nietzsche

Introduction

The time for me has not come yet. Some are born posthumously.
                                        —Nietzsche (EH III:1)

Nietzsche's Timeliness

Nietzsche was certainly right when he wrote these words in
1888, shortly before the collapse that ended his productive life. He did
not find the readers and fellow "new philosophers" he sought during his
own lifetime; and it is doubtful whether he would have been happy with
most of those who were attracted to him for long afterward. But today, a
century later, he might well be at least somewhat more heartened, not
only by the extent but also by the nature of the interest that is coming to
be taken in his thought and efforts. His time may at last be arriving; and
as we move toward the turn of both this century and the millennium, he
may well turn out to have been right as well when (in his subtitle to
Beyond Good and Evil) he proclaimed his kind of philosophy to be a
"prelude to a philosophy of the future."

In any event, Nietzsche certainly has attained a place of significance in
the history of modern philosophy second to none; and I believe that he
will prove to have more staying power, and to be of greater interest in the
years to come, than almost any of his rivals. But time will tell. Meanwhile
there is much to be done by way of midwiving this birth of a Nietzschean
"philosophy of the future"; for ours is still a time in which misunderstand-
ings and abuses of his thought abound, and its future is by no means
assured. Controversy rages over what is to be made of it—and while this
is to some extent not only inevitable but healthy, its constructive appropriation and just assessment continue to be hindered by the predilections
and prejudices of many parties to the fray and onlookers alike.

Making sense of Nietzsche is a tricky business. Some have made a
kind of sense of him that is pretty horrendous. Others have made such
sweet and shallow sense of him that, if their versions of him are accepted,
he would best be left to the apostles of self-improvement. Marginally
better sense used to be made of him by taking him to have been a

proto-existentialist. More recently, it has become fashionable to make sense of him by representing him as a sometimes stumbling but notable forerunner of analytic philosophy, or as a largely welcome precursor and partial corroborator of Freud. And there long have been and still are others, of the most diverse persuasions, who make a kind of sense of him by making nonsense of him, taking him to be oblivious to conventional philosophical standards of sense-making—in some cases with derision, and in others with applause.

I would hope that the inadequacies of all such ways of dealing with Nietzsche are clear. He deserves a better fate than any of these. My way of making sense of him gives him far more credit, and makes him out to be far more interesting and significant—not only in his own time but for philosophy today, and tomorrow as well. He did like to think of himself as a philosophically radical bomb-thrower bound to outrage the establishment; and he certainly did have a penchant for saying outrageous things. Philosophers have long responded accordingly; and this image continues to shape the expectations of many, who then react with disappointment when it is suggested that the thought behind the image belies it. It also continues to affect the ways in which Nietzsche is interpreted, by new friends and foes alike. In my view, however, the way to make the most of Nietzsche philosophically, and to do the greatest possible justice to him, is to try to figure out what he is up to, with all the patience and care and responsibility to his texts that he asks of his readers (e.g., in the last section of his Preface to his *Genealogy of Morals*).

This much at least must be admitted by all who take the trouble to read him and pay attention. Nietzsche was interested in what and how we (both as human beings and as human types—and as philosophers too) have come to be. This interested him more than what we were in the first place—although he was interested in that as well, particularly because of its relevance to these other matters. But he was more interested still in what may yet become of us—and not only in what is likely, but also in what we could and might do best to make of ourselves, and what it would take to get from here to there. Hence all of his talk of "becoming those we are," of a "higher humanity" and "order of rank," and of the "enhancement of life" and the means to it. These notions all point beyond the "all too human" as well as the original "human animal," beyond the "European of today" and our already attained varieties of humanity, and beyond "the type *Mensch*" generally as well.

All of these matters are of evident and great importance to Nietzsche, and are prominent among the concerns of the kind of philosopher he both calls for and tries to be. Taken together, their treatment requires both *interpretation* and *evaluation*. They further are matters to be *comprehended;* and this evidently means not only making some sort of sense of them, but making sense of them in a way that does the fullest possible justice to them. Nietzsche undeniably thinks about them, and seeks to persuade kindred spirits to do likewise. And in doing so, he directs his (and our) interpretive and evaluative efforts to the task of going beyond commonplace and misguided ways of thinking about them, and of figuring out how to grasp them as clearly and thoroughly as is humanly possible.

This task, as he so often insists, requires all of the honesty, courage, analytical astuteness, sensitivity, and rigor that we can muster. Without these all too rare but occasionally realizable traits, we will never get any clearer about these things than most people have and do—most philosophers formerly and today included. But precisely because this task requires going beyond ordinary and received ways of thinking (which are all too much colored and shaped by "all too human" circumstances and motivations), it also requires more than such resoluteness, discipline, and skill. It requires a rare but humanly possibly kind of intellectual creativity as well, to be able to come up with alternatives to these ways of thinking and ways of expressing them. It requires insightfulness, to be able to latch onto significant features that are not readily apparent. And it requires another quality of mind as well, of responsiveness (akin to a developed aesthetic sensibility) to the qualitative differences between alternative forms of attained and attainable human life.

This understandably perplexes those whose idea of comprehension is modeled too closely and strictly upon the paradigm of scientific thinking. It also poses a problem for those who depart from the latter only to put in its place the paradigm of coherent narrative—not to mention those wedded to an idea of comprehension that refers everything to be grasped to facts of ordinary language usage, with all of the grace of Procrustes. The kind of comprehension and sense-making to which Nietzsche aspires goes beyond all of these paradigms, even if it avails itself of them along the way.

Bewilderment about what he is up to is further compounded by the fact that Nietzschean comprehension is not only backward-looking, attentive to the regularities and narrative threads that may be discerned among events hitherto, but also forward-looking, addressing itself to alternative possibilities for which all that has transpired only prepares the way. It draws upon diverse reflections on each—past developments and future possibilities—to help make sense of the other, and so of both together, frequently reversing the direction of their reckoning.

All of this gives Nietzsche's thinking and kind of philosophy an untidy character. For him and his purposes, however, this untidiness is unavoidable.

And it is only if these features of his thought are recognized that one can gain a proper appreciation of the place of notions like the "enhancement of life" and the "revaluation of values" in it, and of the relation between his reflections upon them and his "genealogical," "psychological," and other such particular types of inquiry. Such inquiries are indispensable to prepare the way for larger considerations of the former sort, but do not suffice to deal with them, and derive their chief significance from their preparatory role in relation to them.

During the thirties and forties, Nietzsche seemed to be the property of the Nazis. With his appalling sister's lamentable blessing, they claimed him as their philosophical inspiration; and many British and American philosophers believed them. Even after the Second World War, it was still common to think of Nietzsche as a proto-Nazi, whose idea of the death of God and vision of the *Übermensch* heralded the rise of fascism and the day of the Stormtroopers. But this was a complete travesty, as should be obvious to anyone who takes the trouble to read his scathing criticisms of virtually everything that came to be associated with the Nazis.

Then in the fifties, Walter Kaufmann and others began to change this image. Kaufmann even sought to make Nietzsche seem not only respectable but a really Good Guy — not the father of Nazism but the apostle of secular humanism and humanistic existentialism. He may have overdone it, but what he did with Nietzsche was a needed and welcome corrective. (I consider it not ironic but altogether fitting, I might add, that Nietzsche was rehabilitated in America by an out-of-step philosopher who was born a Jew, and whose family was victimized by the Nazis. Nietzsche was a much more kindred spirit to the Kaufmanns than to the Nazis of this world.)

By the early sixties, Kaufmann had had considerable success. His existentialist-humanist Nietzsche had replaced the proto-Nazi Bogie Man — but this was a mixed blessing, because neither existentialism nor humanism had the slightest philosophical respectability in that heyday of analytical orthodoxy. That is why few academic philosophers in the English-speaking world in those days would talk about Nietzsche and take him seriously. Some admitted that they "liked" to read him — but more for fun than for philosophical profit. Others of the older generation recognized that he might have something to say, but couldn't bring themselves to deal with him. Wartime associations were too strong, even if they were recognized to be unfair.

By 1970 though, things had begun to change again. Arthur Danto had written a book proclaiming Nietzsche to be (of all things) a precursor of *analytic* philosophy. This shocked everyone — and gave some currency to the idea that he just might be a real philosopher after all. Interest in Nietzsche remained strong among members of the "Continental philosophy" underground (in their eyes, a kind of valiant Resistance movement fighting the occupation-army analytic Establishment, which had invaded our shores from England and had retaken the colonies). But it also began to grow among those like myself who wanted to overcome the split between analytic and Continental philosophy. During the past decade a number of us of the bridge-building persuasion have done what we could to bring Nietzsche and the mainstream of contemporary philosophy not only within shouting distance but close enough for real conversation to begin.

At the same time, another wave of "New Nietzsche" interpretation made its appearance, reinforcing the former contingent. It owed its inspiration both to the later Heidegger and to various recent French philosophers like Derrida and Foucault, who have tried to appropriate Nietzsche to their new brand of radical philosophy (or anti-philosophy), seeking to overthrow and replace the entire classical modern philosophical tradition. This has set up the current debate about whether Nietzsche made important contributions to the treatment of a variety of long-standing philosophical questions about truth and knowledge, value and morality, art and science, and human nature and human life—or whether he wanted to blow the whistle on the entire enterprise, bury it, and replace it with something altogether different.

Then there is the new theme heard from a good many influential defenders of the Western philosophical and intellectual tradition, to the effect that Nietzsche is the Darth Vader of modern philosophy, who must be reckoned with as the scary Dark-Force alternative to the forces of Light, rationality, morality, and human value. In their eyes, Nietzsche is *not* Kaufmann's champion of secular humanism, but rather a kind of philosophical monster posing a deep threat to everything "we" hold dear, and invoked to frighten people back into the fold of traditional Western philosophical (and religious) principles and values. He needs to be reckoned with, on their view, as a kind of test or ordeal, which one must undergo and survive if one is to earn one's philosophical laurels.

While I am glad to see Nietzsche granted such importance, I am not at all happy to see him cast in this role of bugbear again. For while I agree that he poses a serious challenge to many things philosophers have taken for granted, I do not see him as a philosophical Dark Force at all. On the contrary: I regard him as a champion in the front rank of those who realize that night is falling as the old sun is setting for good—and who would rather light a candle than curse *or* welcome the darkness.

I also am not comfortable to see him lionized by the friends of certain recent French philosophical fashions, as the father of deconstruction and herald of the death of philosophy as we have known it from Plato to Kant and analytic philosophy. I agree that he finds much to criticize in the Western philosophical tradition; but I do *not* see him as someone who wants to subvert philosophy and replace it with an intellectual free-for-all, in which the name of the game is no longer anything like truth and knowledge, but rather only entertaining intellectual pyrotechnics or amiable conversation. What a sorry pair of ways for philosophy to end — either with meaningless bangs or idle whimpers. The Nietzsche I know would not be pleased.

I see Nietzsche as a philosopher intent upon reforming philosophy, and upon changing the ways in which we deal with philosophical questions, in order to do a better job of dealing with them than empiricist, materialist, rationalist, idealist, and other traditional types of philosophers have done — and better also than their latter-day analytical, Marxist, phenomenological, *and* existentialist successors have done.

In short: I see Nietzsche *as a philosopher.* He may have been other things as well, but he deserves the name of philosopher as much as any thinker in the history of philosophy. And, to employ one of his own distinctions, he is no mere *philosophical laborer,* working away within someone else's way of thinking, to elaborate and refine and apply it. Rather, he is a *genuine philosopher* — one of those rare thinkers whose thought opens the way to new understanding of things of great importance. But what sort of philosopher is he? What kind of philosophy is Nietzsche's kind of philosophy? In the essays in this volume I try to suggest and make a case for an answer to these questions.

A Way with Nietzsche

Nietzsche was a thinker, figure, and influence about whom many sorts of books have been and can and should be written. He had many sides and moments, and has had many audiences with differing sensibilities and interests; and no single work can be attuned to all of these sensibilities, or satisfy all of these interests. His thought moreover does not have a sharp and clear shape and structure, nicely laid out for all to see and systematically developed for all to follow. It acquires contours only in the course of interpretation. The "perspectivism" of which he speaks is not without a certain application in this context. The vantage points from which — and the eyes with which — he is viewed by different interpreters may complement each other to good effect.

My *Nietzsche,* published ten years ago in Routledge & Kegan Paul's "Arguments of the Philosophers" series, is an examination of Nietzsche's philosophical thinking. In writing it (for that series, at that juncture), I was guided by two basic aims: first, to do something at least approaching justice to the range, manner, and expressions of his philosophical endeavors; and second, to render his efforts accessible, intelligible, and interesting to philosophers and to philosophically minded readers more generally in the English-speaking world, regardless of their particular philosophical orientations and prior acquaintance with him. Each chapter of that study is devoted to one of Nietzsche's major philosophical concerns, and deals with his thinking with respect to the various issues these concerns subsume.

It is only if one takes account of the many different things Nietzsche has to say on these issues in his widely scattered discussions of them that one can do anything approaching justice to him; for his thought on these matters is in many cases much more subtle, complex, and compelling than one might gather if one were to consider only the remarks he makes in some few places. As anyone who has read him is aware, he does not provide systematic treatments of each of the matters with which he deals, but rather touches upon them and returns to them on many different occasions, seldom if ever setting down anything that might be considered his definitive position concerning any of them. Consequently, it seems to me that understanding him requires drawing together the many strands of his dispersed and unsystematic reflections upon each of them, and attempting to discern what they add up to.

I have long been guided in my interpretation of Nietzsche by a conviction arising out of years of living with his writings. It is that, although he was not a systematic writer *or* thinker, his mature thought is fundamentally coherent, both with respect to particular issues and in general; and that what he says on some occasions is best construed in the light of what he says on others, rather than in a manner that would saddle him with numerous basic inconsistencies (as many commentators and interpreters, both unsympathetic and sympathetic to him, have been all too quick and happy to do).

It undeniably was part of Nietzsche's method to approach problems and issues from a variety of different angles, and to experiment with different formulations (often of a one-sided or oversimplified nature) in dealing with them, even though this might result in at least the appearance of confusion and even contradiction. It seems to me that it is a legitimate way of reading him — and also a very fruitful one — to take him thus to have been working toward and working out a set of interconnected positions that his various remarks and reflections collectively serve to indicate and elaborate, qualifying and complementing each other. To be sure, it is not possible to reconcile everything he says in this way, even if attention is confined to his writings from the latter half of his productive life. But in many cases this can be done; and in my view the results do him a greater measure of justice than is done him otherwise, and are of considerable interest as well.

Philosophy today is again—or perhaps still—in something like the condition Nietzsche discerned over a century ago, as he reflected both upon it and upon our culture more generally; and he could well prove helpful in our attempt to reorient our thinking, in its aims, its manner, and perhaps even its substance. For anything like this to become a real possibility, however, or even for him to have a more modestly fruitful impact upon current and future philosophical endeavor, Nietzsche the philosopher must be brought into focus. This is what I sought to do in my previous book; and the limits, organization, and procedure of that study all flowed directly from this intention. The same intention underlies and motivates this volume.

"Arguments," as most philosophers tend to think of them, are rather few and far between in Nietzsche's writings. Most of what he has to say, whether of a critical or of a constructive nature, does not fit the standard model of philosophical argumentation at all well. To deal only with that in Nietzsche's writings that readily fits it would be to leave out most of what is interesting and important in his thought. And to force his philosophical thinking into this mold would be to treat him in the cruel and perhaps fatal manner of Procrustes.

It seems to me, however, that while Nietzsche does have his faults, it is the mold itself that is the greater problem—as he himself insisted. It has its uses, but also its limitations; and one of Nietzsche's great services is to help us to see this, and to loosen its grip upon philosophical thinking. At the same time, however, I do not take him (as some do) to have been a thinker willing and eager to break completely with the entire philosophical enterprise as well. The Nietzsche I know proposed and attempted to carry on something like this enterprise in a rather different sort of way. It is a way that might still be considered to involve argument, but only if the notion is extended and modified in accordance with an understanding of philosophy as a fundamentally *interpretive* affair, in which the chief tasks are the criticism, development, and substantiation of interpretations of what obtains and transpires in the world and in human life.

In dealing with Nietzsche as a philosopher, one owes it to him to begin by considering what sorts of issues and problems he believed it to be possible and important to deal with as interpreters (and as analysts and critics of prevailing modes of interpretation along the way). One likewise must attempt to understand what he did and did not think interpretation of the sort he practiced and preached involves and amounts to. This applies with respect not only to "life" and its demands and conditions, and to art and the creativity it involves, but to knowledge as well, as it traditionally has been and also alternately may be conceived. I thus consider it imperative to "rescue" the Nietzschean conception of interpretation —insofar as it is his avowed task and that of the "new philosophers" he heralds—from its all-too-common reduction *either* to the status of a mere handmaiden of "life," whose only significance is a matter of its "value for life" as a tool of the "will to power," *or* to the level of a fundamentally "artistic" affair, the proper assessment of which can only be aesthetic. He himself certainly said a good deal about interpretation along both of these lines; but it by no means follows—either in point of fact or (on my reading) for him—that it cannot amount to anything more.

To effect this rescue-operation, it is necessary to look closely at what Nietzsche had to say not only directly about interpretation, but also about philosophers and philosophy, and about truth and knowledge; and the success of the operation also requires that one follow him as he proceeded to get down to cases both in his critiques of various "metaphysical errors" and moral and valuational views, and also in his own treatment of a broad range of substantive matters, relating to life and the world, human nature, value, and morality. These are among the things I sought to do in my earlier study of his philosophical thought, and have continued to do subsequently—attending at once to the manner of his philosophical thinking and to the positions and views that emerge as he engages in it. I readily grant that in construing him as I do, "this too is only interpretation"; and I am not at all surprised when others try their hands at putting the pieces together (or at taking them apart) and come up with very different pictures of what Nietzsche thinks and is up to. I have learned and expect to continue to learn from them. But I continue to believe that there is no substitute for this kind of confrontation with his texts in interpreting him.

One of the things of which I have become convinced, and would urge others to heed, is that it is crucial in interpreting Nietzsche to learn to distinguish the different forms and levels of discussion in which he engages in dealing with various topics, and the different ways in which many philosophical terms function in his texts. This warrants brief elaboration, even though the points I shall make have already been touched on above. Failure to heed them is all too common in discussions of him, both friendly and critical, and has unfortunate consequences.

1. Nietzsche does not always use terms like "philosophy," "truth," "knowledge," "value," "morality," "art," "life," "world," and "man" in the same ways. On some occasions he uses them to suggest what he takes to be their usual traditional philosophical meanings; on others, to invoke their commonplace ordinary senses; on further occasions, to refer to what these things usually amount to; and on others still, to designate the

fundamental natures of these things as he would have them understood, or to special cases of what they might and perhaps sometimes do amount to. Such differing uses require sorting out; and the various remarks and discussions he offers in which such terms occur, used in these differing ways, likewise require sorting and careful interpretation. To do justice to him, one must be attentive to his differing meanings and points, while at the same time attending to the relations between them.

2. Nietzsche does not always approach and address topics and problems from the same point of view, or always deal with them on the same level of analysis. He favors the adoption of differing standpoints and perspectives, and shifts—often without warning, and in his published writings as well as in his notebooks—from one level of analysis to another. His discussions of "truth," "value," "morality," and "man" are cases in point; and there are many others. These differences must be noted and taken into account, if serious interpretive errors are not to be made. On the other hand, these differing approaches and levels should not be supposed to be entirely disjointed. Indeed, I am convinced that they are meant to complement and supplement each other, and are to be taken together and utilized together as so many particular strategies devised and pursued in the service of a larger "will to knowledge," which in Nietzsche is master of them all, aiming at a comprehensive grasp of these matters and their fundamental interconnection.

3. Nietzsche frequently does not trouble explicitly to qualify his remarks and extend discussions in any of the above respects, specifying neither their intended scope nor the ways in which he means the terms he uses to be understood, nor the perspectives or levels of analysis from which they are made. Often, however, what he says is subject to implicit qualifications along these lines; and these qualifications must be detected and taken into account if he is not to be misunderstood. The best rule of thumb to follow, in my view, is to suppose that the many different things he says in dealing with something like "truth" or "value" or "morality" are to be taken as qualifying each other, collectively revealing the scope and limits and level of analysis of his particular remarks. Any of them taken in isolation from the rest is bound to be misleading. None wears its proper interpretation on its sleeve, and none by itself is the key to the interpretation of all the rest. The key to interpreting them is the methodological key of seeking to make collective sense of them. And the fact that one *can* make collective sense of them—and good and interesting sense at that—is reason enough to consider warranted the supposition that they are subject to implicit sense, scope, and level qualifications.

I deal with Nietzsche as I do because I am convinced that this sort of treatment is needed both in order to do justice to aspects of his thought that cannot otherwise be adequately discerned and appreciated, and also to facilitate a wider recognition of their interest and relevance in relation to contemporary philosophical inquiry. And I might add that I further find this way of dealing with him more fruitful for my own philosophical thinking than any other, and wish to commend it by example, thereby to encourage others at least to make the same experiment in their reading and consideration of him.

Yet we must be candid with ourselves about one thing: in envisioning and calling for his "new philosophers" Nietzsche did not have in mind *Nietzsche-scholars*. We will be truest to him if we undertake to philosophize in the spirit of his thinking—working on portions of his philosophical agenda, as we might see fit to adapt and appropriate them, rather than restricting ourselves to the exploration and interpretation of what he wrote and thought. It may be well for us to immerse ourselves in the interpretation of his writings long and deeply enough to come to terms with him, and to acquire the best sense we can of that spirit, and that agenda, and where he got with it. It may also be well for us to keep him with us as philosophical companion, critic, and inspiration, as we go on. But if we have it in us to do so, we *should* attempt to go on; and this surely is as he himself would have it.

With what, however, are we to go on, if we are prepared to do so? I do not expect general agreement about this; but I shall mention a number of things I have come to think are parts of his philosophical agenda we would do well to place on ours today, on which he made promising and important beginnings but carried out far from completely or satisfactorily. One is a reconsideration of the history of philosophy, and of the nature of philosophy both as it has been and commonly is and also might better be carried on. Another is the double endeavor of the development of a comprehensive "naturalistic" theory of value, and of the reevaluation of all existing values in light of it. Another, related to this one, is an analysis and critical assessment of moralities and ethical views along the lines of Nietzsche's multifaceted treatment of them, and reflection on what alternatives to them might deserve consideration. Another is the elaboration of an epistemology—including a theory of truth and a philosophy of science—that would be "naturalistic" not simply in the sense coming to be current in the analytical literature today, but in the deeper and also subtler way that was Nietzsche's. Another is a Nietzschean philosophy of art.

Another is consideration of whether, beyond what we may learn from the natural sciences about life and the world, it is possible to interpret them philosophically in something like the way Nietzsche tried to do (even if perhaps not in the same terms), and in doing so gain insight into them beyond the knowledge of them the sciences are capable of affording. Another is consideration of the same sort of question where human social life and social institutions are concerned. And the last I shall mention is the development of what is sometimes called a philosophical anthropology, along the general lines suggested and partly fleshed out in Nietzsche's many reflections on human nature, human life, and human possibility.

It is this last concern I feel most strongly inclined to make my own. I would like to have plenty of company; but I also hope that many others will be drawn to the various other parts of this agenda, as well as to yet other Nietzschean philosophical tasks and ventures. It is in this way that Nietzsche's thought is most likely to have a strong, lasting, and important impact upon the present and future course of philosophy. And that would be a very good thing indeed.

Nietzsche Introduced

Friedrich Wilhelm Nietzsche was a classical philologist by training and academic profession. His philosophical efforts—deriving chiefly from the last dozen years of his short productive life—were little heeded until long after his physical and mental collapse in 1889 (at the age of only forty-four). Yet he subsequently emerged as one of the most controversial, unconventional, and important figures in the history of modern philosophy. His influence upon European philosophy in the twentieth century has been profound; and he has belatedly come to receive considerable attention in the English-speaking world as well, as the shadow cast by the travesty of his appropriation by the Nazis and Fascists has receded, along with the sway of philosophical fashions inhospitable to his kind of thinking and writing. He gave his *Beyond Good and Evil* the subtitle "Prelude to a Philosophy of the Future"; and in this he may well have been prophetic.

Nietzsche's philosophical enterprise grew out of his background as a philologist schooled in the study of classical languages and literatures, his deep concern with issues relating to the quality of life in the culture and society of his time, his conviction that the interpretive and evaluative underpinnings of Western civilization are fundamentally flawed, and his determination to come to grips with the profound crisis he believed to be impending as this comes to be recognized. He sought both to comprehend this situation and to help provide humanity with a new lease on life, beyond what he called "the death of God" and "the advent of nihilism" following in its wake. He deemed traditional forms of religious and philosophical thought to be inadequate to the task, and indeed to be part of the problem; and so he attempted to develop a radical alternative to them that might point the way to a solution.

Nietzsche was born on October 15, 1844, in the town of Röcken in the Prussian province of Saxony. His father, who died when Nietzsche was only five, was a Lutheran minister. While the young Nietzsche for a time considered following the same calling, his education centered upon classical studies, with music (piano and composition) as his other main early interest and pursuit. He excelled in both areas, and both remained close to his heart throughout his life. He had no formal philosophical training. His introduction to philosophy came through his discovery of Schopenhauer's *The World as Will and Representation* while studying philology at the university at Leipzig. This encounter with Schopenhauer's thought profoundly influenced him, as can be seen in his first book *The Birth of Tragedy* (1872), which he published soon after being appointed to a professorship of philology at Basel University (at the astonishingly early age of twenty-four, before he had even been awarded his doctorate).

Nietzsche was early convinced of the soundness of Schopenhauer's basic conception of the world as a godless and irrational affair of ceaseless striving and suffering; but he was repelled by Schopenhauer's starkly pessimistic verdict with respect to the worth of existence in such a world, and sought some way of arriving at a different conclusion. In *The Birth of Tragedy* he made his first attempt to do so, looking to the Greeks and their art for guidance, and to Wagner (with whom he had become acquainted and enthralled) for contemporary inspiration. His attachment to Wagner subsequently gave way to disenchantment and then to scathing criticism (culminating in his late polemic *The Case of Wagner*), and he gradually emancipated himself from Schopenhauer as well; but the fundamental problem of how nihilism might be overcome and life affirmed without illusions remained at the center of his concern throughout his life.

Nietzsche's brief academic career ended in 1879, owing to the drastic deterioration of his health. His only significant publications after *The Birth of Tragedy* prior to its final year were the four essays he subsequently gathered together under the title *Untimely Meditations*, of which *The Uses and Disadvantages of History for Life* and *Schopenhauer as Educator* (both 1874) are of the greatest interest. Then, in 1878, he published the first of a series of volumes of aphorisms and reflections under the title *Human, All Too Human*. It was followed during the next few years by two supplements that became a second volume under the same title, by *Daybreak* in 1881, and then by the initial four-part version of *The Gay Science* in 1882. In these works, which he described as "a series of writings . . . whose common goal is to erect *a new image and ideal of the free spirit,*" Nietzsche found his way to his kind of philosophy.

It was only in 1886, however, with the publication of *Beyond Good and Evil,* that he pursued it further in something like the same manner. In the interval (1883–85) he published only the four parts of his great literary-philosophical experiment *Thus Spoke Zarathustra.* A mere three more years remained to him prior to his collapse in January of 1889, from which he never recovered. (He died eleven long years later, on August 25, 1900.) During this brief but phenomenally productive period he wrote prefaces to new editions of most of his pre-*Zarathustra* writings, added a fifth part to a new edition of *The Gay Science* (1887), published *On the Genealogy of Morals* in the same year, and then in the final year of his active life (1888) wrote *Twilight of the Idols, The Case of Wagner, The Antichrist,* and his autobiographical *Ecce Homo* — all the while filling many notebooks with reflections and thought experiments. (The significance of this *"Nachlaß"* material is much debated. After his collapse and death, selections from it were gathered into a volume published under the title *The Will to Power.*)

From his early essays to these last works, Nietzsche showed himself to be an astute, severe, and provocative critic on many fronts. Cultural, social, political, artistic, religious, moral, scientific, and philosophical developments and phenomena of many kinds drew his polemical attention. Everywhere he looked he saw much that was lamentably "human, all too human," even among those things and thinkers generally held in the highest regard. This has given rise to the common impression that the basic thrust and upshot of his thought is radically negative, contributing greatly to the advent of nihilism that he announced (and of worse things as well).

This impression, however, is deeply mistaken. Nietzsche actually was a profoundly positive thinker, concerned above all to discover a way beyond the nihilistic reaction he believed to be the inevitable consequence of the impending collapse of traditional values and modes of interpretation, to a new "affirmation" and "enhancement" of life. His critical fire was only a means to this end, preliminary to the twin philosophical tasks of *reinterpretation* and *revaluation* he advocated and pursued with growing explicitness and determination from *The Gay Science* onward.

As a further means to this end, and likewise preliminary to these tasks, Nietzsche developed and undertook a variety of forms of analysis, of which the kind of "genealogical" inquiry exemplified by his investigations in *On the Genealogy of Morals* is one notable and important example. His analytical acumen was as extraordinary as his critical astuteness; and his writings both before and after *Zarathustra* contain a wealth of cultural, social, psychological, linguistic, and conceptual analyses from many different perspectives, upon which he drew not only in his critiques but also in his reinterpretive and revaluative efforts. His recognition of the importance of engaging in and drawing upon a multiplicity of such analyses in philosophical inquiry is reflected in his insistence that such inquiry is inescapably perspectival—and that this circumstance is by no means fatal to it, if one can learn to capitalize upon the possibility of bringing a variety of perspectives to bear upon many of the matters with which it may concern itself. This is his practice as well as his prescription, in his explorations of issues ranging from moral and religious phenomena to aspects of our human nature and to knowing and reasoning themselves.

The form of Nietzsche's philosophical writings both before and after *Zarathustra,* which for the most part consist of collections of relatively brief aphorisms and reflections on such issues rather than sustained systematic lines of argument, is well suited to this multiply perspectival tactic. It greatly complicates the task of understanding him; but it also makes his thinking far more subtle and complex than is commonly supposed. He returned to problems repeatedly, in one work after another, approaching them from many different angles; and it is only if account is taken of his many diverse reflections on them that anything approaching justice to his thinking about any of them can be done. Even then he can be—and has been, and no doubt will continue to be—interpreted in quite different ways. Precisely for this reason, however, and because he has so much of interest to say (on almost any such interpretation) about so many things, he is certain to continue to attract, deserve, and reward philosophical attention.

Nietzsche was greatly concerned with basic problems he discerned in contemporary Western culture and society, which he believed were becoming increasingly acute, and for which he considered it imperative to try to find new solutions. He prophesied the advent of a period of nihilism, with "the death of God" and the demise of metaphysics, and the discovery of the inability of science to yield anything like absolute knowledge; but this prospect deeply worried him. He was firmly convinced of the untenability of the "God-hypothesis" and associated religious interpretations of the world and our existence, and likewise of their metaphysical variants. Having also become persuaded of the fundamentally nonrational character of the world, life, and history, Nietzsche took the basic challenge of philosophy to be that of overcoming both these ways of thinking and the nihilism resulting from their abandonment. This led him to undertake to reinterpret ourselves and the world along lines that would be more tenable, and would also be more conducive to the flourishing and enhancement of life. The "de-deification of nature," the tracing of the "genealogy of morals" and their critique, and the elaboration of "naturalistic" accounts of knowledge, value, morality, and our entire "spiritual" nature thus came to be among the main tasks confronting him and the "new philosophers" he called for.

Unlike most philosophers of importance before him, Nietzsche was openly and profoundly hostile to most forms of morality and religious thought. He declared "war" upon them, on the grounds that they not only are indefensible and untenable, but moreover feed upon and foster weakness, life-weariness, and *ressentiment,* poisoning the wellsprings of human vitality in the process by "devaluing" all "naturalistic" values. He further rejected not only the "God-hypothesis" (as a notion utterly without warrant, owing its acceptance only to naivete, error, need, or ulterior motivation), but also any metaphysical postulation of a "true world of 'being'" transcending the world of life and experience, and with them the related "soul-" and "thing-hypotheses," taking these notions to be ontological fictions reflecting our artificial (though convenient) conceptual shorthand for products and processes. In place of this cluster of traditional ontological categories and interpretations, he conceived of the world in terms of an interplay of forces without any inherent structure or final end, ceaselessly organizing and reorganizing themselves as the fundamental disposition he called "will to power" gives rise to successive arrays of power relationships among them.

Nietzsche construed our human nature and existence naturalistically, insisting upon the necessity of "translating man back into nature," in origin and fundamental character, as a form of animal life among others. "The soul is only a word for something about the body," he has Zarathustra say; and the body is fundamentally an arrangement of natural forces and processes. At the same time, however, he insisted upon the importance of social arrangements and interactions in the development of human forms of awareness and activity, and moreover upon the possibility of the emergence of exceptional human beings capable of an independence and creativity elevating them beyond the level of the general human rule. So he stressed the difference between "higher types" and "the herd," and through Zarathustra proclaimed the "overman" (*Übermensch*) to be "the meaning of the earth," representing the overcoming of the "all-too-human" and the attainment of the fullest possible "enhancement of life." Far from seeking to diminish our humanity by stressing our animality, he sought to direct our attention and efforts to the emergence of a "higher humanity" capable of endowing existence with a human redemption and justification.

Nietzsche proposed that life and the world be interpreted in terms of his conception of "will to power"; and he framed his "Dionysian value-standard" and the "revaluation of values" he called for in terms of this interpretation as well. The only positive and tenable value scheme possible, he maintained, must be based upon a recognition and affirmation of the world's fundamental character, and so must posit as a general standard the attainment of a kind of life in which the assertive-transformative "will to power" is present in its highest intensity and quality. This in turn led him to take the "enhancement of life" and creativity to be the guiding ideas of his "revaluation of values" and development of a naturalistic value theory.

This way of thinking carried over into Nietzsche's thinking with respect to morality as well. Insisting that moralities as well as other traditional modes of valuation ought to be understood and assessed "in the perspective of life," he argued that most of them are contrary rather than conducive to the enhancement of life, reflecting the all-too-human needs, weaknesses, and fears of less-favored human groups and types. Distinguishing between "master-" and "slave-moralities," he found the latter increasingly to have eclipsed the former in human history, and to have become the dominant type of morality at the present time, in the form of a "herd-animal morality" well-suited to the requirements and vulnerabilities of the mediocre who are the human rule, but stultifying and detrimental to the development of potential exceptions to that rule. He further suggested the possibility and desirability of a "higher" type of morality for the exceptions, in which the content and contrast of the basic "slave/herd-morality" categories of "good and evil" would be replaced by categories more akin to the "good and bad" contrast characteristic of "master-morality," with a revised (and variable) content.

The strongly creative flavor of Nietzsche's notions of such a "higher humanity" and associated "higher morality" reflects his linkage of both to his conception of art, to which he attached great importance. Art, as the creative transformation of the world as we find it (and of ourselves thereby) on a small scale and in particular media, affords us a glimpse of the possibility of a kind of life that would be lived more fully in this manner, and constitutes a step in the direction of its emergence. In this way, Nietzsche's mature thought thus expanded upon the idea of the basic connection between art and the justification of life that was his general theme in his first major work, *The Birth of Tragedy*.

A Life in Brief

Prelude: Early childhood (1844–49)
    First-born of a Lutheran minister and his wife, living in a small provincial town in what is now eastern Germany.

The precocious youth (1849–58)
  Bright, serious boy of many talents (musical as well as scholastic), left
  fatherless at five, raised in an adoring all-female household.

The brilliant student (1858–69)
  Classics student excelling in his studies, first at an elite boarding
  school and then at the universities at Bonn and Leipzig; aspiring
  composer and fine pianist; discovers Schopenhauer and meets Wagner.

The rebellious professor (1869–79)
  Prodigy in classical philology, a professor at Basel at twenty-four;
  unconventional interests and writings, antagonizing his colleagues; an
  avid Wagnerian (still composing music himself); cultural critic becoming a philosopher, while struggling with academic frustrations and
  debilitating illnesses.

The nomad philosopher (1879–88)
  Pensioned retiree at thirty-four; plagued with recurring severe health
  problems; alienated from academic life and nearly everything else;
  living alone in Swiss and Italian boarding houses—and proceeding
  from "free-spirited" reflections to *Zarathustra,* and on toward a
  "philosophy of the future" and a "revaluation of all values."

The insane invalid (1889–1900)
  Mere shell following a complete physical and mental collapse (probably
  of syphilitic origin) in early 1889—at the age of only forty-four; a
  decade of empty madness before the final curtain.

Chronology

1844	Friedrich Wilhelm Nietzsche born on October 15 in Röcken, in the Prussian Province of Saxony.
1849	Father dies (at the age of thirty-six).
1858–64	Attends the classics-oriented boarding school Schulpforta. (Plays the piano and composes on the side.)
1864	Enters Bonn University to study classical languages and literatures.
1869	Appointed associate professor of classical philology (before even completing his Ph.D.) at the Swiss university at Basel.
1870	Full professor at Basel. Enlists as a medical orderly in the Franco-Prussian war, contracting serious illnesses.
1872	First book *The Birth of Tragedy* appears—his only major

classical studies publication. (It is met with scholarly derision.)

1873–74   Publishes the first three *Untimely Meditations,* including the essays *On the Uses and Disadvantages of History for Life* and *Schopenhauer as Educator.*

1876   Writes a fourth *Meditation* in homage to Wagner, but his enthusiasm for Wagner cools.

1878   The first volume of *Human, All Too Human* (638 aphorisms) appears. Wagner sends him *Parsifal,* and their estrangement deepens.

1879   Resigns (with pension) from his position at Basel, incapacitated by his health problems. Begins spending his summers in the Swiss Engadine region, and his winters in northern Italy, living in boarding houses.

1879–80   Writes two sequels to *Human, All Too Human,* subsequently published as the two parts of its second volume (another 758 aphorisms).

1881   Publishes *Daybreak* (575 more aphorisms). Alternative periods of depression and exhilaration. First summer in Sils Maria, where the idea of "eternal recurrence" comes to him.

1882   The year of his intense but short-lived relationship with Lou Salome, which ends badly. Publishes the initial four-part version of *The Gay Science* (342 aphorisms and reflections).

1883   The first two parts of *Thus Spoke Zarathustra* are written and published. Wagner dies. Estrangement from family and friends; depression. Resolves against living in Germany.

1884   Completes and publishes the third part of *Zarathustra.* Breaks with his sister, unable to endure her anti-Semitic, pro-"Teutonic" fiancé Bernard Förster. (She marries Förster the next year, to Nietzsche's disgust and distress, accompanying him to Paraguay, where he sought to found a Teutonic colony.)

1885   The fourth part of *Zarathustra* is written, but is only privately printed and circulated. Health worsens.

1886   *Beyond Good and Evil* (296 aphorisms and reflections in nine parts, plus a poem "Aftersong") is published. New editions of most pre-*Zarathustra* works are prepared and supplied with prefaces.

1886–87	An expanded second edition of *The Gay Science* is prepared and published, with a new preface and fifth part consisting of forty-one additional reflections, and an appendix of poetry, "Songs of Prince Vogelfrei."
1887	*On the Genealogy of Morals* appears, consisting of a preface and three "essays" (of seventeen, twenty-five, and twenty-eight numbered sections, respectively). Completes orchestral score for *Hymnus an das Leben*. Begins working on magnus opus, to be called *The Will to Power*.
1888	*The Case of Wagner* is published; and *Twilight of the Idols, The Antichrist, Nietzsche contra Wagner, Dionysian Dithyrambs* (a collection of poems), and *Ecce Homo* are all written. *The Will to Power* project is dropped, in favor of a projected four-part *Revaluation of All Values*. Condition deteriorates.
1889	Collapses in early January in Turin, at the age of forty-four. (Never recovers, living his final eleven years in invalid insanity in the care of his mother and sister.) *Twilight of the Idols* is published in the same month.
1892	First public edition of the fourth part of *Zarathustra* appears.
1893	Sister returns from Paraguay, and—under the name Elizabeth Förster-Nietzsche—assists their mother in the management of her brother's affairs.
1895	*The Antichrist* and *Nietzsche contra Wagner* are published.
1897	Mother dies, leaving complete control of his care—and of his literary estate—to his sister, who exploits his growing fame and fosters the assimilation of his thought to right-extremist political purposes during the next four decades.
1900	Nietzsche dies, on August 25, in Weimar.
1901	Sister publishes an arrangement of selections from his notebooks of 1883–88 under the title *The Will to Power*, in his name.
1908	*Ecce Homo* is finally published (twenty years after it was written).
1910–11	First edition of Nietzsche's collected works is published under the supervision of his sister—including a greatly expanded edition of *The Will to Power*.
1935	Sister dies, triumphant in the knowledge that her brother had come to be regarded by Hitler and Mussolini (and many others) as the philosophical inspiration of National

Socialism and Fascism—a travesty that would plague Nietzsche's reception for the next half-century.

1967–84   Publication of the *Kritische Gesamtausgabe* of Nietzsche's writings.

Part One

SKIRMISHES

CHAPTER ONE

Nietzsche as Menace? Nietzsche and Allan Bloom's Nietzsche

The great popular success of Allan Bloom's *Closing of the American Mind*[1] is one of those phenomena I wish H. L. Mencken could have lived to see, and to remark upon. After the Bible, it may be the most widely unread best-seller of modern times. Every college and university administrator in the land probably has at least one copy; but those who have actually read it through probably are outnumbered by those who are happy in their work.

Quite apart from any impact it may have on academia, for the better or for the worse, one effect of the book has been to help make Nietzsche a household name. Bloom has probably done more to convince more people in this country that Nietzsche somehow *matters* in an important way than have all of us in the Nietzsche business put together. The manner in which he has done so, however, makes this a mixed blessing, even for us. We have been working for some decades now to try to get our fellow philosophers and others to recognize that Nietzsche *does* matter, in important ways, within academic philosophy and also beyond it. In this respect, Bloom has done us a considerable favor. And his version of Nietzsche is infinitely more worthy of serious attention than was the lamentable caricature of Nietzsche figuring so prominently in the news a half-century ago.

On the other hand, Bloom's Nietzsche comes across as a specter of a different but no less sinister sort. Those who suppose that Bloom may be relied upon at least where Nietzsche is concerned are likely to conclude that Nietzsche matters chiefly as a kind of deadly virus of modern thought, posing the most awful threat, and who must somehow be vanquished at all costs. Bloom may protest that he esteems and admires Nietzsche as one of the very greatest of philosophers, around whom (he even says) the modern world revolves.[2] With such friends, however, Nietzsche does not need enemies. For Bloom, everything depends upon mounting a counter-offensive against Nietzsche and all of his works before it is too late—even if this means having to read Locke.

Bloom exemplifies a tendency that has become increasingly common among Anglo-American philosophers in recent years: to recognize that Nietzsche represents the culmination of the movement of modern thought away from the articles of faith of the Enlightenment—and then to recoil from the consequences of this development, as though he were its reductio ad absurdum, and to suppose that some alternative *must* be found. This is usually done by reverting with the fervor of the "born-again" either to these articles of faith or to others yet older. The line of thought seems to be: These developments lead to Nietzsche. It would be too horrible if Nietzsche were right. Therefore Nietzsche must be wrong. Therefore modernity must have gone astray somewhere. Something must have been rejected that should have been kept, among these abandoned articles of older philosophical or religious faith, and had better be revived and embraced.

But what if Nietzsche and others are right about their untenability? What if intellectual conscience and philosophical integrity require that we make no such retreat, and instead bid farewell to all such articles of faith once and for all? Would the philosophical and human outlook then really be as bleak as Bloom and other philosophical conservatives old and new suppose? Would the result necessarily be the dark night of nihilism, either European-style or American-style, ending in no new dawn, but rather only in the abyss, as Bloom scarily warns? Or is he posing a false forced choice in order to frighten the straying flock back into the old fold? In a word: Does he sell Nietzsche short? Indeed he does—but in a way that is instructive as well as lamentable. His treatment of Nietzsche is worth our attention not because it is so very important or illuminating in itself, but rather because it so nicely exemplifies the above-mentioned tendency, and because it serves to raise these questions so vividly.

Bloom actually presents us with a number of Nietzsches. There is the American "pop cult" Nietzsche, to be found (though happily without Nietzsche's name attached) in the widely prevalent ways of modern popular thinking Bloom so despises. There is the "lit crit" Nietzsche, of whom he thinks no better. There is the New Left Nietzsche, whom he considers a kind of bastardized bad joke. There are the two second-generation half-Nietzsches, Freud and Weber, both of whom he respects somewhat more, but still regards as offspring of dubious legitimacy and worth. And then there is Bloom's Nietzsche himself—a far more formidable figure and one of the greatest of modern philosophers, but also the most dangerous of them, who purportedly was fatefully wrong on the issues that matter most, however brilliant and insightful he may otherwise have been.

I shall focus upon the last of these Nietzsches, and shall pass over the others with but a few brief remarks. Bloom professes to be intent upon saving the real Nietzsche (his own Nietzsche) from the fate of being reduced to these other sorry forms—even if only to preserve him for the different fate Bloom himself has in mind for him, of a proper and honorable execution by philosophical firing squad. Yet he gives the strong impression of wanting to tar Nietzsche so completely with the brush of responsibility for these unwelcome fruits that anyone who shares Bloom's distaste for them will be ill-disposed toward their source as the final battle commences. Bloom heaps much scorn upon those who have turned Nietzsche's dynamite into pablum, and repeatedly points to various purportedly characteristic shortcomings of Americans as deserving the blame for what has become of Nietzsche's ideas over here. At the same time, however, he seems to want to persuade us that all of this ultimately is really Nietzsche's fault, for having sown the seed of it in the first place. But this is as absurd as blaming Nietzsche for what the Nazis did with him—which Bloom at times also comes close to doing.

Even if there is something to the history of it all that Bloom relates, moreover (and there probably is, though not nearly as much as he thinks), that would cut no ice with respect to the question of whether Nietzsche's positions on the actual issues are sound. It also has no bearing on how his thinking with respect to these issues is to be interpreted. Nietzsche worried a great deal about the way in which his ideas would be taken. He was acutely concerned that most people were not ready (as he put it) for his truths. But he was convinced that it is unworthy of a philosopher (as he also put it) to do anything other than try to get to the bottom of these issues, and to work out the consequences of doing so unflinchingly, at least while in philosophical company and with one's philosophical hat on. One who respects him as Bloom *says* he does should meet him on *this* ground, and should seek to come to terms with his thought accordingly, rather than by way of its uses and abuses.

What, then, are we to make of Bloom's Nietzsche, in relation to the Nietzsche we may find in *his own* writings? It must be acknowledged at once that, especially in his chapter on "Values," Bloom often captures the concerns and thrust of Nietzsche's thinking on various matters quite well, and conveys them better than many other writers who take notice of him do. Indeed, he does so well enough that it rings very oddly when, after a dozen pages of rather harrowing exposition, Bloom steps back and remarks: "Not all that Nietzsche asserted is plausible, but its charm is undeniable."[3] *Charm?* A more lightly dismissive term could hardly have been chosen; and Bloom uses it again in the same way a page later ("For all the charms of Nietzsche"),[4] as if to make sure that the reader will not miss the put-down. His intention is probably to assure the reader that there is no need to be alarmed, and that he knows a way out. But this is no way to take a formidable rival seriously.

Something strange is also going on when Bloom cites Nietzsche as the source of the "alien views and alien tastes" by which "democracy has been corrupted,"[5] and then proceeds, a few pages later, to complain that Nietzsche rejects the universalism of Greek and French philosophy, and with it the associated quest for real truth and real goodness. He replaces them, we are told, with mere "values"; and "For Nietzsche and those influenced by him, values are the products of folk minds and have relevance only to those minds."[6] In the first of these passages, Bloom sounds as though he is in the camp he mentions in the second, seeming to suggest that Nietzsche's "alien views" may be fine for the "folk mind" of which they are the product, but have no place over here in the Land of the Free. In this case, however, it is Bloom rather than Nietzsche who has abandoned universalism; for Nietzsche surely did not think that what he had to say about truth, morality, and values had no application outside of German-speaking Europe.

Nietzsche might well have allowed that most American minds even today (including Bloom's) are not yet ready fully to comprehend and appreciate what he has to say—as he observes with respect to most of his contemporaries. He clearly thought, however, that it was twilight-time for all the old idols not only in Europe but throughout Western civilization, and wherever else a comparable sophistication might be attained. It is almost as if Bloom wishes he could close the American mind to Nietzsche's challenge, and dreams of a Fortress America in which his Socratic and Enlightenment faith in reason's power to disclose the Good, the True, and the Beautiful can be preserved from all subversion from abroad. But that is an impossible and misguided dream; and attempts to achieve it can only enfeeble those they would protect, with consequences more serious than those Bloom associates with the closing he discusses.

Bloom is a splendid latter-day example of the kind of phenomenon Nietzsche takes Kant (among others) to represent. Nietzsche is very hard on Kant because he sees him as having devoted his efforts to mounting a brilliant, desperate rear-guard action to save the Socratic-Christian faith from final interment. This faith is also Bloom's. It is the faith in eternal verities and a transcendent "true world of being," to which our minds or souls most truly belong, and to which they may by proper application lead us. The "death of God" that Nietzsche proclaims is the demise of this faith, as one that might still be plausibly held worthy of belief. For Socrates and Kant, reason was the key; for Christianity, it is the acceptance of Divine Revelation.

For Nietzsche, both are real enough as human phenomena; but they neither derive from nor are capable of leading us into any such Promised Land. The faith of Socrates, Kant, and Bloom may be strongly motivated, but is generally so motivated (Nietzsche suspects) for all-too-human reasons. On his view, we must learn to live without it, because it cannot withstand the scrutiny of the intellectual conscience to which it itself has given birth. And we must also distance ourselves from it because it is nihilism in disguise, setting us up for a fall into the abyss of despair and paralysis by its radical devaluation of everything that has no grounding and validation in the absolutes it postulates. Those who fight rear-guard actions on its behalf only make all the more difficult the necessary shift to a new conception and appreciation of ourselves and our world by which we might yet manage to live and flourish, beyond the transitional nihilistic rebound that disillusionment is likely to bring in its wake.

Like so many of his kindred spirits, Bloom can see only what must be given up if Nietzsche is right. He recoils from the prospect, and blames the messenger for the message. And like so many others, he either ignores or belittles what Nietzsche proposes to put in place of the idols whose twilight is at hand, portraying him (as Spiro Agnew might have put it) as nothing but a nattering nabob of nihilism. He sees Nietzsche as a nihilist, who "with the utmost gravity told modern man that he was free-falling in the abyss of nihilism."[7] (The pun on "gravity" and "free-falling" is a nice one, whether or not it was intended; but if it *was* intended, it is another way of—pardon the further pun—making light of Nietzsche.) Bloom gives little weight (pardon again) to Nietzsche's professed intent to *overcome* nihilism, to attain a newly and more truly affirmative relation to life in this world, and to promote the emergence of a redeeming higher humanity that would be "antinihilist" as well as "Antichristian," and thus "victor over [both] God and nothingness."[8] For Bloom cannot see the rejection of absolute truth discoverable by reason— especially with respect to morality and the good life—as anything other than nihilistic.

Bloom takes Nietzsche to have supposed that "the reconstitution of man" in the aftermath of the death of God "requires the sacrifice of reason," in opposition to our Socratic and Enlightenment heritage, in which reason is "at the center" and is supposed to be capable of leading us into all truth. He strangely has little to say about Nietzsche on interpretation in this connection. What he stresses instead is that Nietzsche replaces talk about the *discovery of truth* with talk about the *creation of values,* which are "not discovered by reason,"[9] leaving "no place for the theoretical man to stand."[10] In place of Socratic and Enlightenment rationalistic faith in the power of reason to give us true knowledge of the highest things, Nietzsche is said to offer us "cultural relativism," which relates values to cultures and so to merely human invention, advocates "culture while knowing it is not true," and thus paradoxically and self-defeatingly "teaches the need to believe while undermining belief."[11]

Bloom's picture of Nietzsche has a good deal to be said for it. It is fairly close to the mark in many respects, at least as far as it goes. It is even with some justice that he sums it up, toward the end of the book, by saying that "*the* issue for Nietzsche" is that "Socrates is alive and must be overcome."[12] It suffers, however, from Bloom's all-or-nothing stance and disposition, which Nietzsche regarded as a recipe for disaster, far more dangerous than the determination to push down and out of the way what is misguided and falling, and then to get on with the task of reconsidering and making the most of what we may find available to work with.

So, for example, in undertaking to develop an account of interpretation and of how some interpretations may be superior to others in the comprehension they afford, Nietzsche seeks to do much more than merely sweep away traditional ideas about truth and knowledge. He attempts to give us something to take their place, that will still serve (and indeed serve better) to guide inquiry. In making so much of questions of value and the revaluation of values, he seeks to do much more than merely devalue traditional notions of the good life and inquiry into what really matters, leaving us stranded in a pure cultural relativism that knows no standard and undermines itself, thus plunging us into nihilistic free-fall and free-for-all. Rather, he attempts to discern a new standard and "center of gravity" enabling us to find our feet again, and to proceed to discover the possibility of an enhancement of life that would redeem humanity without recourse to fundamental illusion.

Further: in subjecting morality to genealogical analysis and searching criticism, Nietzsche seeks to do much more than merely subvert it, opening the way to a manner of existence "beyond good and evil" that knows no restraint. Rather, he attempts to develop a new way of thinking about morality that would endow it with significance within the context of a naturalized conception of life and its enhancement. In undertaking to translate humanity back into a de-deified nature and to dethrone reason as a faculty transcending the circumstances of our mundane existence in its origins, he seeks to do more than simply sacrifice it on the altar of culture and creativity. Rather, he attempts to comprehend how we have come to be more than mere creatures of nature through the very circumstances of our naturalistic genealogy, and to do justice to the achievement our reason represents and to the more modest but nonetheless significant ability it may give us to attain forms of knowledge that are not to be despised or underestimated.

Bloom sells Nietzsche short because he misses all of this. He sees only the Nietzsche who threatens everything that he holds dear. He and many others who shrink from letting go of their attachment to the faith in absolutes and in the power of reason to discover them thus regard him as their mortal foe. They do not perceive that he is actually perhaps their best *ally* in their resistance to a nihilism that would plunge us into the abyss of radical meaninglessness, in the darkness and emptiness of which our humanity and all distinctions would disappear. Nietzsche does insist that a price must be paid, which Bloom and his kindred spirits are loath to pay, for at least the chance of passage to the other side: namely, the abandonment of the old faith and its idols, so prominently displayed in Bloom's book. But I believe, with Nietzsche, that if life and philosophy are to have a non-nihilistic future, this future is to be found on the far side of the disillusionment that Bloom condescendingly dismisses as "Continental despair."

Bloom is certainly right in claiming that the other Nietzsches he identifies are sorry creatures, on which we would be ill-advised to stake our fortunes. But Nietzsche is certainly right in claiming that there is likewise no hope of avoiding the abyss if we can do no better than huddle with Bloom by the altar of the old Socratic-Enlightenment faith. If there is a live alternative that promises any real hope of escaping the nihilistic catastrophe that both deem to threaten, it is neither that of Bloom's Nietzsche nor that of Bloom himself, but rather something like that of the counter-nihilist Nietzsche who picks up where Bloom expires in bankruptcy and Bloom's Nietzsche leaves off.

Bloom quite rightly and commendably recognizes that the cluster "culture-values-creativity" is central for Nietzsche, as the heart of his conception of our humanity and its possible enhancement, and indeed of what he has Zarathustra characterize as "the meaning of the earth." But Bloom regards this cluster as a poor substitute for the rival cluster of "knowledge-morality-reason" more immaculately conceived, which for him is the true locus of our humanity and worth, in the spirit of Socrates and the Enlightenment. He takes modern philosophers and other intellectuals to task for capitulating to Nietzsche in this respect, with greater or lesser degrees of sophistication, rather than rallying to the defense of his traditional trinity. This is what he takes the failure and impoverishment of higher education fundamentally to involve and reflect. Nietzsche, however, would consider the real failure and impoverishment to be that of those like Bloom, who lack either the sophistication, the intellectual honesty, or the courage to recognize the untenability of the traditional claims made for his trinity, and to turn to the task of reinterpreting our humanity (and his trinity along with it). For if that is not done, we and our students and the rest of modern humanity will be left empty-handed and despairing, in the aftermath of the impending overdue final demise of Bloom's faith and quest.

Moreover, Nietzsche is by no means intent upon persuading us that when culture, values, and creativity are brought to the fore the elements of Bloom's trinity must be abandoned altogether or so marginalized that they cease to be of any significance. On the contrary, he finds that when they are demythologized and reinterpreted they acquire a new lease on life—no longer immaculately conceived, to be sure, but with a significance that is far from negligible. This is true of knowledge, which turns out for Nietzsche to be a genuine human possibility after all, when properly understood, with respect to the host of matters Nietzsche examines in *The Gay Science* and elsewhere. It should be plain to anyone who reads him that he himself was deeply committed to its pursuit, and attached great importance to it. This is even true of morality, not only in the form of that "higher morality" he took to be both appropriate and needful for exceptions to the human rule in the service of their realization of the possibility of a "higher humanity," but also where more ordinary forms of morality are concerned. Indeed, he considers them to have a crucial function in human life more generally—past, present, and future. His denials of the appropriateness of a single morality for all human beings, and of the absoluteness and autonomy of moral principles, should not be allowed to obscure these points.

In view of the great fuss Bloom makes about reason, it is particularly important to stress that the same observation also applies with respect to Nietzsche's treatment and assessment of it. What upsets Bloom most about Nietzsche is that he is supposed to have "required the sacrifice of reason." "For all the charms of Nietzsche," according to Bloom, this sin is unforgivable, and fatally flaws his thought.[13] But *does* Nietzsche "require the sacrifice of reason"? Not at all. What he requires is the acknowledgment that our human reason is no pristine faculty with which we are endowed from on high, unconnected with the rest of our biologically, socially, and historically conditioned existence and practical dealings with each other and our world. Rather, it is a capacity we have gradually acquired and now possess to a greater or lesser extent, that has emerged as one of the more remarkable outgrowths of the interplay of these elements and circumstances. So to understand it, however, is not to require its sacrifice.

Moreover, as Nietzsche observes, the human and even all-too-human, very maculate origins of a thing or capacity do not settle the questions of what may be done with it once it has been engendered, and of what its worth and significance may prove to be. And in the case of reason, notwithstanding his insistence upon its limits and links to our affective constitution and practical needs and interests, he thinks that a great deal may be done with it, and that its importance is likewise great. It may be no substitute for creativity, which he for good reason takes to be more important still. He considers both to be indispensable, however, to all genuine philosophy, to the advancement of science, to the comprehension of everything humanly comprehensible, and indeed—now that the point of no return has long passed in our exchange of blind and unwavering instinct for consciousness—to the preservation, flourishing, and enhancement of human life as well. In short, far from sacrificing reason, Nietzsche would have us make the most of it.

To be sure, Bloom is right to observe that for Nietzsche the kinds of values that give life its savor and culture its content "are not discovered by reason," but rather require to be "created."[14] Bloom overstates the case in suggesting that Nietzsche supposes reason to have nothing whatever to do with the discovery of value, since he acknowledges it to be one of Nietzsche's views—presumably arrived at by means of thought—that "the very idea of culture carries with it a value: man needs culture and must do what is necessary to create and maintain cultures."[15] On this level, at any rate, and also in carrying out his "revaluation of values," Nietzsche undeniably is employing reason in the elaboration and application of his value theory. Moreover, he considers reason to have an important role in the ascertainment of the kinds of values—and even the kinds of morality—that are and are not conducive to the flourishing of various types of human beings under diverse conditions of existence. But he also clearly and reasonably holds that reason by itself does not suffice to establish the values that give cultures their identities and human lives their direction.

It is hard to see, however, why Bloom should find this so troubling. It is no objection to a philosopher of art if he maintains that works of art and the values they engender are not to be discovered by reason, but rather require to be created, and that they have nothing to do with truth. And it is surely no objection to Nietzsche that he holds that the same points apply with respect to cultures as well. The sticking point for Bloom would appear to be that Nietzsche proposes to extend them further, leaving no room beyond their scope for an independent, purely rational determination of the content of the One True Morality, and of the lineaments of the One True Good Life. To this, however, we and Nietzsche might well reply that the burden is on Bloom and anyone else who may care to join him to make sense of these notions, and to show how such a program can be carried out, rather than upon Nietzsche to demonstrate the impossibility of doing so—and that one would be well advised not to hold one's breath until they deliver.

Meanwhile, while they are off pursuing their Holy Grail, we would do well to turn our attention to the task of seeing what mileage we can get out of the phenomena at hand, mindful of those relating to values, cultures, and creation, as well as those our scientific brethren contemplate. That is what Nietzsche sought with such determination and urgency to do, in works such as *The Gay Science, Beyond Good and Evil,* and *On the Genealogy of Morals.* It seems to me that his enterprise, pursued in this way, is a much more promising one than the one Bloom urges upon us. And it further seems to me that, in trying to persuade American readers that they should disdain Nietzsche's "alien views and alien tastes" in favor of our (native?) Socratic and Enlightenment heritage, Bloom not only is being rather silly, but also misguidedly seeks to close the American mind to a valuable import. Even if he is right about what happened when Nietzsche first "came to America"—"the goods," he says, "got damaged in transit"[16]—it would be bad policy to deny him a visa today. For he deserves a serious hearing—and a better one than Bloom has given him. Fortunately, the attention Bloom draws to him may help to bring about that very result, to Bloom's philosophical disadvantage, and our gain.

Notes

1. Allan Bloom, *The Closing of the American Mind* (New York: Simon & Schuster, 1987).
   2. Ibid., 148.
   3. Ibid., 206.
   4. Ibid., 207.
   5. Ibid., 148.
   6. Ibid., 153.
   7. Ibid., 143.
   8. *On the Genealogy of Morals* II:24.
   9. Bloom, 143.
   10. Ibid., 202.
   11. Ibid.
   12. Ibid., 307.
   13. Ibid., 207.
   14. Ibid., 143.
   15. Ibid., 202.
   16. Ibid., 226.

CHAPTER TWO

Nietzsche and Nihilism: Nietzsche and Danto's Nietzsche

Was Nietzsche a nihilist? It is widely thought that he was; and Arthur Danto, in his book *Nietzsche as Philosopher,*[1] subscribes wholeheartedly to this view. Indeed, Danto claims that "Nihilism" is "the central concept of his philosophy."[2] He attributes to Nietzsche "a deep and total Nihilism"[3] — one which "is not an ideology but a metaphysics."[4] Nietzsche, he states, makes "unbridled claims in behalf of this extreme Nihilism";[5] and he asserts that "Nietzsche's philosophy is a sustained attempt to work out the reasons for and the consequences of Nihilism."[6] In short, according to Danto, "Nietzsche's is a philosophy of Nihilism."[7]

Is Danto right? There are several ways in which one might attempt to answer this question. First, one might examine Nietzsche's own assertions about the nature of nihilism, and see whether he explicitly subscribes to it as he himself conceives it. Second, one might consider the way in which "nihilism" as a philosophical doctrine is standardly defined, and then determine whether or not the definition is applicable to Nietzsche's philosophical views. "Nihilism" in the philosophical sense of the term may be defined either as the doctrine that nothing true can be said about reality, or (more narrowly) as the doctrine that there are no objectively valid axiological principles. Nietzsche might thus legitimately be termed a "nihilist" if it were the case that he subscribes to either (or both) of these doctrines (Danto claims that he subscribes to both).

It is my contention that, whichever way one chooses to approach the question, the answer is that Danto is wrong; and that Nietzsche (or, at any rate, the mature Nietzsche, i.e., from *Zarathustra* — 1883 — onward) was not a nihilist, either as he himself conceives of "nihilism," or in either of the senses of the term mentioned above. I shall attempt to show this, first by considering what he himself has to say about nihilism, and then by showing that his actual views are such that the term "nihilism" cannot be applied to them in either of the senses indicated.

1

"At times," Danto says, Nietzsche "spoke of his philosophy as Nihilism."[8] Is this true? And is it true, moreover, that Nietzsche makes "unbridled claims in behalf of this extreme Nihilism"?[9] Nietzsche does say: "it is the measure of strength to what extent we can admit to ourselves, without perishing, the merely *apparent* character [of things], the necessity of lies. To this extent, nihilism, as the denial of a truthful world, of being, might be a divine way of thinking" (WP 15). He does say that "Nihilism . . . can be a sign of strength: the spirit may have grown so strong that previous goals . . . have become incommensurate" (WP 23). He does speak of "nihilism as the necessary consequence of our valuations so far" (WP 69n). He does say that "It could be the sign of a crucial and most essential growth . . . that the most extreme form of pessimism, genuine *nihilism,* would come into the world" (WP 112). He does say, in a note of 1887, "That I have hitherto been a thorough-going nihilist, I have admitted to myself only recently" (WP 25). And, in a passage intended to serve as the preface to a work he planned to entitle *The Will to Power,* he does refer to himself as "the first perfect nihilist of Europe" (WP P:3).

But can these passages support the weight of Danto's claims? Two facts ought to give one pause at once. First, these passages are very nearly the only ones in the entire corpus of Nietzsche's writings that could be cited in direct support of these claims. And second, all of these passages are taken from Nietzsche's notebooks, which he himself never published. In his published writings, he never refers either to himself as a "nihilist," or to his philosophy as "nihilism." In *Ecce Homo,* in which he is nothing if not candid about himself, he refers to himself not as a "nihilist" but as an "immoralist"—an expression that itself actually applies to him only in a restricted sense, since he does not repudiate all forms of morality, but rather only certain ones, associated primarily with the Judeo-Christian tradition.

Further, even in the passages cited above, he may scarcely be said to make "unbridled claims" on behalf of "extreme Nihilism." On the contrary, most of them either are quite tentative or are qualified by subsequent remarks. In the last passage cited, for example, after referring to himself as "the first perfect nihilist of Europe," he goes on to refer to himself as one "who, however, has even now lived through the whole of nihilism, to the end, leaving it behind, outside himself" (WP P:3). And he immediately proceeds to characterize the relation of his philosophy to nihilism as follows: "For one should make no mistake about the meaning of the title that this gospel of the future wants to bear, '*The Will to Power:* Attempt at a Revaluation of All Values'—in this formulation a *countermovement* finds expression, regarding both principle and task: a movement that in some future will *take the place of* this perfect nihilism" (WP P:3: emphasis added).

Finally, in the earlier note of 1887, Nietzsche does not assert that he *is* a nihilist, but rather only that he has "hitherto been" one (WP 25). And, while this consideration does not rule out the possibility that he *might* still have thought himself to be one, his wording provides little support for this interpretation; indeed, it would seem to weigh against it. (He does *not* say, "That I *am* a thoroughgoing nihilist.")

Thus the case for the mature Nietzsche's having conceived his position as one of nihilism is weak, to say the least, even if one considers only those passages that provide the strongest support for it. It becomes completely untenable, however, when one considers the sustained critical analysis to which "nihilism" is subjected in the large body of notes that make up the first book of *The Will to Power*. It is to this analysis that I now shall turn.

Consider, first, the following remarks: "A nihilist is a man who judges of the world as it is that it ought *not* to be, and of the world as it ought to be that it does not exist" (WP 585A). Again: "Nihilism represents a pathological transitional stage (what is pathological is the tremendous generalization, the inference that there is no meaning at all)" (WP 13). Again: "It is in one particular interpretation, the Christian-moral one, that nihilism is rooted" (WP 1). Again: "The nihilistic movement is merely the expression of physiological decadence" (WP 38). Again: "We can abolish either our reverence [for traditional values] or ourselves. The latter constitutes nihilism" (WP 69n). Again: "The belief in . . . aim and meaninglessness, is the psychologically necessary effect once the belief in God and an essentially moral order becomes untenable. Nihilism appears at that point. . . . One interpretation has collapsed; but because it was considered *the* interpretation, it now *seems as if* there were no meaning in existence at all" (WP 55: second emphasis added).

And from Nietzsche's published writings: "there may actually be puritanical fanatics of conscience who prefer even a certain nothing to an uncertain something to lie down on — and die. But this is nihilism and the sign of a despairing, mortally weary soul" (BGE 10). Again: "Some have dared to call pity a virtue. . . . To be sure — and one should always keep this in mind — this was done by a philosophy that was nihilistic and had inscribed *negation of life* upon its shield" (A 7). Again: "Nihilism and Christianity: that rhymes, that does not only rhyme" (A 58). And finally:

This man of the future, who will redeem us not only from the hitherto reigning ideal [i.e., Christianity] but also from that which was bound to grow out of it, the great nausea, the will to nothingness, nihilism; this bell-stroke of noon and of the great decision that liberates the will again and restores its goal to the earth and his hope to man; this antichrist and antinihilist; this victor over God and nothingness—*he must come one day.* (GM II:24).

In the light of these and other similar passages, it is difficult indeed to see how anyone could conclude that Nietzsche considered himself a nihilist. For in them nihilism is regarded as a phenomenon deriving from and related to others that he associates with "decadence," and also as a danger, against which he directly and strongly reacts, and which he considers it imperative to overcome. What requires explanation is: given that these passages express his basic stance in relation to nihilism, how is one to understand those of his other remarks pertaining to nihilism that have led Danto and others to conclude that he embraced it? In some of these remarks, he attempts to show that "the advent of nihilism" is at hand, and is indeed inevitable, and to explain why. In others he suggests that while it may prove disastrous, its advent may also in certain circumstances be a good sign; and to this extent, he regards it positively. In neither case, however, do his remarks imply an unqualified affirmation of nihilism, which would conflict with the attitude expressed in the passages cited above.

"Nihilism," Nietzsche says, "stands at the door" (WP 1). The advent of nihilism is inevitable. What is this nihilism of which he speaks? "What does nihilism mean? *That the highest values devaluate themselves"* (WP 2). *"Radical nihilism* is the conviction of [the] absolute untenability of existence when it comes to the highest values one recognizes" (WP 3). Why is the advent of nihilism held to be inevitable? Because "We have measured the value of the world according to categories that refer to a purely fictitious world" (WP 12B). When this is recognized—as it is coming to be—the world will appear valueless and meaningless to those who cannot conceive of its value and meaning in any other terms. When it is recognized that the world cannot be understood in terms of the categories that traditionally have been applied to it, those who cannot conceive of it in any other terms will despair of being able to comprehend it at all. This is only natural; indeed, according to Nietzsche, it is psychologically unavoidable. And those in question include all of us—not excepting Nietzsche himself—at least for a time. "The categories 'aim,' 'unity,' 'being' which we used to project some value into the world—we *pull out* again; so the world looks valueless" (WP 12A).

The world *looks* valueless. But that does not mean that it *is* valueless, and is essentially incomprehensible. With the collapse of our traditional world view, a period of nihilism must follow. But that is not, for Nietzsche, the end of the line. "The universe seems to have lost value, seems 'meaningless'—but that is only a *transitional stage*" (WP 7). For it is not the intrinsic meaninglessness and incomprehensibility of the world itself that he holds to be the source of the coming nihilism. Rather, its source is held to be the collapse of an (erroneous) *interpretation of* the world: "It is in one particular interpretation, the Christian-moral one, that nihilism is rooted" (WP 1). Nietzsche goes on to observe that "the untenability of one interpretation... awakens the suspicion that *all* interpretations of the world are false" (ibid.). Nihilists, after all, do not stop with a repudiation of the previously accepted interpretation of the world; they generalize, denying the possibility of any alternative. This generalization, however, is not only not logically warranted, but is also, according to Nietzsche, "pathological"; nihilism, on his view, is not simply a transitional stage, but moreover "a pathological transitional stage (what is pathological is the tremendous generalization, the inference that there is no meaning at all)" (WP 13).

Of course, the logical illegitimacy of the generalization by itself does not serve to establish that some other interpretation of the world is in fact either possible or correct; and it remains to be seen what Nietzsche intends to propose along these lines. But it should be clear that in his prophecy and explanation of the advent of a period of nihilism he does not commit himself to the position that nihilism is a doctrine that is both final and correct.

Given that Nietzsche holds a period of nihilism to be inevitable following the collapse of "the Christian-moral" interpretation of the world, the question arises of his attitude toward it. The answer to this question is twofold, because his attitude toward it depends on whether it has the character of epilogue or prologue. He considers it necessary to distinguish between two types of nihilism, only one of which is transitional in a positive direction. It, however, is held not to be the "expression" of "decadence," as the other is, but rather a symptom of the fact that the fictions of the traditional world view are no longer *needed:* "Nihilism ...can be a sign of strength: the spirit may have grown so strong that previous goals... have become incommensurate" (WP 23). Thus Nietzsche writes: "Nihilism: It is *ambiguous:* A. Nihilism as a sign of increased power of the spirit: as *active* nihilism. B. Nihilism as decline and recession of the power of the spirit: as *passive* nihilism" (WP 22).

Nietzsche is profoundly contemptuous of nihilism of the latter sort; as, for example, in the note: "*The perfect nihilist.* —The nihilist's eye idealizes in the direction of ugliness" (WP 21). Still, it deeply worries him. He thinks of "the nihilistic catastrophe that finishes Indian culture" (WP 64);

and fears that a similar fate may be in store for the West. So, for example, in the paragraph in which he speaks of "the advent of nihilism," he states: "For some time now, our whole European culture has been moving as toward a catastrophe" (WP P:2). And, in the Preface he added to *On the Genealogy of Morals,* he says: "I understood the ever spreading morality of pity . . . as the most sinister symptom of a European culture that had itself become sinister, perhaps as its by-pass to a new Buddhism? to a Buddhism for Europeans? to—nihilism?" (GM P:5).

Nietzsche's attitude toward nihilism of the former sort, on the other hand, is quite different. He says: "It could be the sign of a crucial and most essential growth, of the transition to new conditions of existence, that the most extreme form of pessimism, genuine *nihilism,* would come into the world" (WP 112). For this reason, he does not view "the advent of nihilism" as an unmitigated disaster. It must come, as the traditional world view must go, if a new world view is to take its place; and the fact that it is coming may be due at least in part to the fact that some feel strong enough to try to do without the traditional world view.

Still, Nietzsche considers "nihilism as the necessary consequence of our valuations so far" to be *"the danger of dangers"* (WP 69n). And he regards it as "the danger of dangers" because he holds that no one can do without *any* world view indefinitely. Unless we are able to achieve a new world view in relation to which we may orient ourselves—one that is more tenable than the traditional one—even the strongest will not be able to endure. "The time has come," he writes, "when we have to pay for having been Christians for two thousand years: we are losing the center of gravity by virtue of which we have lived; we are lost for a while" (WP 30). The question is: are we to remain lost, or can we find a *new* "center of gravity"?

Faced with the advent of nihilism, this question profoundly worried Nietzsche; and his great anxiety in the face of the former possibility was the source of the urgency with which he attempted to realize the latter. He felt it to be imperative, if at all possible, not merely to avoid "passive nihilism," but moreover to go beyond the stage of "active nihilism" that must be expected to follow the demise of the traditional world view, "leaving it behind" (WP P:3) in favor of "a countermovement . . . [that] will take the place of this perfect nihilism." And in fact he holds not only that this *is* possible, but moreover that in his philosophy—and more specifically, in his conception of "the will to power"—this "counter-movement finds expression" (WP P:4).

While Nietzsche does see something positive in one type of nihilism, therefore, he is far from embracing it unreservedly and unconditionally. He does at times speak highly of it in *The Will to Power*—as, for

example, when he says that it can take the form of a courageous denial of
the existence of any "true world" apart from this one; and that "To this
extent, nihilism . . . might be a divine way of thinking" (WP 15). But he
qualifies his approval even as he gives it, with the words "to this extent."
A nihilism of strength compares favorably in his eyes with the blind
acceptance of what he regards as the lies and deceptions associated with
the traditional world view. Further, it constitutes progress; it is a step in
the right direction, in relation to the traditional world view. But it is *only*
that; *only* a "transitional stage." Nietzsche himself does not want to stop
there, with a No to traditional morals and values and a denial of traditional metaphysics; and he is anxious that *we* do not stop there either. He
wants us to see that they are untenable, and that they are going to have to
be abandoned, whether we like it or not. But he is just as concerned—
indeed, more so—that something else should take their place. "My style,"
he says, "is *affirmative,* and deals with contradiction and criticism only as
a means" (TI VIII:6).[10]

2

It remains to be determined, however, whether or not the affirma-
tions Nietzsche makes are sufficient to refute the claim that he *in fact*
was a nihilist. For, to be sure, it does not refute *this* claim simply to
show that he did not consider himself to be one, and that he regarded
his philosophy as a "countermovement" to nihilism, which went beyond
it. I shall now attempt to show that this claim too is wrong; and that
Nietzsche does not hold, as Danto contends he does, that "there is
nothing about reality to be said (or, about reality, there is only *that*
to be said)."[11] I shall argue that, on the contrary, he holds that there
are positive general truths, both about the nature of reality and in the
matter of value, which can be stated, and which ought to be recognized,
at least by those who are strong enough to live with an awareness
of them.

Nietzsche's views on these matters do entail a rejection of the basic
tenets of most traditional metaphysical and axiological systems; but they
are of such a nature that he could be termed a nihilist only if it were to be
arbitrarily stipulated that everyone is a nihilist who is not a Platonist, a
Christian, a Rationalist, or an adherent of some other such traditional
philosophical or religious world view. If, on the other hand, nihilism is
understood—I believe it should be—to involve the claim that neither the
world nor values are such that anything both positive and objectively true
may be said about them, then Nietzsche most emphatically is *not* a
nihilist. In support of this contention, I shall first consider some of his

basic views about reality generally, and about human nature; and then some of his main points concerning axiological matters.

According to Danto, "if we take 'true' in [the] conventional sense of expressing what is the case," then it is Nietzsche's position that "nothing is true and everything is false."[12] He takes Nietzsche to be saying that men have not discovered "the truth" about the world, not because anything has kept them from it, but rather because "there is none to discover."[13] Consider, however, the following passages from *Ecce Homo:* " 'We strive for the forbidden': in this sign my philosophy will triumph one day, for what one has forbidden so far as a matter of principle has always been—truth alone" (EH P:3). Again: "I was the first to *discover* the truth by being the first to experience lies as lies" (EH IV:1). Again: "the truth speaks out of me.—But my truth is *terrible;* for so far one has called *lies* truth" (EH IV:1). Again: "How much truth [can] a spirit *endure,* how much truth does it *dare?* More and more that became for me the real measure of value" (EH P:3; cf. BGE 39).

In *Ecce Homo,* Nietzsche also frequently speaks of "truth" in connection with both the person and the message of his Zarathustra. He refers to his work, *Thus Spoke Zarathustra,* as "born out of the innermost wealth of truth" (EH P:4). "Zarathustra," he says, "is more truthful than any other thinker. His doctrine, and his alone, posits truthfulness as the highest virtue; this means the opposite of the cowardice of the 'idealist' who flees from reality" (EH IV:3). And he writes: "what Zarathustra wants: this type of man that he conceives, conceives reality *as it is,* being strong enough to do so" (EH IV:5). Innumerable similar passages could be cited, from this and other published works, as well as from his notebooks. They clearly indicate that, far from holding that "nothing is true," Nietzsche in fact holds that there *is* such a thing as "truth"—truth about the nature of things and ourselves; and not only that it *may* be discovered, but moreover that it *has* been discovered, and that he himself has discovered it (or elements of it). But what is it that he has discovered, which he refers to repeatedly as "the truth"?

Many things, of course; but most importantly, in his eyes, one thing in particular. In the last lines of the last note in *The Will to Power,* he states his fundamental "discovery" and his most profound interpretive "truth" as follows: "*This world is the will to power—and nothing besides!* And you yourselves are also this will to power—and nothing besides!" (WP 1067). Nietzsche is by no means prepared to regard his conception of the world as "will to power" as merely one more world interpretation alongside others—the Platonic, the Christian, the Kantian, the Hegelian, the mechanistic, and so on—that is no less but also no more ultimately sound than they are. On the contrary, he argues at length that each of the others is *false;* and he further argues at length that his is *true.* In *Beyond Good and Evil,* for example, it is set forth, not as a poetic vision, but rather as a serious hypothesis, the validity of which is to be determined by its explanatory power. "Suppose," he says,

> we succeeded in explaining our entire instinctive life as the develop-ment and ramification of *one* basic form of the will—namely, of the will to power, as *my* proposition has it; suppose all organic func-tions could be traced back to this will to power and one could also find in it the solution of the problem of procreation and nourish-ment ... then one would have gained the right to determine *all* efficient force univocally as—*will to power.* The world viewed from inside, the world defined and determined according to its 'intelligible character'—it would be 'will to power' and nothing else. (BGE 36)

In this passage the matter is stated hypothetically; but it is quite clear, from other passages in this work and elsewhere, that Nietzsche is quite convinced of the truth of his hypothesis. "Life itself," he states categorically elsewhere in the same book, "is will to power" (BGE 13; also 259). And, in a note in *The Will to Power:* "But *what is life?* Here we need a new, more definite formulation of the concept of 'life'. My formula for it is: Life is will to power" (WP 254). All of the phenomena associated with life, according to Nietzsche, from the "lowest" to the "highest," are to be understood in these terms. "In the case of an animal," he says, "it is possible to trace all its drives to the will to power; likewise all the functions of organic life to this one source" (WP 619; see also 658).

Nietzsche also extends the application of this concept beyond the phenomena associated with life. "Life," he states, "is merely a special case of the will to power" (WP 692). He refers to the "will to power" as that "in which I recognize the ultimate ground and character of all change" (WP 685). "The victorious concept 'force'," he says, in terms of which science has come to understand all things, "still needs to be completed: an inner will must be ascribed to it, which I designate as 'will to power'" (WP 619). He even goes so far as to say that "the innermost essence of being is will to power" (WP 693). These and other similar passages suggest that Nietzsche is committed to a definite if rather unorthodox world interpretation; and that he intends his statements of it to be taken, not as false, but as true—and as true not merely in a relative or perspectival sense, but as true in the sense of being fairly accurate and adequate expressions of the way the world really is.

He further holds a number of other, though related, cosmological propositions to be true. The one for which he is perhaps best known is the proposition that all events recur eternally. Even Danto is compelled to admit that Nietzsche commits himself to the truth of his doctrine of the eternal recurrence of the same events. At times, to be sure, he seems less concerned with the truth of the doctrine than with the cultivation of an affirmative attitude toward life so great that one not only could *endure* the thought of an eternal recurrence of the same series of events that has produced and is the existing world, but moreover could *desire* such a recurrence. To *will* the eternal recurrence of the same events is for Nietzsche the ultimate expression of an affirmative attitude toward life. So, for example, in *Beyond Good and Evil,* he puts forward "the ideal of the most high-spirited, alive, and world-affirming human being who has not only come to terms and learned to get along with whatever was and is, but who wants to have *what was and is* repeated into all eternity" (BGE 56).[14]

At other times, however, that with which Nietzsche is concerned is the demonstration of the *truth* of the proposition that the same series of events that has occurred must recur eternally. And that he should have both concerns is not unreasonable. After all, there is nothing self-contradictory in both maintaining the truth of a doctrine and desiring that people should have an attitude toward life so positive that they can embrace it gladly. Indeed, once Nietzsche became convinced of its truth it is only reasonable that he should have become all the more concerned with the problem of our responses to the idea of eternal recurrence, and that he should have continued to regard one's reaction to the idea as a decisive test of one's attitude toward life; for he knew, from personal experience, that the idea could appear terrible indeed. In moments of pessimism and weakness he found the idea unendurable; while in moments of exuberance and strength, he embraced it enthusiastically. And this suggested to him both that he himself was still "human-all-too-human," and what a better man than himself would in part be like. He undoubtedly had the doctrine of eternal recurrence in mind when he wrote the passage in which he asks: "How much truth [can] a spirit *endure,* how much truth does it dare?" (EH P:3).

That Nietzsche does hold this doctrine to be true is clear. One of the notes in *The Will to Power* consists of an outline of a projected discussion of it, which reads, in part, "*The eternal recurrence.* . . . 1. Presentation of the doctrine and its *theoretical* presuppositions and consequences. 2. Proof of the doctrine" (WP 1057). He never completed, let alone published, the systematic discussion he here contemplates; but his basic line of reasoning is indicated clearly enough in a number of other notes in *The Will to Power.* In one he states: "The law of the conservation of energy demands *eternal recurrence*" (WP 1063). In another: "Our presuppositions: no God; no purpose; finite force" (WP 595). Nietzsche does not think it necessary to argue for the first of these "presuppositions." He spells out and argues for the second as follows: "If the world had a goal, it must [already] have been reached. If there were for it some unintended final state, this also must have been reached" (WP 1062). He takes it to be obvious, however, that no such goal or final state *has* been reached. This argument itself presupposes, first, that an infinite time has preceded the present moment—a presupposition Nietzsche considers incontrovertible; and second, the third of the presuppositions cited above—"finite force"— about which he says: "The world, as force, may not be thought of as unlimited, for it *cannot* be so thought of; we forbid ourselves the concept of an infinite force as incompatible with the concept 'force'" (WP 1062). Assuming the validity of these presuppositions, Nietzsche thus states his argument for the truth of the doctrine of eternal recurrence as follows:

> If the world may be thought of as a certain definite quantity of force and as a certain definite number of centers of force—and every other representation [of it] remains indefinite and therefore useless—it follows that, in the great dice game of existence, it must pass through a calculable number of combinations. In infinite time, every possible combination would at some time or another be realized an infinite number of times. And since between every combination and its next recurrence all other possible combinations would have to take place, and each of these combinations conditions the entire sequence of combinations in the same series, a circular movement of absolutely identical series is thus demonstrated: the world as a circular movement that has already repeated itself infinitely often and plays its game *in infinitum.* (WP 1066)

Now, it is by no means my intention to argue for the validity either of Nietzsche's presuppositions or of his reasoning from them; on the contrary, I would argue that several of his presuppositions are in fact questionable at best, and that his reasoning is fallacious. I would only contend that these passages clearly show him to have been convinced of the truth of the doctrine of eternal recurrence and of its demonstrability; and that this provides a further illustration of the fact that, whatever the merit of the specific positions he takes may be, his philosophy cannot be considered *nihilistic* in the sense under consideration.

Innumerable other illustrations of this fact may be found in his extensive discussions of the many more specific phenomena to which he directs his attention, both in his published writings and in the notes that make up *The Will to Power.* I shall not develop any others at length; but perhaps it would be well to cite a few, simply in order to indicate some of the other matters about which he considers it possible to discover and state facts and truths, and to uncover and refute illusions and falsehoods.

First, on life and living things: "Physiologists should think before putting down the instinct of self-preservation as the cardinal instinct of an organic being. A living thing seeks above all to *discharge* its strength — life itself is *will to power;* self-preservation is only one of the indirect and most frequent *results*" (BGE 13). Again: "The influence of 'external circumstances' is overestimated by Darwin to a ridiculous extent: the essential thing in the life process is precisely the tremendous shaping, form-creating force working from within which *utilizes* and *exploits* 'external circumstances' " (WP 647). And: "A *species* comes to be, a type becomes fixed and strong, through the long fight with essentially constant *unfavorable* conditions" (BGE 262). And finally:

> Life itself is *essentially* appropriation, injury, overpowering of what is alien and weaker; suppression, hardness, imposition of one's own forms, incorporation and at least, at its mildest, exploitation. . . . 'Exploitation' does not belong to a corrupt or imperfect society; it belongs to the *essence* of what lives, as a basic organic function; it is a consequence of the will to power, which is after all the will of life. . . . If this should be an innovation as a theory — as a reality it is the *primordial fact* of all history: people ought to be honest with themselves at least that far. (BGE 259)

Next, on ourselves: "In man *creature* and *creator* are united: in man there is material, fragment, excess, clay, dirt, nonsense, chaos; but in man there is also creator, formgiver, hammer hardness, spectator divinity, and seventh day: do you understand this contrast?" (BGE 225). And: "man is the *as yet undetermined* animal" (BGE 62). Again: "I distinguish between a type of ascending life and another type of decay, disintegration, weakness" (WP 857). And: "What determines rank, sets off rank, is only quanta of power, and nothing else" (WP 855). Again: "For it is our energy that disposes of us; and the wretched spiritual game of goals and intentions and motives is only a foreground — even though weak eyes may take them for the matter itself" (WP 995). And: "All 'purposes,' 'aims,' 'meaning' are only modes of expression and metamorphoses of one will that is inherent in all events: the will to power" (WP 675).

Further: "We think that . . . everything evil, terrible, tyrannical in man, everything in him that is kin to beasts of prey and serpents, serves the enhancement of the species 'man' as much as its opposite does. Indeed, we do not even say enough when we say only that much" (BGE 44). In this connection Nietzsche says, "today's ears resist such truths" (BGE 202); and he speaks of the emergence of a new breed of "investigators and microscopists of the soul" — of whom he considered himself to be the first — "who have trained themselves to sacrifice all desirability to truth, *every* truth, even plain, harsh, ugly, repellent, unchristian, immoral truth.—For such truths do exist" (GM I:1).

When one considers passages such as these, and Nietzsche's many other substantive assertions and denials in connection with issues in philosophical psychology and the philosophy of mind, and on such matters as the nature and origin of conventional morality, religious belief, and social and political institutions, it is difficult to believe that Danto is talking about the same person when he attributes to Nietzsche the view that, "if we take 'true' in [the] conventional sense of expressing what is the case," then "nothing is true and everything is false."[15] These passages make it quite evident that Nietzsche does *not* hold this view. If, therefore, a nihilist is one who takes this position, then Nietzsche clearly is not a nihilist.

At this point one might begin to wonder what possibly could have led Danto and others to attribute this position to Nietzsche. The reason would appear to be that Nietzsche does say some things that might *seem* to warrant this attribution, which commentators like Danto have seized upon and have used to support their interpretation of him. In fact, however, Nietzsche does not mean what they have taken him to mean when he says these things; and, consequently, their interpretation of him is based on a misconstrual of his actual points. For example (and most importantly, for present purposes): Nietzsche says, quite a number of times, both in his published writings and in his unpublished notes, that there is no "true world" in connection with which the term "truth" has an application (which application moreover has often been held to be its only proper philosophical one). In saying this, however, he does *not* mean that it is meaningless to speak of "reality" at all, or that nothing true can be said about it. Rather, what he means is that there is no world or reality or realm that *transcends* that in which we live, and with reference to which *this* world is unreal, illusory, a mere appearance, or merely phenomenal.

Philosophers and religious thinkers throughout history, according to Nietzsche, have been led, by their distaste for the conditions of life and their longing for stability and order, to invent the idea of a world other than this one that is more conformable to their desires; and to assert that this other world is the *true* or *real* world. Further, in their hands "truth" has come to be understood in such a way that it has application only to such a world, or only under conditions that could not obtain except in such a world. And since, by traditional metaphysical and theological convention, the expressions "true world" and "truth" have become associated with this "other world," one of the ways in which Nietzsche felt it appropriate to deny the existence of such an "other world" was to assert that there is no "true world," and thus no "truth"—*in this sense.* But *only* in this sense; and the fact that Nietzsche intends his denial of the existence of a "true world" and of "truth" to be understood as subject to this restriction is to be seen in the fact that he usually either places the expressions in scare-quotes, italicizes them, or else links them explicitly with such expressions as "other world," "thing-in-itself," "world of forms," and "metaphysical world" (the last mentioned referring to what is represented as "reality" in traditional metaphysical systems).

His denial of the existence of a "true world" and of "truth" in this sense, however, is by no means tantamount to the assertion that it is meaningless to speak about "reality" at all, or that there are no fundamental truths about reality that may be discovered and expressed. In *Twilight of the Idols,* for example, Nietzsche writes: "*First proposition.* The reasons for which 'this' world has been characterized as 'apparent' are the very reasons which indicate its reality; any other kind of reality is absolutely indemonstrable. *Second proposition* . . . : the 'true world' has been constructed out of contradiction to the actual world" (TI III:6). And, at the conclusion of the section that follows, entitled "How the 'True World' Finally Became a Fable," he states: "The true world—we have abolished. What world has remained? The apparent one perhaps? But no! *With the true world we have also abolished the apparent one"* (TI IV). That is, with the abolition of the idea of a "true world" apart from the actual world, the actual world ceases to seem merely to be an apparent world, and comes to be recognized as reality; for it was only by contrast to the fictitious other world that was regarded as the "true world" that the actual world was taken to be merely apparent.

Nietzsche recognizes that nihilism is the natural first response to the discovery that the "true world" of traditional theology and metaphysics is a mere fiction: "the untenability of one interpretation of the world, upon which a tremendous amount of energy has been lavished, awakens the suspicion that *all* interpretations are false" (WP 1). It "awakens the suspicion"—but does it *follow* that "*all* interpretations are false"? Obviously not. And, more important for present purposes, is it Nietzsche's conclusion that it follows? Clearly, no. In this same note, he speaks of the "rebound from 'God is truth' to the fanatical faith 'All is false' "—a "fanatical faith" that Danto seems to think Nietzsche shares, but that it should be obvious he does not from the very way in which he refers to it. And, if that is not decisive, his attempt to establish that reality can and should be understood in terms of the concept of "the will to power" is.

In short, Nietzsche can be considered a metaphysical nihilist only if his remarks about the untenability of conceptions of "the true world" of the sort associated with traditional theology and metaphysics are taken to apply to all possible interpretations of the world, his own included; and only if he is held not to have gone beyond the nihilistic reaction that he describes as the "rebound" or natural initial response to the discovery of the untenability of these traditional conceptions and world views. It seems to me, however, that to understand him in this way is to misunderstand him completely; and that the passages cited in this section demonstrate this conclusively.

3

To show that Nietzsche is not a metaphysical nihilist, of course, is not to show that he is not an axiological nihilist; for one who cannot be considered a nihilist with reference to his views on the nature of reality might nonetheless quite consistently hold that there is no objective basis in reality for value determinations. The question therefore arises: Is Nietzsche a nihilist in the latter respect? Danto claims he is, asserting that it is "Nietzsche's view" that "values have no more application to the world than weights do to numbers."[16] And, on this point, the consensus of popular opinion is if anything more strongly behind Danto than on the previous one.

In the light of the foregoing, Danto's argument for this conclusion has little force; for it consists, in effect, in merely pointing out that if Nietzsche is a metaphysical nihilist, he must a fortiori be a nihilist with reference to values. If nothing true can be said about reality, then obviously there can be no substantive and positive assertions pertaining to values that have an objective basis in reality. Danto's reasoning is sound; but since, as I believe I have shown, his major premise is false, his argument does not establish his conclusion. Of course, the falsity of his major premise does not suffice to establish the contrary conclusion; the matter must be settled by looking at what Nietzsche actually has to say about value. I would contend, however, that Danto is wrong here too; and that Nietzsche is no more an axiological nihilist than he is a metaphysical nihilist.

It must be admitted at the outset that Nietzsche does frequently characterize himself as an "immoralist"; that he openly declares war on what he often simply terms "morality" and "the moral interpretation of the world"; and that he denies the existence of any divinely ordained moral principles or self-contained "moral facts." Yet it does not follow from this that he therefore holds all values to be completely conventional and without objective basis in reality. Indeed, a quite different conclusion is suggested by such remarks as these: "One has deprived reality of its value, its meaning, its truthfulness, to precisely the extent to which one has mendaciously invented an ideal world" (EH P:2). Again: "to us the democratic movement is . . . a form of the decay, namely the diminution, of man, making him mediocre and lowering his value" (BGE 203). Again: "all . . . ways of thinking that measure the value of things in accordance with *pleasure* and *pain*, which are mere epiphenomena and wholly secondary, are . . . naivetés on which everyone conscious of *creative* powers . . . will look down not without derision, nor without pity" (BGE 225). Again: "my problem . . . : under what conditions did man devise these value judgments good and evil? *and what value do they themselves possess?*" (GM P:3).

Again: "The world does not have the value we thought it had. . . . [But] the world might be far more valuable than we used to believe; . . . and while we thought that we accorded it the highest interpretation, we may not even have given our human existence a moderately fair value" (WP 32). Again: "destruction of the world of being: intermediary period of nihilism: before there is yet present the strength to reverse values and to deify becoming and the apparent world as the only world, and to call them good" (WP 585A). And: "*Fundamental innovations:* In place of 'moral values,' purely naturalistic values" (WP 462). Again, in connection with the idea that all events are transitory: "To me . . . everything seems far too valuable to be so fleeting: I seek an eternity for everything" (WP 1065). And finally, Nietzsche speaks of "a Dionysian value standard for existence" (WP 1041), and says: "Dionysus is a *judge!* —Have I been understood?" (WP 1051).

Unfortunately, Nietzsche has not been understood by all too many writers who—in spite of these and many other similar passages—maintain that he is a nihilist and a complete relativist in the matter of value. In point of fact, he holds that there is a single, ultimate, value standard, by reference to which the value of everything else can and should be determined: namely, the quantitative and qualitative enhancement of life, and in particular, of what he frequently refers to as "the type 'man,' " culminating in the ideal of a "union of spiritual superiority with well-being and an excess of strength" (WP 899). And he further holds that this value standard is grounded in the very nature of things. It is not divinely ordained; but neither is it a mere human convention or invention. It derives directly from a consideration of the very essence of life as Nietzsche conceives it: namely, as "will to power." He writes: "For this is the doctrine preached *by life itself* to all that has life: the morality of development. To have and to want more—*growth*, in one word—that is life itself" (WP 125; emphasis added). And because of the connection Nietzsche envisages between this ultimate value and the essential nature of things, there is, on his view, an objective basis for his particular value determinations. He says: "There is nothing in life that has value, *except the degree of power* — assuming that life itself is the will to power" (WP 55; emphasis added).

Nietzsche thus is far from holding, as Danto says he does, that "values have no more application to the world than weights do to numbers."[17] On the contrary, he holds that the fundamental nature of things and their ultimate value are to be conceived in precisely the same terms; and the values of actions, practices, institutions, and the like are to be determined, on his view, precisely in terms of the extent to which they enhance or detract from the (quantitative and qualitative) degree of power of the beings under consideration — their "quanta of power" being just what they essentially *are* for Nietzsche. He thus is a naturalist in the matter of value, as he himself states he is; but he clearly is no nihilist. Indeed, it is difficult to imagine any stronger version of the thesis that value determinations have an objective basis in reality than his.

On a more general level, there are several basic considerations that ought to suggest, even to the casual reader, that Nietzsche is not an axiological nihilist. The first concerns his program of a "revaluation of values," of which he constantly speaks, and to the implementation of which he devotes a great deal of attention. The point may be stated quite simply. Nietzsche could not have undertaken such a project, or even have conceived it, if he himself did not hold that there is some value standard by reference to which the traditional values he proposes to consider could be "revalued."

He does not propose simply to show that traditional values are nothing more than conventions, with no objective basis in reality. It is not his intention merely to *devalue* these values, while maintaining that there are no others that have been overlooked, which ought to be set in their place. On the contrary, his contention is that certain things have been regarded as absolute values whose *actual* value is only derivative, or even — in some cases — precisely the opposite of what it has been taken to be; and that there *is* an ultimate value, which *ought* to be recognized, by reference to which the *actual* value of these traditional values *can* and *should* be determined. And it is on the basis of this conviction that he proceeds to pose and consider "the problem of the value of truth," in the first part of *Beyond Good and Evil,* and the question of the value of such things as religion, conventional morality, social institutions, knowledge, and art in subsequent writings.

On these issues he states his general point as follows: "Man has repeated the same mistake over and over again: he has made a means to life into a standard of life; instead of discovering the standard in the highest enhancement of life itself" (WP 354). When he speaks of "the highest enhancement of life," once again what he has in mind is: "union of spiritual superiority with well-being and an excess of strength" (WP 899). And with this standard of value in mind he proceeds to assess the actual value of traditional values—and also of men. Thus he says: "If [an individual] represents the ascending course of mankind, then his value is in fact extraordinary. . . . [While] If he represents the descending course, decay, chronic sickening, then he has little value" (WP 373).

The second consideration is even more general. It pertains to Nietzsche's basic concern, which led him to undertake the investigations and to write the things he did; and I would suggest that no one with any feeling for this basic concern of his could possibly consider him a nihilist in the matter of value. Few philosophers have been motivated in their philosophical efforts by a stronger fundamental concern; and few have felt that more depended upon the success of their philosophical enterprises.

It seemed to Nietzsche that humanity as we know it is at the crossroads. The fundamental assumptions about ourselves and the world, associated with our Judeo-Christian-Socratic heritage, which have given structure and meaning to life in the Western world for the past 2500 years, are being called into question. Indeed, they have been undermined by the spirit of truthfulness, which has exposed their foundations and has made them untenable any longer. And Nietzsche felt that unless a new world interpretation was developed, in terms of which life could once again be seen to be meaningful and desirable, the West would go the way of the East, and mankind thus would sink into a degenerate and ultimately moribund condition. He saw Schopenhauer as the first modern European to exhibit and explicitly embrace this latter sort of development; and while Schopenhauer was not taken seriously by most of his contemporaries, Nietzsche regarded him as the herald of things to come, if no one could show any other way.

If Nietzsche had been a nihilist where values are concerned, he should have been content at most simply to describe this situation. For what would it matter to someone if growth and development gave way to stultification and decline, if he held that nothing really had any value anyway? In fact, however, Nietzsche hardly viewed the situation he contemplated with indifference. On the contrary, he viewed it with alarm, at least as great as that with which Plato viewed the collapse of traditional values in the Greece of his day. He sensed impending disaster, and the increasing urgency with which he wrote, and the relentlessness with which he drove himself, were expressions of the intensity of his concern. He did not sit down, in a cool hour, and say to himself: "Values have no more application to the world than weights do to numbers. And now, there is this matter of the enhancement versus the decline of life: shall I simply describe the situation, and let things take the course they appear to be taking? Or shall I take sides, on one side or the other, even though there is really nothing to choose between the two?"

This was not at all the way in which Nietzsche approached the matter. He could allow that weak souls like Schopenhauer will quite naturally find life too disagreeable to be worth living on the only terms it offers them. But he was far from indifferent to the possibility of the whole human race coming to be like Schopenhauer, and of Schopenhauer's ideal of the termination of all life becoming a reality. He was not content simply to observe that the strong will be able to find life endurable and even desirable in spite of its hardships, while the weak will not; and that if no one is strong, then the human race will cease to develop and ultimately to exist. Rather, he held that *this must not happen*; that life ought to flourish, ought to be enhanced, ought to continue to develop; that there ought to be strong, creative types, able to take the hardships of life in their stride; and moreover, that there ought to come to be human beings who are stronger and more creative than any now or previously existing—he himself included. And he did not regard these as his own personal, subjectively determined, objectively groundless imperatives, but rather as imperatives with an objective basis in reality, deriving from "the doctrine preached by life itself to all that has life" (WP 125). The use of the term "objective" in this context is not mine, but his. He writes: "What is the objective measure of value? Solely the quantum of enhanced and organized power" (WP 674).

"Nihilism," in the axiological sense, is characterized by Nietzsche as "the radical repudiation of value, meaning, and desirability" (WP 1). In the same note in which this characterization occurs, he describes his own position as follows: "Against 'meaninglessness' on the one hand, against *moral* value judgments on the other" (WP 1; emphasis added). His formulation of the byword of nihilism is: " 'Everything lacks meaning' " (WP 1). But this byword is certainly not his own. "Now that the shabby origin of [traditional] values is becoming clear," he says, "the universe seems to have lost value, seems 'meaningless'—but that is only a *transitional stage*" (WP 7; Nietzsche's emphasis). His own pronouncement, which he places in the mouth of Zarathustra, is very different: "Behold, I teach you the overman. The overman is the meaning of the earth" (Z P). For Nietzsche, "the earth," and life, *have* a "meaning"—a meaning deriving from the value he takes to be associated with the realization of the ideal of a "union of spiritual superiority with well-being and an excess of strength," the symbol of which is the "overman."

In taking this position, Nietzsche does not consider himself merely to be indicating a personal preference, or giving expression to his own feeling of strength and vitality. He is not saying that he, Friedrich

Nietzsche, has chosen to regard the enhancement of life affirmatively, even though nothing is of any intrinsic value. He is not saying that the "overman" is the meaning of the earth *for him;* but that others, who have conceived its meaning differently, and Schopenhauer, for whom life lacked any positive meaning, have been on equally firm—or weak—ground, since the question of the general validity of such claims does not even arise. Rather, he is saying that Schopenhauer—and Plato, and Christianity, and the rest—have *missed* the *true* meaning of the earth; just as they have missed the fact that the enhancement of life *is* an ultimate value, and is the only ultimate value that does not rest upon illusion, but rather has an objective foundation, in the nature of life itself. For him, these things are true without qualification, and quite independently of whether Schopenhauer or Plato or St. Paul or most people or even anyone at all would concur. Indeed, he recognizes that these men and most others most definitely do *not* concur; but that, for him, does not count against the truth of his claims, or render them merely subjective and personal.

Here it is illuminating to refer again to *Thus Spoke Zarathustra.* Nietzsche has Zarathustra attempt to *"teach"* men that "the overman is the meaning of the earth." The fact that he calls this a "teaching," and tries to teach it to men, implies that he does not regard it merely as an expression of a purely personal value determination. When he has Zarathustra say to his friends: "This is *my* way; where is yours?" he does not mean this to apply to Zarathustra's basic teaching, but rather to the ways in which particular individuals are to live in light of it. Zarathustra's pronouncements would be absurd, and the work itself would have been an absurdity, if Nietzsche had not been convinced that it *mattered* whether or not life flourished and developed. And this could not have mattered to him—as it did, so obviously, and so greatly—if he had felt that the world actually is utterly devoid of meaning, and that there is nothing more to be said for the ultimate value he proposes than there is for the traditional values whose ultimacy and objective validity he denies.

The claim that Nietzsche is an axiological nihilist is thus quite clearly wrong. Like the claim that he is a metaphysical nihilist, it reflects a profound misunderstanding of him. And also like this other claim, the misunderstanding it reflects derives from a misconstrual of a number of things he does say about values and morality.

There are, for example, many passages in his writings that, taken by themselves, would seem to support the view that he is a relativist in the matter of values and holds that all values are merely creations of those whose interests they serve. Nietzsche does frequently speak of changes of values, differences of values, and the "creation of values." For example, he says that the true task of the genuine philosopher "demands that he *create values"* (BGE 211). And he also often says things like, "In valuations are expressed conditions of preservation and growth" (WP 507). But passages like these should not be taken to imply that he holds that even the basic value he affirms, and in terms of which he proposes to "revalue" traditional values, has no objective standing, but rather is merely subjectively determined, reflecting nothing more than his own needs or disposition.

To understand these and other similar passages properly, it is necessary to distinguish between two sorts or orders of values, which Nietzsche treats quite differently. One consists of values that are the creations of particular individuals or groups, whose physiological conditions and natural and social circumstances lead them to esteem certain qualities and to condemn others. These conditions and circumstances vary greatly, and so, consequently, do the valuations to which they give rise. It is values so conceived that Nietzsche has in mind when he discusses those that prevail among the great majority of humankind, on the one hand, and when he urges higher types to create their own values, answering to their own distinctive powers and abilities, on the other.

These values are not thought by Nietzsche to be completely arbitrary or strictly conventional; for he holds that they are strongly correlated with the psychological and ultimately the physiological characteristics of those who affirm them. But he also holds that they are not absolute; that people differ profoundly with regard to the psychological and physiological characteristics to which they are related; and that consequently it is improper to claim universal validity for any set of values that "express conditions of preservation and growth" of one particular individual or group, or to ask which of several competing sets of such values is the "true" or "right" one.

The matter is different, however, with regard to the value by reference to which Nietzsche proposes to carry out his program of a "revaluation of values." This value is one that he regards as objective and ultimate, being grounded in the very nature of things. It is held not to be the value of some particular individual or group, but rather that "preached by life itself to all that has life" (WP 125). It does not "express conditions of preservation and growth" of some one individual or group, but rather pertains to the general *desirability of* "preservation and growth," that is of the quantitative and qualitative enhancement of life, and in particular of "the type 'man,'" conceived in terms of the emergence of a union of the greatest possible physical well-being and strength with the greatest possible spiritual development.

Given this as the ultimate value, and since one person's meat is sometimes another's poison, it follows that different lower-order valuations of various particular things by different types of human beings are entirely in order, and indeed are quite necessary; and that it will further be appropriate for those of exceptional ability to "create" their own particular "values" as a way, and as a means, of enabling themselves — and through them, "the type 'man'" — to attain the highest possible degree of spiritual development. It should thus be clear that this lower-order relativism in the matter of values, upon which Nietzsche insists, is by no means incompatible with the idea of an ultimate and nonrelative standard of value, to which he is equally firmly committed.

There are, to be sure, passages in Nietzsche's writings like the following, from *Twilight of the Idols:* "Judgments, judgments of value, concerning life, for it or against it, can, in the end, never be true; they . . . are worthy of consideration only as symptoms; . . . *the value of life cannot be estimated*" (TI II:2). Passages like this one may seem to pose a serious problem for the interpretation of Nietzsche I am suggesting. It seems to me, however, that they in fact do not. It is quite true that Nietzsche regards judgments about or estimations of the value of life, not as propositions that — at least in principle — might be true, but rather as indications of the sort of stuff the person is made of who makes them. So, for example, in the same section of *Twilight of the Idols,* he observes that, "Concerning life, the wisest men of all ages have judged alike: *it is no good*"; and then says: " 'At least something must be *sick* here,' *we* retort" (TI II:1). And he goes on to suggest that "the great sages are *types of decline*" (TI II:1).

Again, he states, with reference to philosophers according to whom "no ultimate meaning is posited except the appearance of pleasure or displeasure," that "for any healthier kind of man the value of life is certainly not measured by the standard of these trifles" (WP 35). Yet his language in these and other similar passages is significant; for his characterization of certain estimations of the value of life as expressions of "sickness," "decadence," and "decline" certainly suggests that he does not consider them to be on a par with that of "any healthier kind of man." At the very least, the way in which he speaks of them clearly indicates that he thinks there is *something wrong* with them.

However, this does not yet touch the central point, which concerns Nietzsche's meaning in asserting that "the value of life cannot be estimated." In this connection, it is of interest that he goes on to say, "For a philosopher to see a problem in the value of life is thus an objection to him" (TI II:2). I take him to mean that one is mistaken to think that the value of life is *something problematical* — an issue that remains open after the essential nature and conditions of life have been determined, and that is to be resolved by seeing how life fares when measured against a standard of value that has some other derivation. He holds, on the contrary, that the value of life is *not* problematical in this sense. For him, the ultimate standard of value is to be conceived in terms that derive directly from a consideration of the essential nature of life itself; and if the former is given and determined by the latter then the question of the value of life cannot arise and the value of life cannot become a problem. Thus "the value of life cannot be estimated," on his view, not because life is without value, but rather because its essential nature itself determines the ultimate standard of value, and because it itself, in its highest form of development, *is* the ultimate value; and therefore because there is no conceptually distinct value or standard of value in terms of which *its* value can be "estimated."

Similarly, when Nietzsche says that "judgments" concerning the value of life "can . . . never be true," even when they are positive, his point concerns judgments in which life is asserted to be of value *because* it happens to contain certain features to which a conceptually distinct standard of value attributes positive significance. Nietzsche denies that any such judgments are true, because he denies the objective validity of any standard of value of this sort. His contention that life, in its highest form of development, is the ultimate value, on the other hand, is a judgment of a quite different sort—if, indeed, it is even a *judgment* at all. For it does not involve passing judgment upon the extent to which life is capable of satisfying certain antecedently determined conditions, but rather merely accepting it on its own terms, as he understands them.

In short, life, for Nietzsche, is not something the value of which can be judged or determined by reference to any independent criteria. Rather, it is, so to speak, a game, which exists because the world as "will to power" of necessity gives birth to it; in which all of us, however well or poorly we can and do play, are by our very natures engaged; which has rules set not by us, nor by mere chance, but by the essential features of the "will to power" that is constitutive of reality generally; and the very nature of which indicates an ideal that both constitutes the ultimate value and determines the standard of value for everything falling within its compass. When Nietzsche's assertion that "the value of life cannot be estimated" is viewed in this light, it seems to me quite evident that it is not to be construed as a profession of axiological nihilism.

Next, it is necessary to consider Nietzsche's denunciations of what he often refers to simply as "morality" and "the moral interpretation of the world," and his characterization of himself as an "immoralist." These have often been taken to provide a clear indication of the fact that he is a nihilist. In fact, however, this involves a misunderstanding of his meaning, though it is a misunderstanding for which his frequent failure to qualify his use of the terms "moral" and "morality" is partly responsible. Just as, in his denunciations of "metaphysics," what he means to repudiate is those metaphysical systems that traditionally have prevailed in Western thought, rather than the possibility of any metaphysics at all, so also in his denunciations of "morality" what he means to repudiate is those moralities that have prevailed in Western culture up to the present time, rather than morality as such.

Nietzsche is harshly critical of the claims of Christian morality, and more generally, of what he terms "slave" morality or "herd" morality, to absolute and universal validity. He also rejects the similar claims of Plato, Kant, Hegel, and the Utilitarians for their moral theories. He is opposed to so much of what has passed and currently passes for "morality" that he often uses the term descriptively to refer to it, and so refers to himself as an "immoralist." It does not follow, however, that he is opposed to every possible morality in principle. Indeed, the contrary is suggested by the famous passage in which he states that "Beyond Good and Evil ... does *not* mean 'Beyond Good and Bad' " (GM I:17). And it is indicated even more clearly when he states: "*Morality in Europe today is herd animal morality* —in other words, as we understand it, merely *one* type of human morality besides which, before which, and after which many other types, above all *higher* moralities, are, or ought to be, possible" (BGE 202).

Even if Nietzsche is not really an "immoralist" in a strict or absolute sense, however, questions still remain. What, for example, is to be made of his assertion that "there are no moral phenomena at all, but only a moral interpretation of phenomena"? (BGE 108). It might seem to follow from this that Nietzsche holds that there is no objective basis for the assessment of particular moral claims and purported moral principles. In fact, however, all that follows is that Nietzsche rejects the complete *autonomy* of moral principles. That is, he rejects the view that moral principles express a special kind of facts—"moral facts"—that are ultimate in the sense of being independent of facts of any other sort, neither logically presupposing them nor depending upon them in any other way.

It is quite consistent with this position to hold, however, that there *are* moral principles for which there *is* an objective basis, in virtue of their relation to certain *non*moral "facts." And this, I submit, is precisely Nietzsche's position. Certain moral principles, on his view, may be derived from his standard of value, even if they have no objective status independently of it. So, for example, he refers to "the doctrine preached by life itself to all that has life" as "the morality of development" (WP 125).

Nietzsche's morality might fairly be characterized as naturalistic; but naturalism in morality surely is something quite different from nihilism.

Thus he asserts that his "fundamental innovation" in this area is the "Naturalization of morality" (WP 462); and the "naturalization" of morality is by no means equivalent to the complete repudiation of it. Once again, it would be well to recall Nietzsche's exclamation: "Dionysus is a *judge!* —Have I been understood?" (WP 1051). This is not the place to spell out his own morality in detail, but its outlines may be grasped by taking his characterization of it as a "morality of development" together with the statement: "I teach No to all that makes weak—that exhausts. I teach Yes to all that strengthens, that stores up strength" (WP 54). And note well, Nietzsche does not say, "I propose," or "I will," or "I affirm," but—"I *teach.*"

Finally, there is the problem of the interpretation of those passages in which Nietzsche seems to commit himself to a moral relativism. The problem here is similar to that which arises in connection with his apparent commitment to a form of relativism in the matter of values, for he says many of the same sorts of things in this context. For example: "I understand by 'morality' a system of evaluations that partially coincides with the conditions of a creature's life" (WP 256). And he maintains that, since human beings differ radically in terms of what he calls "order of rank," and so have different "conditions of life," a concrete morality that will be appropriate for one sort of human being will differ from that which will be appropriate for another. Thus he says: "Moralities must be forced to bow first of all before the *order of rank*" (BGE 221). And he explicitly denies that he is proposing a single sort of practical morality—a morality of individualism—for adoption by all, saying: "My philosophy aims at an ordering of rank: not at an individualistic morality" (WP 287).

As in the case of his remarks on values, however, no real difficulty is posed by these and similar passages. The solution to the problem they seem to raise once again is to be found by distinguishing between the basic moral principle to which Nietzsche is committed and the differing lower-order "moralities" that are indicated by it when the differing capacities of men are taken into consideration. In brief, Nietzsche's "morality of development" is a consequence of his identification of the greatest possible enhancement of strength and spirituality of "the type 'man'" as the ultimate standard of value. He further holds, however, that human beings are far from equal where the relevant capacities are concerned, and that therefore the enhancement of "the type 'man'" would not be served if all were to live individualistically and self-assertively.

For those who would be unable to endure an existence unstructured by conventions, therefore, and for those whose acts of self-assertion would not be creative, one type of concrete "morality" is indicated. It reflects the only sort of contribution they are capable of making to the enhancement of the "type": namely, what Nietzsche likes to refer to as "herd morality," which corresponds quite closely to prevailing and traditional conventional morality, and the desirability of which he suggests when he says: "A high culture can stand only upon a broad base, upon a strong and healthy consolidated mediocrity" (WP 864). On the other hand, for those who are strong enough to live a life of their own, and who have the capacity to be truly creative, another type of concrete "morality" is indicated. It is an individualistic, self-assertive morality, which reflects the much greater and more direct contribution *they* are capable of making to the enhancement of the "type."

Neither type of "morality" is right or appropriate for all, according to Nietzsche, and neither is wrong or inappropriate for all; but it is important to observe that he further holds that each *is* right for *one* type of human being, and wrong for another. And that this is so is something that is determined by reference to the general "morality of development" to which he is committed, and to the basic standard of value that underlies it. In this way, it is possible for Nietzsche to take a position of moral relativism at one level, while maintaining his commitment to a nonrelative morality at another, more fundamental level.

In short, the widespread view, endorsed by Danto, that Nietzsche is a "nihilist," and that his philosophy is a philosophy of "radical nihilism," is wrong. A careful analysis of his writings shows that he neither considered himself to be a nihilist, nor deserves to be considered one, either metaphysically or axiologically. Far from considering nihilism to be the last word, he actually regards it as a mere "transitional stage," a natural consequence of the discovery of the untenability of certain traditional metaphysical and axiological views—which, however, he himself goes beyond, and to which his own philosophy is a "countermovement." Far from holding that there are no truths about reality that may be discovered and stated, because there is no actual nature of things to discover and describe, he in fact holds the contrary, and has a good deal to say of a substantive nature in this connection. And far from denying objective validity to all value judgments and moral principles as such, he in fact maintains that a certain standard of value and a certain morality have an objective basis in the very nature of things.

To show this, of course, is not at all to show that the substantive positions Nietzsche takes on these matters are correct. I have not been concerned here either to defend or to criticize them, and do not propose to turn to this task now. This task is an important one—much more important, indeed, than that of merely showing that he does take such positions, and what they are. Yet philosophers will not turn to such an undertaking, because they will not even see the need for it, if the erroneous view prevails that Nietzsche is a nihilist, and therefore takes no substantive positions that require evaluation.

Notes

1. Arthur Danto, *Nietzsche as Philosopher* (New York: Macmillan, 1965).
2. Ibid., 22.
3. Ibid., 31.
4. Ibid., 30.
5. Ibid., 33.
6. Ibid., 34.
7. Ibid., 80.
8. Ibid., 22.
9. Ibid., 33.
10. It is interesting to observe that Nietzsche's own understanding of his work, as expressed in this passage, is directly at odds with Danto's contention that: "He was less interested in characterizing the world as it might be in itself than he was in bringing . . . to our attention that what we believe about the world is all wrong. . . . He was less interested in stating what was true than in telling what was false" (98).
11. Ibid., 130.
12. Ibid., 75.
13. Ibid., 93.
14. Indeed, Nietzsche may initially have conceived the significance of the idea of eternal recurrence—and the idea itself—in these terms; that is, as a *test* of the nature of one's attitude toward life. Schopenhauer, in *The World as Will and Representation,* had proposed a similar test: only the result he anticipated is the exact opposite of the one Nietzsche desires. Schopenhauer suggests that one reflect upon the hard facts of life, and upon one's own experience in particular, and then ask oneself which one would choose, if offered a choice between living the same life over again and absolute annihilation; and he contends that "no man, if he be sincere and at the same time in possession of his faculties, will ever wish to go through it again. Rather than this, he will much prefer to choose complete non-existence" (trans. E. F. J. Payne. New York: Dover, 1969. vol. 1, § 59, p. 324).

Nietzsche, who was intimately acquainted with Schopenhauer's work, may initially have intended his affirmation of the idea of eternal recurrence as a response to Schopenhauer, in just the terms Schopenhauer proposes in his test; only he extends them to include not merely the events of his own life but all events that have occurred, and to encompass a recurrence of them not merely once but infinitely many times ("eternally"), to indicate that his response to Schopenhauer's test differs from Schopenhauer's own as radically as possible.

15. Danto, 75.
16. Ibid., 33.
17. Ibid.

CHAPTER THREE

Beyond Nihilism: Nietzsche on Philosophy, Interpretation, and Truth

"Interpretation," according to Nietzsche, has always been the actual — if generally unacknowledged — activity of philosophers and other thinkers, at least to the extent that they have been more than mere philosophical and intellectual "laborers" content to work within and with the framework of interpretations developed by others. And it is his further contention that genuine philosophers — including the "new philosophers" he envisions and calls for — will not and should not abandon interpretation in favor of some more "exact" form of thinking and reasoning, but rather must engage more self-consciously and deliberately and less dogmatically in it. So he characterizes his own philosophical activity as interpretive, despite the fact that this would appear to place his own positions on a par with those he rejects and brands as "lies," "errors," and "fictions." "Supposing that this also is only interpretation — and you will be eager enough to make this objection? — well, so much the better" (BGE 22).

This might lead one to wonder whether, by allowing and indeed insisting that "interpretation" (or more fully, the devising and making of cases for and against various "interpretations") is at the heart of all genuine philosophical activity, Nietzsche does not in fact lower philosophy as he conceives and commends it to the level of the mere mongering of *Weltanschauungen,* thus reducing it to a kind of quasi-literary enterprise of little or no cognitive significance. Some interpreters and many readers have in fact taken this to be precisely his intention, or at any rate the upshot of his treatment of the matter; and they have then proceeded to praise or condemn him, as this conclusion agrees or conflicts with their own sentiments. This is especially common among those inclined to suppose that "interpretation" is a very subjective sort of affair, and that, to the extent that it can be shown to be involved in the development of a position being advanced, its presence undermines any appearance the positions may have of credibility. Once something becomes a matter of one interpretation against another, the idea runs, "it is all relative" —

relative to the feelings and attitudes of those advancing the conflicting interpretations; and thus the discussion has left the ground on which serious argument can alone be based and cognitively significant conclusions reached. *Incipit Zarathustra, exit scientia.*

As I read him, however, this is not at all Nietzsche's view of the matter. "Interpretation" as he understands it is by no means an affair so hopelessly "relative" and "subjective" that to construe philosophical activity in terms of it is tantamount to depriving it of all cognitive import. Indeed, it seems to me that he is on to something important in taking the enterprise of philosophy—properly understood and carried on—to be fundamentally (although perhaps not exclusively) a matter of engaging in the complementary activities of critically examining received or proposed interpretations and developing (and making cases for) others that might improve upon them. And if this is so, the question of what constitutes and counts as a philosophical argument largely becomes the question of what is involved in the establishment of the relative soundness and adequacy of such interpretations.

To be sure, Nietzsche does take the *value* of different interpretations in most human contexts to be primarily a function of considerations of other sorts relating above all to the preservation and enhancement of life. He also suggests that interpretations are of considerable *symptomatic* significance, serving to reveal a great deal about those who advance them. It by no means follows, however, that he holds the relative soundness or tenability of different interpretations to be conceivable only along one or both of these lines. Indeed, an attentive reading of him reveals that he not only allows but moreover insists that some interpretations may be better than others, where "better" is construed not in terms of such cognitively neutral notions as that of "value for life," but rather in terms of soundness and adequacy. This is a matter of considerable importance for the understanding of his entire philosophical enterprise; and so I shall offer some comments upon it, before turning to a fuller characterization of that enterprise as he conceives and engages in it.

1

Can some interpretations conceivably be "better" than others, in the sense of being more illuminating, more adequate, more insightful, and more just than others are? In approaching this question, consider first the "interpretation" of works of art and literature. Here, particularly in the case of the performing arts, it often refers to what performers do with the works being performed—in short, to their adaptions. "Interpretations" of this sort may be considered works of art in their own right, to be evaluated and judged on their own terms, rather than in terms of strict fidelity to a "text" and intentions of its creator. To ask whether one is better than another would thus be to ask something like whether one is aesthetically superior to another. This question, however, is not the sort of question presently under consideration. Nietzsche admittedly does at times suggest that a kind of quasi-aesthetic perspective (from which a premium is placed, e.g., on elegance) is *one* perspective from which the superiority of some "interpretations" to others may be determined—one differing, it may be noted, from that of "value for life." But he quite clearly does not wish to collapse the distinction between truth and beauty (or, more judiciously put, between cognitive and aesthetic significance), as is shown, among other things, by his frequent acknowledgment of the aesthetically repellent features of many matters as he interprets them.

More to the point is another use of "interpretation" in connection with the arts, and also (quite significantly, in view of Nietzsche's training and early career), in philology insofar as it is concerned with the analysis of texts. It refers to the examination of a work with a view to establishing something about its nature that goes beyond the level of what is sufficiently obvious in it to require no comment. Such interpretations, while sometimes offered merely in an attempt to affect the receptivity of others to a work in such a way that they will get something new and different out of their future encounters with it, are often serious attempts to enhance the *understanding* of a work—to show that it has certain features that require to be recognized if one is properly to construe it. Different interpreters, however, will often seize upon different aspects of a work, and sometimes proceed to construe the whole in terms of the part that they have brought to light. And some are only too ready to read their own concerns and commitments into and out of anything that is of interest to others already, thereby to win a wider and more sympathetic audience than they might be able to attract on their own. For these and other such reasons, observers of the fray are commonly inclined to conclude that where interpretations of works of art and literature are concerned, it is pointless to raise the issue of soundness. Interpretations of *Hamlet,* for example, are legion; how could one begin to settle the question of which of them, if any, is to be preferred?

On the other hand, it should be obvious to anyone who has read a fair number of interpretations of such a work that, while none of them may be definitive and completely adequate, some do less justice to the work than others; even though it may be difficult to determine which of several apt and insightful interpretations does more. And this can be so even though there may be important respects in which the work is simply ambiguous, and admits of different "takings" or readings (or "interpretations" in the sense mentioned previously). Indeed, the work may be so constituted as to require – or at least to invite – something of this sort on the part of those who encounter it. And part of what "interpretation" in the sense presently under consideration involves is the ascertainment of the ways and extent to which this sort of thing constitutes part of the nature of the work, when it does.

It further may be that the work has been available and interpreted in various ways for so long that, as Nietzsche remarks with reference to the world we live in, the text has virtually disappeared beneath the interpretations. But it does not follow that nothing on the order of a text remains beneath them – that they as it were float suspended in the void – and that interpretations are all that other interpretations have to deal with, and probe for. It may also be that it is only by developing an interpretation oneself that one can attempt to say anything about a text otherwise interpreted by others. But it does not follow that any new interpretation thus proposed is *merely* "another interpretation," in principle no more adequate to the text than any other. No new interpretation, simply by virtue of its being new (let alone one's own), may legitimately be held superior in point of adequacy or validity to every other; but it cannot be assumed that any standing interpretation, however hallowed by tradition or popular acceptance, is as sound or more so than any other that might be opposed to it could possibly be. There likewise may never be an interpretation of a work so completely adequate to it that the possibility of another more illuminating and doing greater justice to it would be foreclosed. But that does not mean that nothing more is understood of the nature of a work when it is interpreted in one way than when it is interpreted in another.

It is Nietzsche's view that the parallel between this situation and that which obtains in the cases of most other forms of inquiry (philosophy included), while undoubtedly not exact, is at any rate quite close, even though the latter generally do not have to do with things produced as works of art and literature are. Interpretation may quite properly be considered the task of the historian, for example, notwithstanding the fact that it is human events rather than works of this kind with which the historian concerns himself; and the same sorts of remarks would be appropriate in connection with historical interpretation as were made above with respect to the interpretation of such works. Scientific theories too may be considered "interpretations" the status of which is not so radically different from that of literary and historical interpretations as to brook no comparison, despite the evident differences in the relation of the matters with which they respectively deal to the aims and purposes of men. This is a point Nietzsche himself makes much of, insisting that most of what passes for explanation in a science like physics is actually only redescription within an interpretive framework; and that even an idea as basic to it as that of "nature's conformity to law" is "no matter of fact," but rather "is interpretation not text" (BGE 22).

These reflections suggest that many forms of inquiry often taken to be widely disparate in character actually display a kinship—as kinds of interpretation—that is overlooked only at the cost of misunderstanding their actual status and significance, the possible cognitive import of the views advanced by those engaging in them being underestimated in some cases and overestimated in others. And they at least lend greater plausibility to the idea that philosophy may be conceived in terms of "interpretation" without thereby relegating it to the outer darkness of cognitive indifference—analogous to the "night in which all cows are black" disparaged by Hegel—and banishing it from the company of disciplines pursued in sufficient light to render the growth of understanding a possibility.

A different perspective upon what it means (and does not mean) to associate philosophy with the notion of "interpretation" is achieved by considering several of the most important cognitive claims of a *positive* nature of which this association is intended by Nietzsche to be a denial. There are two such claims in particular with which he wishes to take issue; and it is important to see what they are, because they are such strong claims that their rejection, far from stranding one with no coherent alternative position short of a nihilism involving the repudiation of all cognitive aspirations, actually leaves one with a good deal of ground to occupy. One is the claim that the kind of accurate and complete comprehension and conceptual articulation of reality to which metaphysicians long have aspired is a genuine possibility. The other is the claim that the ascertainment of certain irreducible, incontrovertible, unadorned, and unadulterated states of affairs, commonly styled pure *facts,* is such a possibility.

Philosophers convinced of one or both of these possibilities, joined in this instance by many of their critics, are inclined to disparage the cognitive import (at least where substantive philosophical questions are at issue) of anything that might be said that upon examination turns out to be unassignable to—or at any rate not intimately connected with—either category. This disparagement is to some extent understandable; for if it is assumed that only "knowledge" that is either purely factual or "absolute" is truly deserving of the name, it would appear reasonable to hold that what is neither the one nor the other is not entitled to it—at first "strictly speaking," but eventually *tout court.*

Nietzsche emphatically rejects both claims: and one reason why his position concerning the cognitive status of some of what falls into neither category (but is in our power to achieve) is frequently misunderstood is that, in the spirit of one who has discovered value in something others have disparaged, he combatively employs the language used to disparage it in his own references to it even as he lays claim to its actual cognitive significance; while he likewise often uses the terms preempted by those to whom he is opposed in his references to their cherished myths. Thus he maintains that there can be no "absolute knowledge," and that there are no pure "facts"; and that, rather than either, there are *only* "interpretations"—or (even more pugnaciously) only "beliefs." For example: "Against positivism, which halts at phenomena—'There are only *facts*'—I would say: No, facts is precisely what there is not, only interpretations" (WP 481). And he contends that anything on the order of " 'knowledge-in-itself' is as impermissible a concept as is 'thing-in-itself' " (WP 608).

At first reading, such passages as these might seem to have sweepingly nihilistic implications. Upon closer consideration, however, it becomes clear that what Nietzsche is rejecting is the existence of "facts" *as positivists* understand them—a rejection amounting to a good deal less than a denial of any way of distinguishing between what is the case and what is not in various situations. And he likewise is rejecting the possibility of "knowledge" *as absolutists* (and especially as rationalistic metaphysicians) envision it—a rejection falling far short of a repudiation of the possibility of any cognitively significant difference between various alternative accounts of some object of inquiry.

In this connection notice should also be taken of the language Nietzsche employs in remarks of the following sort: "The sense of truthfulness . . . is nauseated by the falseness and mendaciousness of all Christian interpretations of the world and of history; rebound from 'God is truth' to the fanatical faith 'All is false' " (WP 1). And again: "One interpretation has collapsed; but because it was considered *the* interpretation it now seems as if there were no meaning at all in existence" (WP 55). Here he both commits himself to the appropriateness of characterizing a *particular* interpretation as "untenable," "false," and "mendacious," and at the same time quite clearly suggests the illegitimacy of concluding, from the "collapse" of one interpretation discovered to be thus unworthy of acceptance, that any other must be equally objectionable. Indeed, his derisive reference to "the fanatical faith 'All is false' " shows that he is by no means disposed to lump all "interpretations" together as equally "false."

Nietzsche employs similar language in speaking of certain other interpretations as well. Here I shall take note only of something he says with respect to one in particular. He questions "the faith with which so many materialistic natural scientists rest content nowadays, the faith in a world that is supposed to have its equivalent and its measure in human thought and human valuations. . . . That the only justifiable interpretation of the world should be . . . an interpretation that permits counting, calculating, weighing, seeing, and touching, and nothing more—that is a crudity and naivete" (GS 373).

Several points about Nietzsche's many remarks along these lines may be noted. One is that he considers the various interpretations he singles out for attention—from the "Christian-moral" to the "natural-scientific"—to have a definite utility, in the sense of performing a significant practical function in relation to the needs and limitations of various sorts of human beings. And the second is that, this utility notwithstanding, he expressly terms each of them not merely perspectival but *erroneous,* or at any rate naive and superficial. He does suggest that the practical value of an interpretation endows it with a certain sort of validity, and even that it may thus be accorded a kind of (pragmatic) "truth." The fact that he also considers it appropriate to characterize interpretations enjoying this status in these other ways, however, clearly indicates that he not only envisions the possibility of attaining a vantage point from which their contingency can be discerned, but moreover takes it to be one of his accomplishments to have reached a position from which the untenability or inadequacy of such interpretations may be grasped. That he countenanced this possibility, and what he takes its realization to involve, may further be seen in the following passage, which sheds considerable light on much of what he says and tries to do:

> But precisely because we seek knowledge, let us not be ungrateful to such resolute reversals of accustomed perspectives and valuations with which the spirit has, with apparent mischievousness and futility, raged against itself for so long: to see differently in this way for once, to *want* to see differently, is no small discipline and preparation of the intellect for its future 'objectivity'—the latter understood not as 'contemplation without interest' (which is a nonsensical absurdity), but as the ability to *control* one's Pro and Con and to dispose of them, so that one knows how to employ a *variety* of perspectives and affective interpretations in the service of knowledge.
>
> Henceforth, my dear philosophers, let us be on guard against the dangerous old conceptual fiction that posited a 'pure, will-less, painless, timeless knowing subject'; let us guard against the snares of such contradictory concepts as 'pure reason,' 'absolute spirituality,' 'knowledge in itself': these always demand that we should think of an eye that is completely unthinkable, an eye turned in no particu-

lar direction, in which the active and interpreting forces, through which alone seeing becomes *something,* are supposed to be lacking; these always demand of the eye an absurdity and a nonsense. There is ... *only* a perspective 'knowing'; and the *more* affects we allow to speak about one thing, the *more* eyes, different eyes, we can use to observe one thing, the more complete will our 'concept' of this thing, our 'objectivity,' be. (GM III:12)

Notwithstanding his insistence that there is "*only* a perspective 'knowing' " (as opposed to a knowing that would be absolute and independent of all "perspective seeing"), Nietzsche thus is concerned to distinguish "knowledge" from "perspectives and affective interpretations" merely as such, and suggests that it is something that can be sought and can in some measure be achieved. It, no less than that which is employed "in the service" of its attainment, has the character of "interpretation"—but it is "interpretation" with a difference. It has an "objectivity" that is lacking in the cases of the various "perspectives and affective interpretations" it employs and upon which it draws. For when the latter are played off against each other, one ceases to be locked into any one of them; and so it becomes possible to achieve a meta-level perspective, from which vantage point various lower-order interpretations may be superseded in favor of others less narrow and distorting than they. The endeavor Nietzsche describes in this passage may not elevate one to the position of "pure, will-less, painless, timeless, knowing subjects," capable of taking a God's-eye view of reality; but it can at least place one in a position to "seek knowledge," and to "employ in the service of knowledge" many of the very factors that impede understanding under most circumstances. And this is so even if that "knowing" which is thus possible can never be "absolute," but rather only provisional, and even if the "knowledge" which is thus obtainable inevitably has the character of a relation between an interpreter and that which is interpreted.

2

In conceiving of philosophy as a fundamentally interpretive affair, therefore, and in practicing what he preaches, Nietzsche may thus be seen neither to cut the ground from under his own feet nor to place himself beyond the pale of serious discussion. Yet he remains very difficult to reckon with. He often simply says what he thinks, presenting his interpretations of various matters without making cases for them beyond showing that and how they enable one to make sense of the matters in question. He does not subscribe to the view that a philosopher is permitted to say what he believes to be true and advance what he supposes to be an illuminating and sound interpretation only when he can come up with a line of reasoning by which it is (more or less strictly) entailed. Insight and understanding matter more in philosophy as he conceives of it than does the ability to provide this sort of justification; and he further believes them to be attainable where it is wanting or impossible no less than when it can be managed, even though certainty of their attainment may not be. Such certainty might in principle be desirable, but to insist upon it, for Nietzsche, is to blinker and shackle oneself to the point that comprehension in most matters of moment will escape one. And so in his own philosophizing he often follows the lead of certain thinkers to whom he was most strongly drawn from the start, and whom he celebrates in his earliest writings on philosophy: Heraclitus and Schopenhauer.

It is instructive, in this connection, to consider certain of his remarks about each of them. In his early essay *Philosophy in the Tragic Age of the Greeks,* he singles out Heraclitus for special praise, as "a type of prophet of truth" who "knows but does not reckon," having looked deeply into the world and discerned its nature more clearly and profoundly than any of his contemporaries: "In each word of Heraclitus the pride and majesty of truth are expressed—but truth grasped in intuitions, not truth reached by the rope ladder of logic" (PTA 9). To see and give expression to "the truth" is held to have been all Heraclitus deemed it important and necessary to do, requiring insight rather than calculation or "rope-ladder" reasoning. Nietzsche's own subsequent philosophical practice is by no means confined entirely within these limits; but it often undeniably has this general character.

While Nietzsche remained convinced of the indispensability of this sort of thinking, however, and indeed of the impossibility of any other at certain points in philosophical inquiry, he also came to have a strong sense of the importance of supplementing it in several respects. He indicates one of them in the very same passage, associating it with Heraclitus's opposite number, Parmenides. "In his contemporary Parmenides there stands by his side a counter-part to him, likewise representing a type of prophet of truth, but formed of ice and not of fire, pouring cold, piercing light around him" (PTA 9). This "cold, piercing light" is that of reason rather than of intuition; and in its absence Nietzsche recognizes that philosophy is bound to fare poorly. Thus, in *Schopenhauer as Educator,* he laments the neglect of intellectual rigor among his philosophical contemporaries, and even goes so far as to remark that "without doubt what now goes on in the various sciences is more logical, cautious, modest, inventive, in short more philosophical than what is done among the so-called philosophers" (SE 8).

It is not primarily on this count, however, that he lauds Schopenhauer in this essay. He does not consider him to suffer from the above-mentioned general defect; but he conceives Schopenhauer's "greatness" in other terms. It is held to be owing to the fact that he was not overly fastidious on this point, but rather "confronts the picture of life as a whole, in order to construe it as a whole." He did not succumb to the tendency — to which "the most acute minds" are suggested so often to be prone — to "exhaust themselves in conceptual scholasticism," to become preoccupied with "those places in great philosophical edifices where scholarly reckoning and counter-reckoning, rumination, doubt and contradiction are permitted," and to fall victim to the "error" that "painstaking investigations" of various phenomena will yield the best understanding obtainable of the world's nature. On this last point, Nietzsche urges that "only he who has the general portrait of life and existence clearly in view can draw upon the various sciences without any harm," either to himself or to philosophical understanding; for "in the absence of such a guiding total picture they are threads leading nowhere," and have the effect merely of increasing confusion concerning "life's course" and the world's fundamental nature (SE 3).

In taking Schopenhauer's "greatness" as a philosopher to consist in his having "pursued this picture . . . without allowing himself to be diverted, as scholars do," Nietzsche reveals something further about the conception of philosophy with which he began, and which influenced the course and nature of his own subsequent philosophical activity. Much of his later effort went into his own attempt to bring "life and existence clearly in view," and to construe them and the world "as a whole" in a manner doing justice to them. In the course of working out his interpretation of them, he has a great deal to say about many different things. Since what he has to say so often involves simultaneously elaborating this interpretation and bringing these specific matters within its compass, however, extending his line of thinking rather than presenting a line of reasoning, his points frequently admit of no piecemeal assessment.

At times Nietzsche thinks and writes rather in the spirit of a Heraclitean "truth-sayer"; at other times, in the manner of an analytic philosopher. At others still, and most commonly and fundamentally, however, he is most like the sort of philosopher he here suggests Schopenhauer to have been — without, however, ever attempting anything on the order of Schopenhauer's systematic and comprehensive elaboration of his interpretation of the world *als Wille und Vorstellung.* One may to some extent approach and assess him in the manner appropriate to previous and subsequent philosophers in the tradition most familiar to us; but in the end one must adapt one's treatment of him to the character and aims of philosophy as he conceives and practices it. To do otherwise is to deal with him in the untoward manner of Procrustes, and to fail to take him seriously enough. It is ultimately as an interpreter of "life and existence," concerned to reorient our thinking about the world, ourselves, and value, that Nietzsche confronts us, and would have us reckon with him.

3

"I do not wish to persuade anyone to philosophy," Nietzsche writes, for "it is inevitable, it is perhaps also desirable, that the philosopher should be a *rare* plant" (WP 420). The hazards of genuinely philosophical thinking constitute one of his reasons for taking this position, and his recognition of the fact that he has "set up the most difficult idea of the philosopher" ("Learning is not enough!") is another (WP 421). Few people possess the many qualities he takes to be required if one is to be able to measure up to the intellectual standard he sets forth. And fewer are capable of withstanding the rigors of philosophy as he "understood and lived it." For it involves "living voluntarily among ice and high mountains—seeking out everything strange and questionable in existence" —and requires that one be able to "dare" and "endure" much more "truth" than most people can (EH P:3).

It means, moreover, that one must "take his stand *beyond* good and evil" (TI VII:1), abandoning all reliance upon customary modes of evaluation, and dispensing with the guidance and security afforded by belief in the indisputability of certain moral principles. Indeed, it demands that one take nothing for granted and question even one's most cherished assumptions. One must be most wary, and hardest toward oneself, precisely where one may be inclined to "remain stuck"—whether "to a person" or "a fatherland" or "a science," or to "some pity" or "one's own detachment" or even "one's own virtues" (BGE 41). And one must strive relentlessly to escape "from the musty agreeable nooks into which preference and prejudice, youth, origin, the accidents of people and books or even exhaustion from wandering seemed to have banished us" (BGE 56).

To be the sort of philosopher Nietzsche has in mind, one must be able to close one's ears to "the siren songs of old metaphysical bird-catchers" that would flatter and delude one (BGE 23); and to resist the lure of "mystical explanations" that, while "considered deep," actually "are not even superficial" (GS 126). And one must possess and be capable of cultivating a variety of characteristics "that usually destroy a man," but without being destroyed by them. This, he suggests, is "why the philosopher rarely turns out well." For one "must be a brief abstract of man," incorporating "a tremendous multiplicity of qualities," although this carries with it a "danger from antitheses." One further "must be inquisitive in the most various directions: danger of going to pieces." Moreover, one "must be just and fair in the highest sense," but also "profound in love [and] hate" as well, one must be both "spectator" and "legislator." And one must be both "supple" and "firm and hard" (WP 976).

Nor is this all: "The dangers for a philosopher's development," Nietzsche observes, are "manifold today":

> The scope and the tower-building of the sciences has grown to be enormous, and with this also the probability that the philosopher grows weary while still learning or allows himself to be detained somewhere to become a "specialist"—so he never attains his proper level, the height for a comprehensive look.... Or he attains it too late, when his best time and strength are spent.... It may be precisely the sensitivity of his intellectual conscience that leads him to delay somewhere along the way and to be late: he is afraid of the seduction to become a dilettante. (BGE 205)

And to this he adds, "by way of once more doubling the difficulties for a philosopher," that one is ultimately required to come to terms with "life and the value of life" in a way for which there is no method, so that his very intellectual conscience may make him "reluctant to come to believe that he has a right, or even a duty," to do anything of the sort. What is demanded of him is "a Yes or No" with respect to them—a fundamental and general affirmation or denial, which in either case will color and profoundly influence all of his subsequent thinking, and in the absence of which his thought will lack true seriousness.

This decision, for Nietzsche, is one the philosopher does have a "right" as well as a "duty" to make; but he "must seek his way to this right and faith only from the most comprehensive—perhaps most disturbing and destructive—experiences," and thus cannot be expected to arrive at it easily. If he "frequently hesitates, doubts, and lapses into silence," this is not to be wondered at; nor should it be surprising that few will manage actually to attain this right, overcome their hesitation and doubts concerning it, and "risk themselves" by venturing to take such a stand (BGE 205). It is with reference to this view of the basic challenge to which the philosopher must be equal that Nietzsche says of his own thought:

> Such an experimental philosophy as I live anticipates experimentally even the possibilities of the most fundamental nihilism; but this does not mean that it must halt at a negation, a No, a will to negation. It wants rather to cross over to the opposite of this—to a Dionysian affirmation of the world as it is, without substraction,

exception, or selection.... The highest state a philosopher can attain: to stand in a Dionysian relationship to existence—my formula for this is *amor fati.* (WP 1041)

These demands are so many and so hard that they would seem to ensure that the "genuine philosopher" will always be "a rare plant," and that Nietzsche's "philosophers of the future" will never be more than exceptions to the rule in the philosophical community. His insistence that these "new philosophers" must also be "spirits strong and original enough to provide the stimuli for opposite valuations and to revalue and invert 'eternal values'" (BGE 203) has the consequence of limiting inclusion in their ranks still further. And even the basic intellectual standard he sets for the philosopher is very high indeed. It is deserving of further comment here, because it is no less important a part of the portrait Nietzsche sketches than the rest, but tends to be overlooked.

To begin with, one can hardly exaggerate the importance he attaches to "intellectual integrity." There is nothing he finds more objectionable in a philosopher than a lack of it, or the sacrifice of it for the sake of preserving some conviction. "Here, if anywhere, we too are still *men of conscience,*" he writes, "we do not wish to return again to anything we take to be outlived and decaying, to something 'unworthy of belief,'" however painful its repudiation might be. And "we will permit ourselves no bridges of lies to old ideals," however much might stand and fall with them (D P:4). A philosopher must have the liveliest intellectual conscience, and a steadfast determination to tolerate nothing that critical scrutiny reveals to be "unworthy of belief." Nietzsche thus endorses Stendhal's dictum: "To be a good philosopher, one must be dry, clear, without illusion" (BGE 39). He often puts this point in terms of "truthfulness" and "honesty"; and his repeated demand that the philosopher must be "hard" is meant to underscore it. Thus he writes:

Honesty, supposing that this is our virtue from which we cannot get away, we free spirits—well, let us work on it with all our malice and love and not weary of "perfecting" ourselves in *our* virtue, the only one left us.... Let us remain hard, we last Stoics! And let us dispatch to her assistance whatever we have in us of devilry: our disgust with what is clumsy and approximate, our *"nimitur in vetitum"* ["we strive for the forbidden"], our adventurous courage, our seasoned and choosy curiosity, our subtlest, most disguised, most spiritual will to power and overcoming of the world. (BGE 227)

As he here indicates, Nietzsche is well aware that the intellectual honesty he prizes will not take the philosopher very far in the absence of a cluster of other qualities. Those he mentions here are only some of those he further takes to be essential to the making of the sort of philosopher he calls for and himself attempts to be. One crucial trait is the fortitude to dispense with comforting illusions and confront disagreeable truths, to which he refers in suggesting that "the strength of a spirit should be measured according to how much of the 'truth' one could still barely endure" (BGE 39). And another is a determination to "drive one's will to knowledge" far beyond ordinary bounds, and the ability to "liberate oneself from many things that oppress, inhibit, hold down and make heavy" most thinkers at present (GS 380).

There is also a kind of "objectivity" Nietzsche supposes to be necessary in the philosopher differing from that which he takes to be characteristic of the scholarly and scientific type of thinker. " 'Objectivity' in the philosopher," he writes, involves "moral indifference toward oneself, blindness toward good or ill consequences; lack of scruples about using dangerous means; perversity and multiplicity of character considered and exploited as an advantage" (WP 425). Balanced against these traits, on the other hand, is a sense of responsibility that, while not that of the merely "moral" man, is no less demanding and of much higher significance. It extends beyond an uncompromising "will to knowledge," to what Nietzsche terms the enhancement of life. Thus he characterizes "the philosopher as *we* understand him, we free spirits—as the man of the most comprehensive responsibility who has the conscience for the overall development of man" (BGE 61).

He further attaches great importance to the qualities of subtlety and acuteness in the observation and analysis of many different sorts of phenomena, from the linguistic and historical to the social and psychological to the physiological and biological, and ranging over such diverse domains of human activity and experience as art, religion, science, and politics. The philosopher must "be able to see with many different eyes and consciences" (BGE 211). He must be adept at "taking things apart" and "know how to handle a knife surely and subtly" (BGE 210)—or how to "philosophize with a hammer" (in the language of the subtitle of *Twilight*), excelling in "the sounding out of idols" that betray their hollowness when "touched with a hammer as with a tuning fork" (TI P). And he must possess "the courage and hardness of analysis" (BGE 209), and the capacity for "piling stone upon stone, pebble upon pebble," without being "ashamed of such modest work" (HH I:37).

Related to this is another point: while Nietzsche's "philosophers of the future" are to be more than astute critics, "critical discipline and every habit conducive to cleanliness and severity in matters of the spirit will be demanded by these philosophers, not only of themselves" (BGE 210). They are to exhibit that "genuinely philosophical combination . . . of a bold and exuberant spirituality that runs *presto* and a dialectical severity and necessity that takes no false step" (BGE 213). They also "will be men of experiments," whose thinking is characterized by "attempts and delight in attempts" to devise novel hypotheses and interpretations and assessments (BGE 210), but who "certainly will not be dogmatists" (BGE 43). For a further trait of philosophers of the sort Nietzsche has in mind (however odd this may seem to some) is modesty with respect to the status of the issue of their efforts. The modest acknowledgment that no interpretation is unsupersedable, and that at least a "little question mark" is best placed after one's own "special words and favorite doctrines" (BGE 25), is held to be a fitting accompaniment and needed complement to the originality and boldness of mind that philosophical profundity and power presuppose.

Indeed, Nietzsche goes further, joining to this commendation an appeal to the philosopher to avoid the "stiff seriousness that inspires laughter," to which so many of "our philosophers" are disposed (BGE 186). Thus he would have philosophers resist the tendency to "solemnity in gesture, word, tone, eye, morality, and task," even though the stakes for humanity could not be higher than they are here. He does consider the emergence of his new type of philosopher to mark a fundamental turning point, and holds that "it is perhaps only with him that the *great seriousness* really begins, that the real question mark is posed for the first time, that the destiny of the soul changes, the hand moves forward, the tragedy *begins*" (GS 382). But he does not take this to mean that the philosophical enterprise ought therefore to be carried on in a spirit of deadly earnestness. Rather, he constantly stresses the importance of lightheartedness, gaiety, playfulness, and irony. "I would not know what the spirit of a philosopher might wish more to be than a good dancer," he writes (GS 381), in a work whose title expresses his conception of what philosophy ought to be: *The Gay Science.* He associates both Zarathustra and his sort of philosophizing with the beginning of "the great seriousness," and with "tragedy" as well (GS 382); but they are balanced and leavened by the "cheerful and koboldish laughter" of "the spirits of my own book" and thought (GS 383).

To be sure, a task like the "revaluation of all values" cannot be accomplished by one minded only to jest. Nietzsche's point here, however, is that it also cannot be carried through at all well if one fails "to shake off a heavy, all-too-heavy seriousness" and to "maintain cheerfulness" as one proceeds with such "a gloomy affair, fraught with enormous responsibility." And besides, he adds, "nothing succeeds if prankishness has no part in it"

(TI P). One may find it easier to deal with a philosopher whose thought is without such qualities as these; but that by itself is no real mark in his favor. And it is Nietzsche's contention that without them, in matters of real substance, philosophical inquiry will not get very far. "There is something about 'truth,' about the *search* for truth," he writes, such that "when a human being is too human about it," in motivation or in approach, "I bet he finds nothing" (BGE 35).

His own philosophical practice may often fall short of or diverge from the standards and principles he advocates; and the picture of the genuine philosopher and philosophy he sets forth may strike many as uncongenial in various respects. But he would be neither surprised nor disconcerted in either event, and would take neither circumstance to count against the picture itself. And if he proposes a conception of the tasks and concerns of the philosopher that embraces certain things at which many philosophers will look askance (with or without good reason), it must be allowed that this conception incorporates the basic features of any model of the philosopher deserving to be taken seriously. The only real question pertains to the merit of including in it those further features he also stresses. This is a question it may not be possible to settle by argument, or even settle at all. To my way of thinking, however, Nietzsche's conception of philosophy has greater attractions and promise than any other I know. Its issue may not measure up to certain standards of knowledge reflecting the convictions or longings of some philosophers, but Nietzsche with good reason takes it to surpass anything that might otherwise be achieved in acuteness, penetration, and profundity. And for him and others like him, there is more to be said for it as well. So he writes, of the knowledge which he takes it to make possible,

> And knowledge itself: let it be something else for others . . . for me it is a world of dangers and victories in which heroic feelings, too, find places to dance and play. *"Life as a means to knowledge"* — with this principle in one's heart one can live not only boldly but even gaily, and laugh gaily too. (GS 324)

4

I readily admit that there may appear to be a serious difficulty confronting my construal of Nietzsche's thinking with respect to the nature of philosophy and its interpretive character, and of his meaning in speaking of "knowledge" in passages such as this. This apparent difficulty has to do with certain things he has to say about "truth" that would seem at least to place a large question mark beside the suggestion that he takes any sort

of thinking to be capable of issuing in the attainment of anything deserving of this designation, unless its meaning is transformed beyond all
recognition. If *all* truth is and can be nothing more than what he calls
"the kind of error without which a certain species of life could not live"
(WP 493), and if no truths can be anything more than the *"irrefutable
errors"* he says "man's truths" ultimately merely are (GS 265), it would
indeed seem that no sort of philosophy—including his own—would have
anything to do with "truth" in any epistemically privileged or even
significant sense.

It is my conviction, however, that to take this to be the thrust and
upshot of Nietzsche's reflections on truth is to misunderstand him very
seriously, where both truth and philosophy are concerned. The first point
to be made, and stressed, is that he has a great many different sorts of
things to say about and in terms of "truth" and "truths." The two passages
cited above, and others like them, cannot be ignored; they clearly are
intended to make important points and to be taken seriously. But it
should not be supposed to be obvious exactly what these points are, and
what their scope is, and what their implications are if it is agreed to take
them seriously. Moreover, the same Nietzsche also said many other
things, which deserve to be accorded the same serious attention. For
example, he lauds those strong and courageous enough "to sacrifice all
desirability to truth, *every* truth, even plain, harsh, ugly, repellent,
unchristian, immoral truth.—For such truths do exist" (GM I:1). And he
likewise writes: "At every step one has to wrestle for truth; one has to
surrender for it almost everything to which the heart, to which our love,
our trust in life, cling otherwise. That requires greatness of soul; the
service of truth is the hardest service" (A 50).

There are also many other passages in which Nietzsche has things to
say about truth differing significantly from what he says in passages of
either of these sorts. Faced with this situation, one might conclude (as
some have) that he meant some of the things he says but not others; or
that he contradicted himself repeatedly, either out of confusion or by
design; or that he was constantly changing his mind. The most reasonable conclusion, however, seems to me to be that he has a variety of
different things in mind in the diverse multitude of passages in which the
terms "truth" and "truths" appear, which need to be sorted out and
explicated.

Elaborating upon this line of interpretive approach, I would further
observe that good and interesting collective sense can be made of the
many different things he says on these various occasions if one supposes
them not to be meant to apply across the board, but rather to have
application within a variety of contexts of restricted scope, and moreover

to contribute to several distinct levels of analysis of what counts as "truth" and "truths" in these contexts. Clues to these scope restrictions and level distinctions, I suggest, are readily discernible through the juxtaposition of the various sorts of remarks Nietzsche makes and reflection upon the indications he often gives of their focus, referents, or associations.

What emerges from this sort of consideration and interpretation, I have found, is a complex, subtle, and fundamentally coherent treatment of truth that has much to be said for it. In my view it both constitutes a significant contribution to the theory of truth and knowledge and removes the apparent difficulty referred to above—even though it also makes clear that philosophical inquiry must proceed without benefit of any royal road to knowledge. It provides different accounts of a number of categories of "truths," and different assessments of their fundamental epistemic status and place in human life and thought. I cannot elaborate and discuss them here; but I would at least identify them.

The broadest of them, which Nietzsche sometimes characterizes as "man's truths," comprehends a wide range of things that have come to be considered "truths" in various commonplace domains of discourse; and these in turn are seen to admit of differing particular analyses, and also of analysis on several different levels. One of these levels of analysis consists in analyzing what might be termed the "surface conditions" or criteria employed within a particular domain of discourse, in virtue of the satisfaction of which a particular proposition may be considered "true." Another is also descriptive, or at any rate analytically interpretive, but on a deeper level. It consists in attempting to determine what is fundamentally involved—what is going on beneath the surface, conditioning the character of the surface—in the emergence of such forms of discourse and "truth."

The "truths" espoused by metaphysical and religious thinkers wedded to the idea of some sort of reality transcending the world in which we live, on the other hand, are accorded different treatment by Nietzsche and are suggested to have a different sort of status and significance. They thus constitute a category of "truths" importantly different from those he takes to be woven into the very fabric of human life as we do and apparently must live it, and to which he is quite differently disposed. And from both yet a third category is to be distinguished, exemplified at least in intention for Nietzsche by the insights into the character of our human existence and of life and the world he believes himself to have achieved and given expression. They too may be interpretive, but he supposes them to transcend both of the former sorts of "truths," and indeed to stand in marked contrast to them. Here one encounters what Nietzsche takes to be at least the possibility of what might be called "truth and knowledge *with a difference*"; and, briefly put, he proposes that they be explicated and construed in terms of the notions of "aptness" and "justice."

If one avails oneself of these distinctions, one not only can make coherent and interesting sense of the many things Nietzsche has to say about "truth" and "truths," but also can see how it is that he is able to embrace the conception of the nature and potential issue of genuine philosophical thinking set forth above, even while saying the sorts of things he often does about "man's truths" generally and about ideas of the sort long passing as "truths" in philosophical and religious thought. To be sure, one may wonder whether his reasons for granting only "all-too-human" significance to both of the latter kinds of "truths" do not apply with equal force to anything he or his new and genuine philosophers might ever come up with. It should count for something, however, especially among those who derive inspiration from him, that he clearly does not suppose his own interpretive efforts to be on a complete epistemic par with the interpretations and pragmatically conditioned modes of conceptualization upon which he brings his critical guns to bear. And while he might be mistaken about this in the cases of some of the particular conclusions he reaches and views he advances, it seems to me that he is entirely and crucially right to insist upon the possibility of a difference, upon its attainability, and upon its importance. For as he realized and stressed, more than the future of philosophy is at stake.

CHAPTER FOUR

Beyond Deconstruction: Nietzsche's Kind of Philosophy

That I still cleave to the ideas that I take up again in the present treatises today . . . that they have become in the meantime more and more firmly attached to one another, indeed intertwined and interlaced with one another, strengthens my joyful assurance that they might have arisen in me from the first not as isolated, capricious, or sporadic things but from a common root, from a *fundamental will* of knowledge, pointing imperiously into the depths, speaking more and more precisely, demanding greater and greater precision. For this alone is fitting for a philosopher. (GM P:2)

A certain amount of historical and philological schooling, together with an inborn fastidiousness of taste in respect to psychological questions in general, soon transformed my problem into another one: under what conditions did man devise these value judgments good and evil? *and what value do they themselves possess?* Have they hitherto hindered or furthered human prosperity? . . .

    Thereupon I discovered and ventured diverse answers . . . I departmentalized my problem; out of my answers there grew new questions, inquiries, conjectures, probabilities—until at length I had a country of my own. . . . Oh how *fortunate* we are, we men of knowledge, provided only that we know how to keep silent long enough! (GM P:3)

    The Nietzsche speaking here is the Nietzsche of 1887—vintage Nietzsche, by any reckoning, commenting on the thinking beginning more than a decade earlier that led up to (and at that point culminated in) *On the Genealogy of Morals.* In these passages and this whole preface we find much that is of interest and importance in connection with the question of Nietzsche's kind of philosophy. The same is true of the other prefaces he supplied to his earlier and subsequent works during the last few years of his productive life (and of course in his post-*Zarathustra* works themselves).

    It is in this last period commencing with *Beyond Good and Evil,* above all and most unquestionably, that we encounter "Nietzsche as philosopher." Whatever philosophy for him may have been, this is it. In these works and prefaces we find him doing and describing the sort of thing it became for him—even if also perhaps a variety of other things as well, which for him were more or less closely connected with it. I consider it implausible (to say the least) to ascribe views to him about what philosophy is, and about what it can and cannot be, that are at fundamental variance with what he does in these works, and with what he says about what he is doing in his prefaces of 1885-88.

To be sure, Nietzsche has many critical things to say about philosophers and philosophy as they traditionally have been and continue typically to be. He also has much to say about truth and knowledge, reason and language, and interpretation and "perspective" that must further be reckoned with. But it must be granted that he makes much of the possibility of "new philosophers," of the sort he not only envisions and calls for but also himself attempts to be, who would differ from those hitherto of whom he is so critical. And he also makes much of a "philosophy of the future" of which more may be expected than the kinds of philosophical laboring and all-too-human interpreting he belittles and castigates.

Some take Nietzsche's critical remarks about "philosophers" (along with what he has to say about the problematic character of truth and knowledge) as his last word with respect to philosophy, amounting to its abandonment and repudiation in favor of other sorts of thinking purged of all cognitive pretensions. This, in my view, is to fail quite fundamentally to do justice to his intentions and undertakings. It is, in short, to fail to take him seriously, in the very matter about which he himself was most serious, and to which he devoted much effort, above all during the last years of his productive life.

During these last years Nietzsche not only accepted but laid claim to the label "philosopher"; and he both preached and practiced something he did not hesitate to call "philosophy," which he deemed more deserving of the name than what generally passes for it. He further retained and claimed the term "knowledge" in this connection, even though he did emphatically reject the idea that anything attainable along these lines can ever be absolute and final, or indubitable and incorrigible. Moreover, he freely availed himself of the language of "truth" and "truths"—despite his rejection of the ideas of "eternal truths" and of the possibility (or even the meaningfulness) of truth as the correspondence of thought with a "true world of being," and notwithstanding all that he has to say about language, "perspective," and interpretation.

This leads some to suppose that Nietzsche was confused and inconsistent, or to suggest that he simply was unable to free himself of ways of speaking and thinking that his own views preclude and should have brought him to abandon. I would suggest, on the contrary, that these conclusions are unwarranted, and that this should rather prompt a reconsideration of what these views actually were, or came to be as his thinking developed into what we find in his post-*Zarathustra* writings.

1

But was Nietzsche "really" a philosopher? This has often been questioned, and even denied, by those who have wanted to dismiss him as someone who was unwilling or unable to play by the rules of the game of philosophy as they themselves understood and practiced it. More recently, it has also been denied approvingly by others who have wanted to embrace him as a precursor of their own rejection of the traditional philosophical enterprise.

Nietzsche's kind of philosophy and philosopher admittedly differ enough from those of the traditional and contemporary mainstream to provide some grounds for those detractors and admirers who contend that he departs from it. There may be some point to the debate about whether his departure is sufficient to warrant locating him outside of it. But this is not a very illuminating controversy; for it may always be argued (as it was by Nietzsche himself) that the paradigms established by the mainstream are themselves too narrow, or even importantly misguided, and so settle nothing of importance.

A more interesting and fruitful question concerns the character of the kind of philosopher and philosophy Nietzsche himself calls for and shows us in his own efforts, during the last years of his productive life in particular. It is undeniable that in these writings we encounter the mature Nietzsche; and they must be allowed to be the clearest cases of whatever it was that philosophical inquiry meant for him. By examining what he undertakes to do in them, how he goes about doing it, and what he says about what he is doing, one can best discern his kind of philosophy and philosopher. It will mark no small advance in the discussion of "Nietzsche as philosopher" if attention can be brought to bear primarily upon these instances of Nietzsche the philosopher laying his cards on the table and at work.[1]

While these writings generally preserve something of the aphoristic form of Nietzsche's pre-*Zarathustra* works, they have a greater coherence than may be readily apparent. In each of them he takes up a fundamental "problem" or related set of problems, which he proceeds to address in a variety of ways he considers appropriate to them. On the most general level of consideration they all are instances of his engagement in the twin basic tasks of his philosophical enterprise: *interpretation* and *evaluation*. These two tasks are not entirely separate operations, for each draws upon and contributes to the other in a kind of dialectic; but they may be considered somewhat different "moments" of Nietzschean-philosophical inquiry, neither of which reduces entirely to the other. They may be likened to a pair of hands, which are used together to accomplish a united purpose. Their fundamental purpose is that of greater comprehension, involving both understanding and assessment.

While the "problems" Nietzsche sets for himself in these various works may be distinguished and differently characterized, moreover, they too are not entirely separate and unrelated; for they have a fundamental interconnection that enables his treatment of each of them to shed light upon the others, either directly or indirectly. They spring from his basic concern with the *character and quality of human life,* as it has come to be and may yet become, in its very considerable complexity and diversity. These works may be regarded as attempts (or series of attempts) to explore this larger question by approaching it from different angles, each supplementing the others in important ways, as Nietzsche came to see the need for and usefulness of doing so. This required frequent stocktaking, reconsideration, and adjustment. The "perspectivism" he espouses has a number of points and applications, and among them this *methodological* one is of great importance to the understanding of his philosophical practice. (I shall develop this point below.)

This way of proceeding is connected with the "experimental" character Nietzsche ascribes to his kind of philosophical thinking—and also with the avowedly merely provisional and open-ended character of his treatment of these general problems, and of the more specific matters he discusses along the way. The upshot of what he has to say about them in any of these works is never complete and final, for it always remains open to revision when subsequent investigations are undertaken, involving yet other approaches that may shed further light upon them.

This does not mean that for Nietzsche nothing like genuine "comprehension" can ever be attained through such inquiry, and that all interpretive and evaluative efforts are exercises in futility, except as displays of one's creative imagination, or as means in the service of the preservation or enhancement of life. He repeatedly insists upon the distinction between the plausibility and soundness of various ideas on the one hand, and their *"value for life"* on the other (between their "truth-value" and their "life-value," as it were). Although some of his unguarded remarks may seem to suggest otherwise, he inveighs explicitly *against* the conflation of the two—even while *also* arguing that the *value* of all knowledge and truthfulness ultimately must be referred to their "value for life" for human beings with differing constitutions and conditions of preservation, flourishing, and growth, and judged before that tribunal.

2

One who reads these books and prefaces with any care cannot fail to notice that Nietzsche constantly speaks of "problems," "questions," and "tasks." These terms recur over and over again in them, in his statements of what it is that he is doing. It is not enough to observe that philosophy for Nietzsche is an interpretive affair and is fundamentally a matter of interpreting, reinterpreting, and critically assessing received and proposed interpretations. This is certainly and importantly true. But it is no less essential to observe that Nietzsche advocates and engages in these activities in the course of attempts to address a variety of problems, questions, and tasks that he sets for himself, and would have like-minded philosophers join him in addressing.

As has often been observed, Nietzsche was not a systematic thinker and writer; but he was avowedly and quite evidently a *problem*-thinker. His early writings—*The Birth of Tragedy,* the "Truth and Lies" essay, and the four *Untimely Meditations* —are all addressed to things he conceived as "problems" calling for consideration. The same is true of the books he published after *Zarathustra* —although in some cases it is the parts of the books, rather than the entire works, that are organized around the "problems" on which he fixes his attention. The books published in his "middle period" (prior to *Zarathustra*) may appear to be exceptions; but when he wrote new prefaces to them in 1886 (and again when he discusses them in *Ecce Homo*), one of his chief concerns was to point out the "problems" with which he then recognized he had been fundamentally occupied in them.

This point is of no little importance for the understanding of Nietzsche's conception and practice of philosophy. He does seek to broaden and modify the range of "problems" with which philosophers as he conceives of them should be dealing, and does suggest that they require to be dealt with in ways differing from those favored by his predecessors and contemporaries. His repeated references to such "problems" make it quite clear, however, that he does not propose to transform philosophy from the consideration of problems into something altogether different. He does resist the idea that the only sorts of problems with which philosophers ought to concern themselves are those that can be dealt with by "arguments" of a purely logical, conceptual, or linguistic kind, unsullied by anything drawn from other disciplines and forms of observation. But he clearly holds that there are many important problems that cannot be settled or adequately dealt with by either the former or the latter—and that a variety of treatments at least akin to "arguments" are called for in dealing with them.

What are Nietzsche's announced "problems"? An inventory of them reads rather strangely, to one whose idea of a "philosophical problem" is that of a question to which there is supposed to be some neatly distinguishable and articulable set of possible answers, which may be debated on the model of a scholastic disputation. Examples of such standard problems come readily to mind: for example, the problems of the existence of God, the reality of the external world, freedom of the will, the possibility of synthetic a priori knowledge, the derivability of "ought" from "is," and other such common fare of the traditional literature and textbook introductions to philosophy. Problems of this sort characteristically resolve into sets of competing propositions, with the game being to find some way of demonstrating their truth or falsity (or, skeptically, the undecidability of their truth or falsity).

Nietzsche has little interest in such disputations, and indeed would have them abandoned, not only as idle but also as diversions from the genuine tasks of philosophy. Its real problems, for him, involve the identification and assessment of prevailing interpretations and evaluations, and the development and advocacy of alternatives improving upon them. The inventory of his problems loses its appearance of strangeness when one adjusts one's thinking in this way.

So, for example, Nietzsche calls attention to the "problems" of ascetic ideals, *ressentiment,* the bad conscience, the will to truth, and different forms of art, religion, and morality, as well as various forms of romanticism, rationalism, and nihilism (to mention but a few examples). And he makes much of the "problems" of art, science, truth, knowledge, morality, value, and the "problem" of what he calls "the type *Mensch*" more generally—under which may be subsumed the "problems" of consciousness and self-consciousness, logic and reason, the affects and their transformations, "herd" and "higher" humanity, and much else. All of these things, for Nietzsche, are (or pose) problems requiring the kind of attention that he calls (re)interpretation and (re)valuation, and considers to be the main business of his kind of philosophy.

Another important point about Nietzsche's conception and practice of philosophy emerges from the fact that he is not only a "problem" thinker but a "case" thinker. His preferred way of approaching the larger problems with which he is concerned is to do so by way of reflection on various "cases" of figures or developments he believes to be revealing with respect to them. In the many cases he selects for attention, these problems are raised in vivid and concrete ways. Attention to them is suggested to help one get somewhere with the problems; while on the other hand the ideas about these problems that these cases suggest serve to help him interpret and assess the cases.

Nietzsche was drawn to this "case-study" approach to the larger problems that concerned him from his earliest works onward. *The Birth of Tragedy* affords a prime example, and his *Untimely Meditations* provide others: the case of the Greeks and their different art forms—and also the case of Socrates; and the cases of David Strauss, of Schopenhauer, of Wagner at Bayreuth, and of the new fashion of historical scholarship. The cases of the Greeks, Socrates, Wagner, and Schopenhauer continued to fascinate him in his later life; and the cases of Christianity, Plato, Kant, Goethe, Napoleon, the new *Reich,* and a host of others were added to them. Nietzsche's pre-*Zarathustra* aphoristic works are full of small-scale case studies of this sort. In his post-*Zarathustra* works he undertook such studies on an expanding scale. The *Genealogy of Morals, The Antichrist,* and *The Case of Wagner* are particularly obvious examples, with both *Beyond Good and Evil* and *Twilight of the Idols* also featuring a considerable number of them.

Nietzsche's most common strategy in those works is to invoke some such case to raise a problem, and then to employ the examination of this and sometimes other related cases to address the problem. The cases are, as it were, the witnesses he calls to the stand, or, alternately, among the data he introduces, the interrogation and interpretation of which serve to shed light upon the larger problems they exemplify or broach. They also serve the important function of keeping his treatments of these problems from becoming lost in abstract reflections, and of keeping him (and us) mindful that these problems have real relevance to human life and experience.

There is another important sense in which philosophy for Nietzsche has to do with "cases." As he practices it, it involves the *making of cases* for and against various proposed interpretations and evaluations. He does not for the most part present arguments of the sort that we are accustomed to find in the writings of philosophers and that we tend to expect of them.[2] But he recognizes the need to do more than merely say what he thinks in order to make his criticisms stick and his own ideas convincing. On the attack, he typically seeks to *make cases against* ways of thinking he finds wanting by presenting an array of considerations, intended collectively first to make us suspicious of them and aware of just how problematical they are, and then to deprive them of their credibility. He generally does not claim that the considerations he marshals actually *refute* the targets of his criticism. Rather he typically aims and purports to *dispose* of them by undermining them sufficiently to lay them to rest, exposed as unworthy of being taken seriously any longer—at least by those possessed of any degree of intellectual integrity and honesty.

When he turns to advancing alternatives to them, Nietzsche proceeds in a somewhat similar manner, presenting various other supporting considerations—both general and specific—none of which by themselves may be decisive, but which taken together are intended to be compelling. They are purported to establish his "right" to the view he is proposing, notwithstanding the novelty it may have, and the initial reluctance one may feel to entertain and embrace it. Here too he is generally prepared to acknowledge that the cases he makes do not actually *prove* his points, and he couches his hypotheses and conclusions in tentative and provisional language. He also not only admits but insists that they leave open the possibility of other interpretations as well as of subsequent modifications, as further considerations may be introduced. But it is clear that he supposes it to be possible to *make cases for* his interpretations and evaluations, whose positive upshot is strong and clear enough to warrant confidence that he is at least on the right track and has gotten hold of something important. He often does say things to the effect that these are "*his* truths," to which others may not easily be entitled. But this way of speaking may be understood as a challenge to others to *earn their right* to lay claim to understand what he has grasped, rather than as an admission that they are nothing more than figments of his own creative imagination.

Nietzsche's procedure may also be likened to the sort of thing Sartre had in mind when he spoke of the "progressive-regressive method" in his *Search for a Method;* only in Nietzsche's case the movements of his thought are even more complex. He constantly moves back and forth between the consideration of quite particular cases and phenomena and more general reflections upon associated basic features or more fundamental traits of human life and human types—both drawing upon the former to shed light upon the latter and invoking his developing ideas about the latter to contribute to the comprehension of the former. But he further constantly shifts his focus from some such phenomena to others, from some human types to others, and from some features of human life more generally to others.

This at first makes many of his books both before and after *Zarathustra* hard to follow; and it is all too easy to become lost in the wood, failing to see it in its larger contours for all the trees. But there is method in this, rather than a mere lack of any purpose other than to put collections of aphorisms between covers, or to keep us off balance. In a sense, Nietzsche *does* mean to keep us off balance—in the sense, that is, of trying to keep us from settling into any one line of thinking that would become a rut, and so neglecting others that are no less germane to understanding both the more specific and the broader matters under consideration. It is not for nothing that Nietzsche suggests his sort of philosopher must be a *dancer* rather than a plodder, adept at moving quickly from one stance to another, in order not to become frozen in any one of them, and so unable to bring a host of them into play.

The movement of philosophical thought for him must be not only *progressive and regressive* by turns, but also *horizontal* on the levels of both more specific and more general considerations, in order to be able to do anything approaching justice to the tangled complexity and interrelatedness of human affairs. This is what I take to be the basic point of the well-known but seldom fully appreciated passage in the *Genealogy of Morals* in which he writes that "precisely because we seek knowledge," we need to develop "the ability *to control* one's Pro and Con and to dispose of them, so that one knows how to employ a *variety* of perspectives and effective interpretations in the service of knowledge" (GM III:12).

3

What exactly did Nietzsche write, and publish or prepare for publication, in the last years between *Thus Spoke Zarathustra* and his collapse (1885-88)? This may be something everyone knows; but it is something of which we do well to remind ourselves, and it provides a useful point of departure that is surely beyond the realm of the controversial. First he composed *Beyond Good and Evil* — a book with nine parts, proclaimed by its subtitle to be a "prelude" to something that Nietzsche sees fit to call "philosophy" — but a kind of philosophy ("of the future") that is evidently to differ significantly from the sort of thing and thinking that philosophy typically had been in the past and was in Nietzsche's own time. On the other hand, it stands for him in some meaningful relation to that traditional enterprise sufficient to warrant his calling it by the same name. (And indeed a reckoning with this tradition and enterprise is one of its first and continuing orders of business.)

Next, in rapid succession, Nietzsche composed a series of prefaces to works published previously — to both volumes of *Human, All Too Human, The Birth of Tragedy, Daybreak*, and *The Gay Science*. All of these retrospective prefaces were written in 1886, along with a fifth book added to a new edition of *The Gay Science* that was published in the next year. Later in that next year (1887), *On the Genealogy of Morals* appeared. Like the prefaces of 1886 and the fifth book of *The Gay Science*, the *Genealogy* at once hearkens back to work begun earlier (as Nietzsche observes in its preface), and also moves ahead, carrying this work further. The fifth book of *The Gay Science* likewise resumes and advances the treatment of many of the issues he had dealt with in the first four books of this work written just before *Zarathustra*. This con-

tinuation of the project of that work, under the same title, is itself
notable; for it suggests that Nietzsche's heralded "philosophy of the
future" is to involve no turning away from the endeavor he called *fröhliche
Wissenschaft,* but rather is to be the same sort of thing carried further.
The *Genealogy* may likewise be regarded as an example of the kind of
inquiry to be undertaken under both banners.

And then, after the *Genealogy,* there followed the works of 1888 — *The
Case of Wagner, Twilight of the Idols,* and *The Antichrist,* along with
Ecce Homo — all again looking both back and ahead. *The Case of Wagner*
and *The Antichrist,* like the *Genealogy,* have relatively specific targets;
while *Twilight* is more comparable to *Beyond Good and Evil* and *The
Gay Science* in the breadth of the ground it covers. Between them, they
show us Nietzsche's final efforts to practice what he preaches in calling
for a *fröhlich-wissenschaftlich* "philosophy of the future"—or at least of
his prelude to it.

Nietzsche's productive life had begun with a series of books and essays
dealing with art and culture, truth and history, religion and ethics,
philosophy and science, and a variety of related specific topics and
figures from Socrates and his fellow ancients to Schopenhauer, Wagner,
and their fellow moderns. It concluded with his repeated return to them,
in the works just cited, and also with his reflections upon these earlier
works—what he had been doing in them and where he saw himself as
having been going—both in his prefaces of 1886 and in *Ecce Homo.* In
these further discussions of them he not only made increasing use of
certain key notions—such as "the enhancement of life" and "will to
power"—but also brought to the fore several more fundamental problems
he recognized to underlie and encompass them: in particular, the problem of value and the assessment of values, the problem of morality, and
also the problem of "the type *Mensch*" and the understanding of our
attained and attainable humanity, as well as the problems of knowledge
and of philosophy itself, as they have been and might be pursued.

Nietzsche's post-*Zarathustra* works and his later thinking revolve around
these large and fundamental problems. In the course of dealing with
them, he arrived at and makes much of his recognition of the basic
character of the twin tasks of the sort of thinking involved in his kind of
philosophy. They are, once again, interpretation and evaluation—including
the assessment of received interpretations and evaluations, but going
beyond them to advance reinterpretations and to undertake a "revaluation
of values."

These tasks are quite evidently not only "deconstructive" but also and
more importantly *constructive* for Nietzsche; and justice is not done to
his kind of philosophy, as he conceived and sought to practice it, if the

former dimension is stressed to the neglect or exclusion of the latter. One's own philosophical taste and disposition may run only to deconstruction or to analytic inquiry, but that should not blind one to the evidence these writings amply provide that such exercises were for Nietzsche merely points of departure. Kinds of philosophy aspiring to nothing further may amount to *something* more than the mere "philosophical labor" Nietzsche contrasted to "genuinely philosophical thinking," but not much more. He would have been no more satisfied with them than he was of the neo-Kantianism he dismissed as "no more than a timid epochism and doctrine of abstinence—a philosophy that never gets beyond the threshold and takes pains to *deny* itself the right to enter—that is philosophy in its last throes, an end, an agony, something inspiring pity" (BGE 204).

There is yet another general point that emerges from reflection upon what Nietzsche wrote during these last years—what he wrote about, how he wrote about it, and what he wrote about what he wrote—that relates to his fondness for the notions of "perspective" and "perspectivism." These notions are commonly taken to have their primary place in Nietzsche's thought *within* the context of his treatment of perception, knowledge, and valuation, and are then extrapolated (bearing the meaning there accorded to them) to apply to his conception of philosophy and philosophical thinking more generally. This may be to go at the matter in the wrong way, however, and so to mistake the upshot of what Nietzsche has to say along these lines in both respects.

Suppose we take him at his word when he describes his efforts in his various works as attempts to approach certain phenomena—such as forms of art, morality, religion, society, and scientific and philosophical thinking—from "perspectives" in which they are not ordinarily viewed, and from which other insights into them may be gained, leading to their better comprehension. Suppose we further recognize that this not only is what Nietzsche sees himself as having been doing in his earlier works when he comments on them in his prefaces of 1886, but also is what he in fact more self-consciously and deliberately undertakes to do in many of his later works—following strategies that he often announces at the outset of these works or their main parts, and that are readily discernible in them.

Suppose we also take this to make good sense of the fact that Nietzsche returns to such phenomena again and again, to take different looks at them. This is just what would be needful to yield a gradually increasing comprehension of them, if it were to be thought (with Nietzsche) that their complexity and multiply conditioned, relationally constituted, and developmentally layered reality cannot be adequately grasped by any single way of looking at them, but rather only by taking collective interpretive account of what comes to light when they are approached in many different ways, with eyes differently focused. This might well be called a "perspectival" kind of thinking—as Nietzsche himself calls it; but it would not signify the abandonment of the very idea of anything like comprehension as its aim. On the contrary, it would be quite compatible with an aspiration to comprehension, and further would be precisely what its pursuit would require of one who is serious about it—as Nietzsche evidently was.

I would suggest, in passing, that his "perspectivist" pronouncements with respect to knowledge can and should be understood along similar lines. Understanding so conceived and attained may never be either certain or absolute, for it may and presumably will always admit of being improved upon and of needing to be revised to take account of what comes to light as further different relevant perspectives are hit upon. But the kind of comprehension afforded in this way may nonetheless still be deemed worthy of being called knowledge, even if (as Nietzsche suggests) its distinction from error would not for the most part be a simple black-and-white affair.

An illustration of what I am talking about, in claiming that the "perspectivism" to which Nietzsche is committed has most fundamentally to do with the strategy or method of his kind of philosophy, may be helpful. Consider for a moment two things he says in his 1886 preface to *The Birth of Tragedy*, by way of articulating his understanding at this point of what he was already fundamentally doing in that earliest of his published works. At the end of section 2 he remarks of it: "how strange it appears now, after sixteen years—before a much older, a hundred times more demanding, but by no means colder eye which has not become a stranger to the task which this audacious book dared to tackle for the first time: *to look at science in the perspective of the artist, but at art in that of life.*" And a little later, at the end of section 4, he writes: "It is apparent that it was a whole cluster of grave questions with which this book burdened itself. Let us add the gravest question of all. What, seen in the perspective of life, is the significance of morality?"

In his prefaces to *Human, All Too Human* and *Daybreak* from the same year, Nietzsche recognizes that his efforts in these works had been directed to further consideration of the same questions—but with the dawning awareness of another and even more fundamental problem, to which they were merely preparatory: "the problem of the order of rank." That, he says, is *"our* problem, we free spirits." (HH I P:7) This point is made again in his preface of the next year to the *Genealogy*.

To mention but a few salient further examples: in two of his other early works, the "Truth and Lies" essay and the second *Untimely Meditation* on history, Nietzsche clearly undertakes to look at various kinds of "knowledge" in what again may loosely and broadly be called "the perspective of life," and more specifically in the context of what certain sorts of basic human needs require. Both early and late, he also turns his attention to such phenomena as Wagnerian and other forms of art, Christianity and other religions, the thinking of philosophers like Socrates, Schopenhauer, Plato, and Kant, various cultural and political tendencies, asceticism and *ressentiment,* and much else. What light can be shed upon them, he asks, and what light upon other related matters can be shed, by looking at such things from a variety of perspectives upon them relating to the larger contexts within which they have arisen, the interests they may serve and reflect, and their consequences for human life?

All such perspectival assessments, for Nietzsche, ultimately culminate in that of what he calls "the perspective of life" and the value problem of "rank." The larger reinterpretations and revaluations they make possible and suggest, however, are arrived at by way of many diverse and more specific perspectival analyses, through which particular features of the matters under consideration are discerned. It is here that one of the most important applications of Nietzsche's avowed "experimental" manner is to be found. Another of its applications is in connection with attempts made to take the further step of trying out various ways of integrating and making collective sense of the results obtained when some phenomenon is considered from a variety of narrower and more limited perspectives. But Nietzsche devotes at least as much effort to the search for specific "perspectives" from which something new may be learned about various phenomena that have attracted his attention and to experimentation with such perspectives when he has hit upon them.

This, I would suggest, is what he was already doing—more by predilection than by design—in his pre-*Zarathustra* works, as he recognized when he wrote his prefaces of 1886. It also is what he undertook to do with greater self-consciousness, deliberateness, and strategy in his later works, from *Beyond Good and Evil* onward. Conjoined with it, at least partially motivating and warranting this "perspectival" way of proceeding, was his emerging realization (or conviction) that the phenomena with which he was concerned are themselves conditioned and engendered by complex relations. This circumstance makes such an approach at once necessary and possible. For at least in dealing with things human, we may gain access to and insight into their relationally constituted natures by learning to look at them from perspectives attuned to these relations, with eyes become sensitive to them. (Hence the celebrated passage in GM III:12.)

4

A consequence of the perspectival approach Nietzsche favors is that one must employ models and metaphors drawn from whatever resources are available to one in conceptualizing and articulating what may be discerned from the perspectives adopted—and indeed, that these perspectives themselves are to no little extent framed only by means of such resources. This point may be usefully elaborated by way of a few remarks about what Alexander Nehamas has termed Nietzsche's "aestheticism," and the "life as literature" thesis Nehamas advances in connection with it.[3] It is obvious that Nehamas is on to something in stressing that Nietzsche draws heavily and frequently upon such resources from the domain of artistic-aesthetic activity and experience. In singling out literature and (even more specifically) literary characters of a certain sort, however, it seems to me that Nehamas goes astray in two respects. First, Nietzsche avails himself at least as much of models and metaphors from *other* parts of this domain as he does from this one. And second, this is only one of a fair number of domains upon which he draws in undertaking his perspectival experiments, and is by no means exclusively privileged among them.

It is undeniable that Nietzsche often avails himself of notions like "text," "sign," and "interpretation," which certainly derive from discourse about literature, and have to do more generally with things written and otherwise expressed in language—all of which were very much on his mind throughout his career, as philologist and then philosopher.[4] But it is also undeniable that he further often avails himself of notions having to do with arts *other* than literature, such as music, painting, and even architecture and sculpture, along with the more general forms of human experience and phenomena to which *they* are related, as literature is to language. Properly formulated, it would seem to me that if one is to speak of "Nietzsche's aestheticism" at all, it should be construed to refer to his tendency to think of life and the world on the models provided by the *various* arts—including but not uniquely privileging literature among them. (Indeed, while his heavy use of "interpretation" is evocative of literature, it is also importantly associated with music; and it is the other—and in particular the *plastic*—arts that are invoked by his equally prominent use of the notion of "perspective.")

Even in this more generalized version, however, the "aestheticism" thesis cannot be sustained, if it is taken to mean anything more than that the domain of the arts is *one of* the sources from which Nietzsche draws his models and metaphors. For he draws—heavily and significantly— upon a good many others as well. The natural sciences constitute another, prompting some interpreters to make as much (for example) of his "biologism" as Nehamas makes of his "aestheticism." But biology is no more exclusive among the sciences in this respect than literature is among the arts; for Nietzsche draws upon the new physics and cosmology of his day, and even upon neurophysiology and chemistry, in much the same way.

Nor is this the end of the matter. Nietzsche takes his models and metaphors not only from the various arts and natural sciences, but also from the domain of what we now would call the social and behavioral sciences, from economics to psychology. (One need only think of the extensive use he makes of notions such as "value," "social structures," and "affects" to appreciate this point.) And he further avails himself of conceptual resources and images drawn from a multitude of other domains of discourse, including law, medicine, linguistics, and even theology.

My concern here is not merely to make the negative point that in this light little remains of the thesis of "Nietzsche's aestheticism" beyond the sound observation that the arts are among the things to which he looks for the models and metaphors he employs and develops. My larger point is a positive one; and it has an important bearing upon the question of how his "perspectivism" is to be understood, and how it works. Nietzsche derives his models and metaphors from many and diverse sources, and avails himself of the different ways of thinking associated with and suggested by them, precisely *in order to play them off against each other,* and to avoid becoming locked into any one or particular cluster of them. They afford him the means of discovering and devising an expanding repertoire of perspectives upon the matters with which he was concerned, and so of developing and sharpening what he calls the many and different "eyes" needed to contribute to a growing and deepening comprehension of them.

As Nietzsche thinks with and through them, experimenting with them, the models and metaphors he employs are themselves modified, as are the provisional versions of the interpretations he frames by means of them and elaborates to connect and integrate them. This requires both the "agility" and the ability to achieve a "comprehensive look" he asserts to be needful for his kind of philosopher. It also requires the capacity and readiness to learn (see GS 335), and further the conceptual and interpretive creativity, that set his kind of philosopher apart from all mere "dogmatists" and "philosophical laborers" alike. And to these qualities must also be added the demands he makes of uncompromising "honesty" and intellectual integrity, and what he is prepared to call "a *fundamental will* of knowledge, pointing imperiously into the depths, speaking more and more precisely, demanding greater and greater precision" (GM P:2).

This neither contradicts Nietzsche's "perspectivism" nor signifies its retraction—nor does his "perspectivism" require the abandonment of all such effort. On the contrary, the upshot of these remarks is an indication of how his "perspectivism" is most fundamentally to be understood. It characterizes his strategy in setting about to tease out aspects of the "truth" about the many matters that concern him, which (as he observes in his preface to *Beyond Good and Evil*) has not yielded itself to philosophical dogmatists in the past, and will continue to elude all those who approach them in a similarly heavy-handed and plodding, blinkered way.

5

Another indication of what Nietzsche's "perspectivism" does and does not involve is provided by the language he uses in referring to different sorts of perspectives he distinguishes. This language is frequently far from neutral with respect to their epistemic status. So, for example, in speaking derisively of the "popular valuations and opposite values on which the metaphysicians put their seal," he suggests that they may well be "merely foreground estimates, only provisional perspectives, perhaps even from some nook, perhaps from below, frog perspectives, as it were, to borrow an expression painters use" (BGE 2). In the following sections of this work, and often elsewhere, he contrasts such narrow, short-sighted, lowly, and merely "provisional perspectives" with others that would not only be different but also broader, more far-sighted, better situated, and less problematic than the former. He constantly advocates making attempts to *position oneself* for a view—of things like values, moralities, religions, kinds of art, and ways of thinking typical of scholars, scientists, and metaphysicians—that will be more comprehensive, less superficial and naive, less skewed by all-too-human motivations, freer of the fashions and preoccupations typical of one's own time, and more honest than those most people and philosophers are all too willing to settle for, or are unable to rise above. In this connection he frequently makes use of the metaphor of the desirability of viewing things "from a height" to which one finds ways to ascend. A vivid example is to be found in the following passage from the 1887 fifth book of *The Gay Science:*

> Thoughts about moral prejudices, if they are not meant to be [mere] prejudices about prejudices, presuppose a position *outside* morality, some point beyond good and evil to which one has to rise, climb, or fly. . . . That one *wants* to go precisely out there, up there, may be a minor madness, a peculiar and unreasonable "you must"—for we

seekers for knowledge also have our idiosyncrasies of "unfree will"
—the question is whether one really *can* get up there.
    This may depend on manifold conditions. In the main the question
is how light or heavy we are—the problem of our "specific gravity."
One has to be *very light* to drive one's will to knowledge into such a
distance and, as it were, beyond one's time, to create for oneself eyes
to survey millennia and, moreover, clear skies in these eyes. (GS 380)

This last remark is well worth noting. It suggests the attainability
under certain conditions of a sort of perspective ("create for oneself
eyes") Nietzsche clearly takes to be privileged ("beyond one's time,"
"clear skies in those eyes"), making possible a comprehensive and more
discerning view of such things; and these conditions include not only
strength but "lightness," together with a special sort of motivation (which
he characterizes both here and elsewhere as a "will to knowledge").
However problematic that motivation may be *in terms of its "value for
life,"* and however mundane and maculate its genealogy may be, Nietzsche
evidently does not take these circumstances to have the consequence that
nothing deserving of the name of knowledge can be attained.
    It may be that for Nietzsche the attainability of such a more elevated
and comprehensive perspective will not suffice to enable one to discern
the basic features of all of reality (if indeed it has any such features).[5] But
even if that is so, it would by no means follow that *there is nothing* of any
significance to be comprehended. For he clearly considers the forms of
morality that have arisen in the course of human events to admit of
better-than-ordinary comprehension if approached in this manner and
spirit. And he would appear to suppose that the same applies to a broad
range of other such phenomena that are to be encountered within the
compass of human life, history, and experience—and indeed to our
attained and varying human reality itself, down to its basic character and
general conditions. Even if we can go no further than this, the domain
that thus presents itself to our attention will be quite enough to keep
Nietzsche's kind of philosophers busy for a good while, and should have
quite enough significance to sustain their interest (see GM P:3).
    As long as Nietzsche remained a kind of Kantian, or an ex-Kantian on
the rebound, his comments about knowledge and its possibility have a
distinctly negative character where most matters of both metaphysical
and everyday interest are concerned. They are frequently accompanied
either by laments about what we cannot have, or by brave words about
our ability to get along without it, or by longings for something (for
example, new and compelling myths) that might replace it, psychologically
if not truthfully. On the other hand, they typically have a more positive

and hopeful character in those contexts in which the sciences can and do operate. Had Nietzsche remained such an agitated quasi-nihilistic and quasi-positivistic neo-Kantian, his thinking and his kind of philosophy would have been of only modest interest—as one rather complex variant of this post-Hegelian stance, reflecting and anticipating several familiar tendencies in the history of philosophy in the past century that were subsequently carried further by others under diverse banners on both sides of the English Channel.

But I do not believe that Nietzsche stopped there. At first hesitantly, in the works of the years immediately prior to *Thus Spoke Zarathustra,* and then with greater boldness and assurance in his post-*Zarathustra* works, I see him as having extricated himself from this unsatisfactory predicament. Freeing himself from the limitations of this heritage, he found his way to a very different understanding and appreciation of the world in which we find ourselves, of our existence in it and access to it, and of the nature and possibility of humanly attainable knowledge of ourselves, our human world, and our environing world as well.

In this final stage of his development the character of Nietzsche's comments about knowledge and its compass changed. They became less negative and more affirmative as he reconsidered the views, concepts, and contrasts he had earlier accepted in framing his thinking about them. His respect for the sciences—as far as they can go—was in some respects not only preserved but deepened; but his enthusiasm for them, as privileged and paradigmatic where attainable human knowledge is concerned, waned. Their limitations had long been apparent to him; but he also came to be convinced that they do not represent the best that we can do in dealing with many of the matters with which he and even they are concerned.

As Nietzsche reconsidered the "appearance-reality" distinction and relation, and worked his way to the conclusion of the development he sets out in his account of "How the 'True World' Became a Fable" in *Twilight of the Idols,* the notion of "knowledge" (beyond that which the sciences by themselves can afford) received a new lease on life for him, in modified but nonetheless significant form. Rather like a latter-day Vico, he seized upon the idea that it is humanly possible to comprehend at least something of that which has been humanly constituted. He came to take this idea quite seriously, concluding that it has important implications for the possibility of knowledge and that its scope is very wide indeed. For what he calls "the world that concerns us"—which includes ourselves—consists in phenomena that are in various and very real respects "our doing."

Nietzsche thus in effect proposed to replace both the Holy Grail of an ultimate reality conceived along the lines of a transcendent deity or "true world" of "being," and also the quest for it as the proper mission and picture of true knowledge, with a different paradigm of reality and associated conception of comprehension. Suppose we take as our paradigm the sort of reality in which human life and the world of our activities and experience consist, and conceive of knowledge in terms of the kind of comprehension of them of which they admit and we are capable. Making them our point of departure, we then can consider how far it is possible to go by expanding the scope of their application into the world with which we find ourselves confronted—while devoting our main efforts to the exploration of those things that are to be encountered *within* the realm of the human, and to the devising of the strategies of inquiry that will be most appropriate to their comprehension. If in this way we manage to achieve some measure of understanding of the kind of world in which our human reality has emerged and taken the various forms and associated expressions it has, so much the better. But even if we cannot do much more than comprehend ourselves and things human, this will at least be something—and something quite significant and well worth achieving at that.

6

I have attempted to show that the kind of philosophy Nietzsche called for and engaged in—especially during the final period of his productive life—is an interpretive and evaluative affair, of which good and important sense can be made. I have presented it as a *sense-making* activity, affording the prospect of enhancing not only "life" but *comprehension* —notwithstanding its avowedly "experimental" and always merely provisional character, and not only despite but actually by way of its "perspectival" manner of proceeding. I shall conclude with a few general remarks on this score.

Interpretation and evaluation for Nietzsche are pervasive and indeed inescapable human activities that take many forms and perform many functions. Both may be considered activities through which human beings *make sense* of things; and making sense of things is a feature of human life so central and basic that it may be deemed one of the hallmarks of our humanity. In a Nietzschean manner of speaking, one might go so far as to characterize *der Mensch* as "the sense-making animal."

Sense may be made of things in many different ways, standing in a problematic relation to what is made sense of; and once made, this sense itself may become further grist for the mill of sense-making. In the course of human events, moreover, a variety of relatively distinct forms of sense-making have emerged and taken shape, each exhibiting manifold and changing varieties, some of which we commonly subsume under such general rubrics as art, religion, morality, and science—all branching off in different directions from ordinary language and discourse (in which this impulse likewise is ever at work), and not infrequently feeding back into them.

All of this does not occur in a vacuum, moreover, but rather within the varying and ever-changing context of human life, and is prompted and conditioned by a multiplicity of human needs, purposes, and capacities— collective as well as individual, and physiological as well as psychological and social. Philosophy is another such activity, and likewise does not occur in a vacuum. As Nietzsche likes to remind us, it always has occurred in this same human context, and always will. This goes for his kind of philosophy as well as any other. All of them are outgrowths, hybrids and cousins of other forms of sense-making, by which they further may continue to be influenced. (The exploration of this vast and complex domain, encompassing virtually all of what transpires in human life beyond the level of the merely physical and biological phenomena underlying it, is among the general tasks of Nietzsche's kind of philosophy.)

The sense-making activities of interpretation and evaluation are fundamentally practical in their operation, even if they need not be and do not remain harnessed to entirely and immediately practical ends. They also are fundamentally *creative* in character, in that they do not passively mirror that of which sense is thus made, but rather *make something of it* —even though at any given time and place little more is usually done than to apply and employ received ways of making sense of what is encountered.

These activities issue in and sustain ways of thinking and valuing that may come to be taken for granted by those who assimilate them; but it is only on a very superficial or provisional level of consideration that they may be accorded the status of "truths" and taken to provide anything deserving of the name of "knowledge." There may be nothing of the kind that is not bound up with activities of interpretation and evaluation of some humanly possible or conceivable sort; but this does not doom all ways of making sense to perpetual parity, none of which may lay any stronger claim to the notions of "truth" and "knowledge" than any others.

As the foregoing remarks imply, these notions too can no longer be conceived in terms abstracting altogether from sense-making activities of the sort of which human thinkers are capable. Once this point is grasped and accepted, however, one may proceed to attempt to differentiate among the various ways of thinking in connection with which they commonly are and might be employed—and to privilege those that draw upon and take account of a wider range of attainable perspectives than others that are bound up with the promptings of particular and narrower "all-too-human" interests.

I consider it to have been Nietzsche's great merit to have battled his way clear of entanglement in more unenlightened and dogmatic ways of thinking, and through the philosophical "dark night of the soul" he came to associate with pessimism and nihilism, and to have arrived at this recognition and risen to this challenge. And even as he did so, he ventured out into the "new seas" with which he thus found himself confronted, learning as he went how to stay afloat and make headway upon them, beginning to chart them, and showing us how we might do likewise and continue their exploration. This is why, for me, he does not mark the end of philosophy, but rather its coming of age. And this is also why, for me as well as for him, what he offers us is indeed a "prelude to a philosophy of the future."

Notes

1. The scholarly controversy over the status of a portion of these efforts — the extensive notebooks he kept during these years as well as previously — may be avoided by restricting attention to what he wrote for publication during this period. I do in fact believe that good use can and reasonably may be made of this *Nachlaß* material in attempting to understand Nietzsche's thinking on a good many issues, including this one; but in order to finesse the vexing question of its status and reliability, nothing I shall say here will be based upon it. The case for my interpretation can be made well enough by reference to his published writings alone.

2. This reflects his early admiration for the intuitive "soothsaying" of Heraclitus as opposed to the "rope-ladder reasoning" of Parmenides, as he puts the contrast in "Philosophy in the Tragic Age of the Greeks" — an unfinished and posthumously published essay written around the time of *The Birth of Tragedy*. This essay, together with *Schopenhauer as Educator*, should be consulted by anyone interested in Nietzsche's early thinking about philosophy, which is of no little relevance to my topic here.

3. Alexander Nehamas, *Nietzsche: Life as Literature* (Cambridge: Harvard University Press, 1985).

4. I would like to note in passing that there would seem to be no good reason to take Nietzsche to have been preoccupied with those writings canonized as "literature" within this larger category, and that this raises further doubts about the soundness of Nehamas's "life as literature" thesis.

5. It may even be that Nietzsche would have us dispense with the very idea of anything of this sort. I remain convinced that he at least seriously entertained the idea that the world does possess a certain basic character that it is possible for us to discern, and that the interpretation of the world he offers in terms of "dynamic quanta" fundamentally disposed in a manner that may be expressed as "will to power" is a fair rendering of it (see my *Nietzsche*, chap. 4). But nothing I say here depends upon this.

CHAPTER FIVE

Beyond Aestheticism:
Nietzsche, Nehamas's Nietzsche,
and Self-Becoming

If Nietzsche had not existed, he would have had to have been invented. The cultural and philosophical crises he so astutely discerned were long in coming, and demanded such a herald and analyst; and the responses to them he explored called for such an imagination and voice. But though Nietzsche did exist, and played these roles with a force and brilliance that have only recently begun to be at all widely appreciated (at least on our side of the English Channel), his discovery has not made his invention unnecessary. For perhaps to a greater extent than in any other instance in the history of philosophy, his discovery is inseparable from his invention, and in a sense demands it. He does not wear his meaning on his sleeve; and the profusion of his writings, written in a bewildering variety of styles and left to us in a perplexing array of states, both requires interpretation and also renders it inconceivable that any particular interpretation offered will ever be definitive.

Indeed, the more attention Nietzsche receives, the more Nietzsches there come to be. It is now widely recognized even in the English-speaking world, as it long has been in Europe, that he was a thinker of great importance. At the same time, however, it is increasingly disputed just what he was up to, and why and how it matters. If general agreement were to be reached about him, his appreciation would be the poorer for it. The growing diversity of interpretations of his thinking signifies not the immaturity of Nietzsche studies, but rather their fuller maturing. To reckon seriously with Nietzsche is in an important sense to invent him anew, making something of what one finds in the awkward wealth of his writings, in response to one's feeling both for him and for what matters philosophically. And if anything can be said about him with assurance, it is that he would not have had it any other way.

Alexander Nehamas's Nietzsche is a welcome addition to the ranks. His *Nietzsche: Life as Literature*[1] presents a version bearing family resemblances to a number of the others; but this Nietzsche also is characterized to no little extent by traits of Nehamas's own distinctive and appealing philosophical personality. With the sensibility of an analytical philosopher, and at the same time a penchant for hyperbole, a delight in heresy, and an underlying concern to come to terms with issues commonly neglected or only superficially touched upon within the analytical mainstream (all of which Nietzsche shared), Nehamas gives us a Nietzsche who can neither be readily embraced nor lightly dismissed — and an interpretation of Nietzsche of which the same may be said.

Nehamas makes much of what he calls "Nietzsche's aestheticism, his essential reliance on artistic models for understanding the world and life and for evaluating people and actions."[2] In the course of developing and applying this idea he has many good and interesting things to say, which undeniably reflect elements of Nietzsche's thought. As Nehamas rather single-mindedly pursues it, however, he is led to say some quite startling and questionable things as well. For example: he not only claims that Nietzsche "showed that writing is perhaps the most important part of thinking," but also goes on to attribute to him "the hyperbolic view ... that writing is also the most important part of living."[3]

Nor is this Nehamas's only interpretive surprise. Another relates to his contention that Nietzsche has no "positive view of human conduct" and refuses "to offer any description of what an ideal person or an ideal life would be like,"[4] but nonetheless proffers a kind of *model* of such a person or life. Indeed, Nehamas suggests that Nietzsche "knows which particular features of his model he wants to project onto life in general,"[5] and even that he "does produce a perfect instance of it."[6] And Nehamas then makes the astonishing claim: "This character is none other than ... Nietzsche himself,"[7] who (in *Ecce Homo* in particular) is held to have made himself into "a creature of his own texts."[8] This is what Nehamas takes to be the culmination of Nietzsche's "aestheticism" and construal of "life as literature." There are a great many problems with this remarkable suggestion; and its main virtue may be its provocativeness. Grandiose as the Nietzsche of *Ecce Homo* was, it is doubtful that even *he* would have presumed to accord himself the status of a "perfect instance" of the "higher humanity" he envisions.

Nehamas's fundamental idea, around which his entire interpretation revolves (hence the book's subtitle), is that "Nietzsche's model for the world, for objects, and for people turns out to be the literary text and its components."[9] His construal of what Nietzsche has in mind in employing such notions as "the will to power" and "eternal recurrence," for example, is tailored to this idea, with surprising results. He takes Nietzsche's talk of the world as "the will to power" to be meant to convey little more than the idea of "the interconnectedness of everything"[10] and "the view that there is no general structure of the world to which any linguistic system can ever be adequate"[11] — even though (paradoxically?) "he likes to think of the world as a text."[12]

As for the "eternal recurrence," Nehamas contends not merely (and plausibly) that the most important thing about this notion is "the psychological use to which he so crucially puts [it],"[13] but moreover that it "is not a theory of the world but a view of the self."[14] This "view of the self" in turn is held to be fundamentally the idea that "the self" is something not *given* but *"created,"* through the "integration" of one's experiences and actions into a single "character." What Nehamas calls "the test involved in the thought of the eternal recurrence" is held to serve as "the final mark of this integration, its limiting case."[15] Indeed, this "testing" is what he takes the notion of the eternal recurrence to *mean* for Nietzsche (its meaning is its use?): "The eternal recurrence signifies my ability to want my life and the whole world to be repeated just as they are."[16]

Among the most striking of Nehamas's interpretive proposals is this singular construal of Nietzsche's "view of the self." He maintains not only that for Nietzsche "the self" has the status of something (to be) "created," but moreover that for him "every single one of my actions is equally essential to what I am."[17] The only "open question" is said to be "how these actions are related to our nature," or whether and how they come to be "integrated," and thus "what nature they actually constitute."[18] This leads Nehamas to suggest that "the self-creation Nietzsche has in mind involves accepting everything that we have done and, in the ideal case, blending it into a coherent whole."[19] Whether good sense can be made of this picture is one important question; and whether this account is faithful and does justice to Nietzsche's thinking with respect to "the self" — both actually and in the ideal case — is another. These will be my chief concerns in the following discussion, for they go to the heart of some of the most important and interesting parts of Nietzsche's thought, as Nehamas recognizes in making them the central themes of the second half of his book.

Before getting down to cases, I would pause to take appreciative note of the basic interpretive strategy (in dealing with Nietzsche) that Nehamas appears to embrace and follow. It is not the only such strategy, but it is mine as well. It involves taking the different things Nietzsche says relating to some topic or other as mutually illuminating and qualifying each other, and so as serving to reveal the outlines and complexities of positions of considerable subtlety and sophistication on the issues addressed.

The maxim of this strategy might be put as follows: interpret Nietzsche's emerging position on any topic to be that in relation to which most of his various particular remarks about it would make sense and become reconcilable—at least until this proves to be impossible, or lands one in absurdity. My experience has been that this experiment not only can be carried through rather successfully in many cases, but moreover is highly rewarding, philosophically as well as interpretively. Nietzsche most certainly was no systematic thinker; but I am convinced—as is Nehamas—that his thought is fundamentally much more coherent than it might at first blush seem to be.

In this connection, I would also draw attention to a companion interpretive principle, to which Nehamas likewise subscribes but is sometimes less attentive than he might be. It is to beware of Nietzsche's different uses of key terms—and especially of those with long and prominent roles in philosophical discussion—in his various remarks in which they figure. Terms like "truth" and "knowledge," "world" and "life," "will" and "power," and "value" and "morality" are all cases in point; and "self" is another. Such terms frequently are freighted with a heavy burden of long-established philosophical, religious, and ordinary-language usages and associations. Nietzsche often allows such terms to bear these traditional philosophical and religious burdens, and to draw along with them their commonplace meanings (which all require to be sorted out). But he also often goes on to make use of them to carry *different* weights, which he himself assigns to them after laundering them of many of their old accretions of meaning, appropriating them for his own purposes. If this is not noticed, he is bound to be misunderstood. It seems to me that Nehamas fails to heed the point sufficiently, in the case of the "self" in particular. He is thereby led to overdramatize and misleadingly explicate both the problem and the way of dealing with it that he attributes to Nietzsche.

Nehamas certainly is right to observe that Nietzsche rejects and seeks to lay to rest the idea of the self or ego as "a metaphysical abiding being" of some sort, whether conceived as substance or as subject. This attack upon what Nietzsche calls "the soul hypothesis" in its various philosophical guises is a major part of his broader campaign against the clutch of hypotheses making up the whole ontological inventory of traditional metaphysics, which also includes the God-hypothesis, the thing-hypothesis, and the postulation of a realm of "true being" beyond this world of "becoming." Nietzsche is no mere agnostic with respect to any of these postulated metaphysical entities, insisting rather that they ought one and all to be repudiated, and that a decisive case against each of them can be made out.

Nehamas recognizes this (as some do not), even though I do not think that Nietzsche's own basic case against the soul-hypothesis is what Nehamas suggests it to be. He also is quite right to seize upon Nietzsche's repeated references to the idea or task of "becoming who (or what) one is" as both a clue and a problem requiring to be considered in reinterpreting the self. But it bears upon *only* a part of what he has in mind; and I would suggest that Nehamas is led to give a questionable account of Nietzsche's thinking along these lines by making too much of this one idea and task.

Nehamas rightly stresses Nietzsche's contention that the subject is to be thought of as a "multiplicity," which has at most only a functional or organizational unity. All entities, for Nietzsche, are unities only as dynamic systems, ordered and maintained through the power relationships obtaining within and among them, and further reflecting the wider power relationships obtaining between them and other systems. Whatever sort of "self" a human being may be said to have (or be, or become) thus possesses an *attained* unity at most for him (and a rather precarious one at that), and is a function of such a system.

"Soul," Nietzsche has Zarathustra say, "is only a word for something about the body."[20] Thus Nehamas also rightly observes that Nietzsche would have us take the body as a clue to the nature of the self, and take the sort of unity the body has as an active organic system as a clue to the nature of the unity the self does or may have. But these are only clues, which Nietzsche suggests we do well to *start* with. Moreover, other perspectives require to be brought to bear upon it as well. One in particular, which Nehamas does not take sufficiently into account, relates to Nietzsche's insistence upon the *social* nature of consciousness. For Nietzsche, at least at a crucial juncture in the emergence and constitution of the self, *social relations* play a very prominent role. Indeed, it is not too much to say that he holds that, at a rather fundamental level, the self is a *social* phenomenon, in relation to which one's psychosomatic constitution is only preliminary. I shall shortly elaborate upon this point.

First, however, it is important to observe that Nietzsche considers it to be a mistake—deriving at least in part from our long habituation to the "soul-hypothesis," and perhaps in part also from the subtle tyranny of language and of society (both of which would have it that everyone is basically *the same* as everyone else)—to suppose that each and every human being has *the same sort of self.* He maintains, on the contrary, that different types of self emerge under different conditions, which have to do both with the differing constitutions and endowments of various human beings, and also with the differing circumstances with which they may be obliged to deal—and further, with what they go on to make of themselves in these circumstances.

So, for example, the socially constituted and shaped self of the sort that is the norm among us is for Nietzsche *one general type* of self, which human beings tend to develop under certain widespread conditions of their existence, and which for most is also the end of the line. But this type of self is further held by Nietzsche to permit of supersedence; just as it is attainable only marginally if at all in the absence of what he terms "the social straitjacket" and the devices of civilization. What human beings are or have, apart from and prior to all such vicissitudes, is no specific sort of "self" at all (except for that which may be defined entirely in terms of their bodily identity), but rather only a somewhat plastic constitution that is capable of development along various lines, and thus is a human variable.

It is with the abovementioned rather special sort of case in mind, I suggest, that Nietzsche invokes the idea and proposes the task of "becoming what (or who) one is." Of course, there is a rather uninteresting sense in which everyone may be said to do so. It is in this sense that (as Nehamas puts it) "what one is . . . is just what one becomes."[21] But on this level it does not make any difference what one does, or how one does it, or even whether one comes to "identify oneself with all one's actions"[22] (which for Nehamas is the intended upshot). For one will be what one becomes in any case.

Surely, however, Nietzsche has something more than this in mind; otherwise he could not have taken his idea of "becoming what one is" to be worth making as much of as he makes of it. A clue is provided by his evident linking of this notion with his conception of the possibility of the emergence of that type of human being he terms "higher," in contrast both to what he calls the "herd" type and also to the "half-human animals" he supposes to have prowled the world prior to the advent of anything deserving of the name of society.

Thus Nehamas does well to raise the question of how we are to understand the idea of "becoming what one is" and the notion of the self that is here invoked. But it should not be supposed that when this question has been answered we will have in our hands all we need to understand Nietzsche's thinking with respect to the general topic of human selfhood in its various permutations. It is only one of many threads which do so, more of which must be gathered and woven together if an account capable of sustaining the weight of that bulk is to be fashioned.

It is noteworthy that Nehamas turns the question of *what the self is* for Nietzsche (in speaking of becoming what or who one is), into the question of how he can continue to attach meaning to the idea of an actual or possible *unity* of the self, given his rejection of its metaphysical unity. *The unity of the self* becomes Nehamas's central theme; and this leads him to construe Nietzsche's injunction to "become what you are" as an injunction to become a *unity* — a unity moreover (and crucially) consisting in "the organization and coherence" of *everything* that one "thinks, wants, and does."[23] He takes this line despite his citation of Nietzsche's remark (in *Schopenhauer as Educator*) that conscience tells one to "Be your self! All that you are now doing, thinking, desiring, is not you yourself."[24]

It may be that Nietzsche does conceive of the possibility of the kind of unity Nehamas characterizes as "a matter of incorporating more and more character traits under a constantly expanding and evolving rubric."[25] Nehamas may also be right to link this idea to Nietzsche's idea of "giving style" to one's character, and to suggest that this involves a kind of "self-creation." But he is on less solid ground when he attempts to yoke this idea to his construal of the self for Nietzsche *as the totality* of what one "thinks, wants, and does."

Does Nietzsche (as Nehamas suggests) "reduce the agent self to the totality of its actions"?[26] Yes and no — and more "no" than "yes." One might, in this connection, recall Sartre's characterization (in *Being and Nothingness*) of human reality as something that "is what it is not, and is not what it is." For Nietzsche, as for Sartre, the only sort of determinate "being" the "agent self" has is to be explicated along the lines Nehamas suggests. That (provisional) totality is what it "is"; and unity here is ascribable to it just to the extent that the "totality" exhibits some measure of coherence. But for Nietzsche as for Sartre, there is another and important sense in which one is *not* what one "is" in *that* sense; one also *is* something one "is not" in that determinate way.

To be sure, Sartre and Nietzsche part company in the way they cash this out. There is no room in Nietzsche's conception of human reality for Sartre's brand of "transcendence" and "nothingness," grounded in the nihilating nature of the ontologically irreducible *"pour soi."* Instead, Nietzsche prefers to think in terms of rather general standing *dispositions* associated with configurations of power-oriented dynamic quanta, which dispositions are mutable and may or may not be well integrated and collectively oriented in some definite direction.[27]

Above and beyond the "totality of its actions," the "agent self" for Nietzsche is to be conceived in terms of the "totality of dispositions" it represents, which indeed may fairly be said to constitute it and whatever *ongoing* unity it may be said to have. And I think it is a mistake to suppose that, in speaking of such dispositions (and of that *Ur*-disposition, the "will to power"), Nietzsche has in mind nothing more than *the set of all actions* which this or that human being in fact happens to perform as it goes along. The "agent self" may be no "being" above and beyond or beneath them; but it does not reduce to them either. Nietzsche seeks a conception of our reality that would dispel the idea that this is a forced choice; and in his talk of power-quanta, power relationships, and "will to power" he attempts to suggest how one might go about framing such an alternative.

Next: in commending "becoming what one is," does Nietzsche really have in mind what Nehamas describes as "a continual process of integrating one's character traits, habits and patterns of interaction with one another"?[28] This sort of "integration" might indeed result in the attainment of a kind of "unity" of a human personality, or "unified self"; but, whether or not it is an "impossible goal," as Nehamas suggests, is he right in claiming that the "perfect unity" in which this process would in principle issue is one that Nietzsche may be taken to advocate?[29] I have my doubts. At the very least, it would seem implausible to suppose that Nietzsche means to commend the attainment of such unity *without any qualification* with respect to the *kind of life* led. Something more than this sort of unity *as such* matters a good deal to him.

It is both helpful and important to distinguish two questions here. First: What is it that Nietzsche repeatedly urges those for whom he is writing (in contrast to the general run of humankind) to *become* — regardless of whether he adds some such phrase as "who you are" or "what you are"? And second: What sorts of unity of the self or person does Nietzsche consider to be attainable by various types of human being? The answer to the first question is clearly that he would have these few, who constitute potential exceptions to the human rule, become the sort of human being he terms "higher," at least approximating to his ideal of the *Übermensch*. This would represent the emergence of a new "artistic" humanity, in connection with which it is appropriate to speak of "great tasks" and the "grand style."[30]

Thus it is not unity per se that Nietzsche commends, but rather *becoming the higher human being one may have it in one to become.* This construal of his injunction is supported, among other things, by calling to mind not only the passage from *Schopenhauer as Educator* cited above, but also some of the main themes of his writings from first to last: the enhancement of life, the transcendence of animality, self-overcoming (especially where the all-too-human is concerned), development, sublimation, transformation, creativity, spiritual superiority, nobility, and the grand style. It is in the context of this cluster of themes that Nietzsche's references to "becoming what one is" have their place and require to be understood. Their prominence suggests that, when potentially "higher" human beings attain to that "higher humanity" of which they are capable, they have "become what they are," *whatever* the relation may be between their attained and previous identities. If they may be said to have followed Nietzsche's injunction in *Schopenhauer as Educator* to "be your self," or even thus to be "true to themselves," this requires to be understood in the above rather unusual sense. For as Nietzsche goes on to say in the same work, "Your true nature does not lie hidden deep inside you but immeasurably high above you, or at least above that which you customarily consider to be your ego."[31]

Consider also Nietzsche's gloss upon his famous statement (in *The Gay Science*) that "we ... *want to become those we are*" (GS 335). He goes on to refer to "human beings who are new" and "who give themselves laws, who create themselves." This likewise indicates that his conception of the "self" that such a human being would come to have (and of its unity) is to be understood rather differently than simply in terms of rendering one's past, present, and future a "coherent whole," in which *all* that one goes on to do and *all* that one has done and *all* of one's previous habits and future dispositions form an "integrated totality," as Nehamas would have it. In any event, this would seem to fit poorly with Nietzsche's emphasis upon self-overcoming, self-transformation, creating oneself, giving oneself one's own laws, and the like.

To be sure, Nietzsche does not suppose that one can escape what one has been altogether. On the contrary, he recognizes that whatever emerges from such developments will bear the marks of their points of departure, and of what there was to be overcome, transformed, and utilized in the process of self-creation. But it still would seem that he looks to the attainment of a *different* self with a *new* specific unity in conceiving of what is to emerge when one "becomes what one is."

The answer to the second question is more complicated. The unity exhibited or attainable by any human being is for Nietzsche to be understood in terms of the integration and organization of that human being's dispositions. But the wealth of human types Nietzsche discerns confronts us with a variety of such possible unities—as well as with a profusion of cases in which no such unities are in evidence. There is, for example, the sort of coordination and hierarchical organization of dispositions characteristic of the "healthy half-human animal," rooted in its basic constitution and unaffected by social constraints. This human type may be no more (or seldom) to be found; but one possible form of unity of the self may be associated with it. Others may be supposed to characterize the "master," "slave," "priestly," and "ascetic" types, at least some of which in various guises are suggested to be with us still.

Another is associated with that human type Nietzsche has in mind when he speaks of the "perfect herd animal." Here too, there is a coordination and hierarchical organization of dispositions; but these dispositions are shaped and formed through social conditioning, in a society so structured that such unified sets of dispositions are strictly cultivated. This, for Nietzsche, while hardly satisfactory, is a development not to be despised, for it lays the foundations of the emergence of any "higher" and different, more autonomous sort of selfhood and responsibility.

I shall elaborate briefly upon Nietzsche's views along these lines, for they are of considerable interest. "To breed an animal *with the right to make promises,*" he writes in the second essay in *On the Genealogy of Morals,* "is not this the paradoxical task that nature has set itself in the case of man?" (GM II:1). What engages his attention here is the fundamental issue of what the possibility of promising (and keeping one's promises) presupposes, and the ramifications in human life of the establishment of this possibility.

Its establishment, Nietzsche contends, required the development of a kind of memory going beyond the (basically animal) capacity to absorb and retain things experienced. "A real *memory of the will*" had to be attained, enabling one to "ordain the future in advance," despite the intervention of many other events and the continuous alteration of circumstances. And he argues that it is in a *social* context that this capacity first was and continues to be acquired. For it was the social necessity of rendering human beings responsible and therefore reliable, and thus of so molding them that they can make and keep promises, that was the original and primary impetus to its development. Nietzsche takes this development to have been of the greatest importance: "Man himself must first of all have become *calculable, regular, necessary,* even in his own image of himself, if he is to be able to stand security for *his own future,* which is what one who promises does!" (GM II:1).

This, on his view, is "the long story of how *responsibility* originated" (GM II:2); but it is a good deal more as well. It also has direct and important bearing on the nature of *personal identity,* as this is usually understood and attained. Such identity is suggested by this account to be a function and consequence of this socially induced transformation, rather than attaching to some sort of substantial (and individual) "self" each of us has or is innately and on our own. What is here at issue is not the sort of identity we each possess by virtue of the spatio-temporal continuity and discreteness of our bodily existence. Rather, it is that which is purportedly characteristic of each human being as a single *person* persisting as the same thinking, feeling, choosing, acting, responsible subject throughout the course of its life. Nietzsche does not dispute that there is something to this idea of personal identity. But he maintains that it requires to be fundamentally reinterpreted.

On a rather rudimentary level, human beings may be said to have (acquired) such an identity to the extent that they have come to have some relatively settled set of rather specific behavioral dispositions. This is a development that goes no little distance toward satisfying the social demand for regularity and calculability in the conduct of members of a social group; and it accordingly may be supposed to be strongly promoted and also guided by societal pressures. But such identity is insufficient by itself to ensure the degree and kind of regularity and calculability required in order for social institutions to develop and function. Assurance is needed of reliability in courses of action reaching far beyond the present, even if one's inclinations and circumstances change, and independently of the desires one might have or come to have. It is only if one learns to think of oneself as having an identity *transcending* one's various desires and dispositions, immediate circumstances and conditions—which remains the same even though all of these may vary, and extends from the present back into the past and on into the future—that one becomes fit for social life.

As long as one's existence is little more than a succession of episodes in which one responds in an immediate way to situations with which one is confronted, in accordance with whatever dispositions and desires are dominant at the moment, this social requirement is not met. If actions are viewed as having their source in nothing beyond so ephemeral a combination of external and internal circumstances, it would make little sense to suppose that anything done upon one ocassion would ensure that something else of a particular sort would be done upon another. A kind of consciousness requires to be established that transcends the immediacy of absorption in these circumstances of the moment, bringing both past and future into view. Links of identification must be forged between episodes in one's life, such that one can feel bound in the present by performances occurring in the past, and bound in the future by what one does in the present. One must learn to *think of oneself,* rather than merely acting and reacting as one is moved in the moment to do—and moreover to think of oneself as somehow being the *same* now as previously, and as being the same in the future as now, notwithstanding changes in one's states and situation.

The basic human purpose of such self-consciousness and self-identification becomes clear only when the idea of agency with respect to one's performances and actions is added to them. It is only with this addition that the social demand is satisfied, of rendering human beings reliable in their dealings with each other beyond the extent to which settled dispositions render them predictable. Our personal identity in its most commonplace form, according to Nietzsche, originated in this socially induced self-identification, as unitary agents in relation to our conduct through time. And while fundamentally a fiction, the acceptance of this idea (under the pressure of our being treated as though it were fact) has the consequence that we not only apprehend ourselves accordingly, but also to a considerable extent cease to *be* creatures of the moment, and *become* such "selves"—at least in a functional sense, if not substantially. Thus Nietzsche contends that, "with the aid of the morality of mores and the social straitjacket, man was actually *made* calculable" (GM II:2). One is brought to *take on* the sort of identity that is the basis of such calculability and social reliability.

But this is not all: a crucial step has also been taken in the direction of the establishment of the human possibility of that more exceptional, extrasocial sort of undertaking Nietzsche has in mind when he speaks of the "great tasks" to which "higher men" may apply themselves. Thus he suggests that, even though the process of transforming human beings in such a way that they may be said to come to have personal identities is a socialization phenomenon in which the "social straitjacket" is employed to render them reliable members of society, it prepares the way for a further development transcending this result. For "at the end of this tremendous process," there emerges its "ripest fruit," which is "the *sovereign individual*, like only to himself, liberated again from morality of custom, autonomous and supramoral," who "has his own independent, protracted will," and whose "mastery over himself also necessarily gives him mastery over circumstances, over nature, and over all more short-willed and unreliable creatures" (GM II:2).

In this way, Nietzsche suggests how the foundation has been laid for the possibility of those he calls "higher" human beings, through a process occurring in response to certain fundamental social demands, and which initially has a very different sort of result. Even the personal identity of such a "sovereign individual" is not to be conceived as the "being" of an unchanging spiritual substance. Yet it is no mere illusion either, but rather a genuine attainment. And it is at this point that Nietzsche's notion of "self-becoming" set forth in section 335 of *The Gay Science* comes into play.

Nehamas's interpretation of this notion culminates in his suggestion that Nietzsche takes *literature*, and more specifically literary *characters*, as his model in conceiving of what such a human being and self would be like. More to the point, however, is Nietzsche's frequent recurrence to something similar but also importantly different in this connection: namely, the phenomenon of *art*, and therewith the artist and the work of art. As early as *The Birth of Tragedy*, he had maintained that in certain respects and circumstances we may be likened to artists, and moreover that we have (or attain) our highest dignity *as* works of art—that is, to the extent that we *become* something of the sort (BT 5). Variations on this theme appear repeatedly throughout his later writings. He even suggests that "the world" may be likened to "a work of art that gives birth to itself" (WP 796); and this in a way is how he thinks of humanity in the various forms it has taken as well.

Furthermore, this is what he would *have* happen, in a less haphazard and more particularized way, in the case of those exceptional human beings who are capable of living beyond and independently of general social and cultural norms. The higher humanity he envisions is styled an "artistic" one, in the sense that those attaining it would be strong and creative enough to make of themselves and their lives "aesthetic phenomena," akin to but transcending those of the sorts artists hitherto have learned to bring about in their various special media. And this is of the greatest importance to him, for, as he puts it in *The Birth of Tragedy,* "it is only as an *aesthetic phenomenon*" that "existence and the world" can be "justified" (BT 5).

This involves doing more with our lives than rendering them unified wholes, in which everything about ourselves is equally essential and a way is found of integrating everything with everything else. For artists are *selective,* and are *transformers* of their material as well. Much must be eliminated, purified, and altered, both in themselves and in the material upon which they work, before they become the artists they have it in them to be, and before anything on which they work attains artistic form. So it is not for nothing that Nietzsche insists upon "hardness" toward oneself, and upon the proper sort of *Bildung,* if the "creator" and "form-giver" in one are to triumph over the merely "creaturely" about one, which he terms so much "material . . . , excess, clay, dirt, nonsense, chaos" (BGE 225).

In *Twilight of the Idols,* Nietzsche argues that art fundamentally is a matter of a compulsion to "transform things . . . into perfection" (TI IX:9), which involves the imposition of form upon that with which one begins, thereby altering its aspect and its character as well. It is "idealizing," not in the sense of "discounting the petty and inconsequential" altogether, but rather in the sense of "bring[ing] out the main features so that the others disappear in the process." And even these "main features" are as much *created* as discovered, because they only emerge as "one lends to things, one *forces* them to accept from us, one violates them" (TI IX:8).

If one returns, with *this* "model" in mind, to a consideration of the sort of self Nietzsche thinks of as being attained and created as one becomes the higher human being one may have it in one to be, it would seem that Nehamas's idea of "perfect unity" should not be read into it. In life as in art, for Nietzsche, "perfecting transformation" does not translate into the establishment of "perfect unity," at least as Nehamas thinks of it. That would be too monolithic, too homogeneous, or at any rate too democratic and harmonious. To construe Nietzsche as taking such unity to be essential to selfhood is to impute to him an attachment to one of the elements of the traditional conception of the self he actually would have us abandon, or at least significantly modify, even as something like a regulative rather than a constitutive idea.

The kind of transformation of ourselves Nietzsche discerns as a possibility, and commends as a task (at least to some), may indeed involve ordering and integration, and issue in a kind of wholeness and unity. But it would have even the appearance of thoroughgoing completeness only from a distance, from which its broad outlines and salient features alone would be discernable. And even then, it would pertain more to a *selected configuration* of one's basic "standing" and emergent "higher-order" dispositions, than to the profusion of one's particular thoughts, desires, feelings, and actions, which this configuration of dispositions would but generally and loosely inform.

"A more perfect union," to borrow a phrase, would not seem to be humanly possible, as Nehamas suggests. But an *"imperfect* union" of *this* sort—that is, a selectively *perfecting* one—*would* seem to be attainable. Nietzsche does go further, in suggesting it to be desirable as well, for reasons relating to his conception of what the "enhancement of life" and "life raised to its highest potency" involve. And this, on my reading of him, is as far as he goes—which, to my way of thinking, is exactly right, and quite enough to make good and important sense of his notion of self-becoming and its significance.

Notes

This essay incorporates a portion of my review of Nehamas's book in *The Philosophical Review,* vol. 97, no. 2 (April 1988), 266–70 (in the first few pages), and some material drawn from 291–94 of my *Nietzsche.* For a fuller discussion of these and related issues, see chapter 5 of that book.

1. Alexander Nehamas, *Nietzsche: Life as Literature* (Cambridge: Harvard University Press, 1985).
2. Ibid., 39.
3. Ibid., 41.
4. Ibid., 8.
5. Ibid., 227.
6. Ibid., 230.
7. Ibid., 233.
8. Ibid., 8.
9. Ibid., 90.

10. Ibid., 80.
11. Ibid., 93.
12. Ibid., 82.
13. Ibid., 142.
14. Ibid., 150.
15. Ibid., 190.
16. Ibid., 191.
17. Ibid., 157.
18. Ibid., 158.
19. Ibid., 188-89.
20. Z I:4 ("On the Despisers of the Body").
21. Nehamas, 191.
22. Ibid.
23. Ibid., 180.
24. Ibid., 171.
25. Ibid., 183-84.
26. Ibid., 172.
27. See my *Nietzsche,* chap. 5, esp. 316ff.
28. Nehamas, 185.
29. Ibid., 195.

30. See my *Nietzsche,* 330-40 and 389-94. In this connection, I would observe that while for Nietzsche such exceptional "higher types" may be thought of as approximations to his ideal of the *Übermensch,* it surely is implausible of Nehamas to suggest that the latter notion amounts to nothing more than "the idea of creating one's own self," as he does when he adds: "or, what comes to the same thing, the *Übermensch*" (174).

31. Nietzsche, *Schopenhauer as Educator,* tr. by William Arrowsmith, in *Unmodern Observations,* ed. Arrowsmith, New Haven: Yale University Press, 1990), 166.

CHAPTER SIX

Beyond Scholasticism: On Dealing with Nietzsche and His *Nachlaß*

We shall forever be in Mazzino Montinari's debt for his enormous labor of love, which left to us what is likely to remain the best possible presentation of Nietzsche's legacy to us. Montinari was a scholar's scholar, and his gift to us is invaluable. It is hard to imagine that it will ever be worth anyone's while to seek to improve upon what he did with all of Nietzsche's writings. He put nearly the whole of Nietzsche's written legacy at our disposal, as faithfully and authoritatively as anyone could. We honor him best by recognizing his astonishing accomplishment for what it is — and then by availing ourselves of it extensively, to the end of coming to terms as best we can with Nietzsche's thought.

As we proceed to do this, Montinari's labors can aid us, but they cannot guide us. Our task is not to follow him, but rather — with the help he has given us — to confront the Nietzsche he so fully made accessible to us. This task itself is not clearly defined for us, by Montinari, or even by Nietzsche himself, let alone anyone else. For in fact there are many ways of taking up this task, and beyond that, many possible ways of carrying them out.

What Montinari made available to us, in definitive form and clearly demarcated fashion, is not merely the body of work Nietzsche published or readied for publication, but also that immense and diverse mass of material he left upon his collapse — in the form of drafts, notes, and letters. The letters were at least intended to be read by those to whom they were sent; but the *Nachlaß* is a different story — and therein lies our problem. What are we to make of this *Nachlaß,* in relation to the rest of what he wrote — and in particular, in relation to what he published or had readied for publication?

There are certain scholarly interests and related standards that understandably accord decisive importance to publication or other evidence of an author's preparedness to say something publicly. But there are also *interpretive* concerns that render it appropriate and desirable to take account of other material as well. And there are further *philosophical* concerns that may prompt one to avail oneself of ideas and arguments a writer has somewhere set down and perhaps worked upon, however unclear the writer's own ultimate commitment to them may be, and indeed even if there is evidence that the writer may have come to have doubts or second thoughts about them, if they prove to be of interest.

I would hope that it need not even be argued that something found in a writer's *Nachlaß* may be taken as grist for one's own philosophical mill regardless of any questions that might be raised about the writer's commitment to it—and further, that with proper qualifications, attribution of it to the writer can and should be made. When it comes to the *interpretation* of something of this sort, however, or of the thought of the writer with respect to the matters to which the material relates, the problem becomes more difficult and is more reasonably contested.

I readily grant that, as a general rule, in interpreting an author's thought primacy should be given to things the author is prepared to say in things intended for publication. Here, however, as in so many other respects, Nietzsche is a rather special case. When one's productive life ends as abruptly as his did, and at such an early age, and especially when his publications so typically consisted of material first developed in the workshop of his notebooks, one should not be too quick to take a purist line.

Suppose I receive the terrible news that a philosophical colleague who was only in his mid-forties has succumbed to a sudden illness that proved fatal—as quickly as Walter Kaufmann's illness did—leaving him no opportunity to decide what to do with the material in notebooks he was known to keep and use as his workshop. Suppose that he was a brilliant and original thinker, and a prolific writer as well, having published extensively and at an increasing rate during the past decade, free from the administrative and other academic duties that slow so many of us down. Suppose that, remarkable though his record of recent publication during the last half dozen years of his productive life may have been, it is discovered that he left a great mass of material in his notebooks from his abruptly terminated final period. And suppose that this material becomes available, through the Herculean labors of a certain scholar, making it possible for those interested in the thought of our lamented colleague to take account of it as well as the things he published and left ready for publication. Suppose further that our colleague wrote rather in the manner of Wittgenstein, and that nearly all of his published and finished works had the character of collections of relatively brief discussions and remarks similar to the material in his notebooks, rather than essays and monographs of the usual sort. And suppose that, even in his published writings, what we find is a philosophical mind at work piecemeal on a variety of topics to which he returns again and again, rather than positions elaborated systematically on one topic after another and seldom reconsidered once they had been committed to print.

Suppose, finally, that we are philosophers who have been greatly impressed by the things our colleague published in his all-too-brief career, and wish to understand his thinking as best we can. What should we do? If he had lived to a ripe old age, it might be reasonable to suppose that he would have had time and opportunity enough to sort out his thoughts and notes, and that anything he had not seen fit to publish probably could and should be given little attention in relation to his published corpus. But this was not so in the case of our hypothetical colleague. He was snatched untimely from us, only a few years after hitting his stride philosophically. His thinking is no less in evidence in his notebooks than in his published works. Would we not consider it our great good fortune to be able to avail ourselves of the former as well as the latter? If it is his thinking that interests us, would we not look to the unpublished material to supplement the indications of his thinking to be found in what he had published? I would, in such a case; and I regard Nietzsche's case as just such a case.

We recently passed the centenary of Nietzsche's *Götzen-Dämmerung.* It would be ironic indeed if we were to celebrate this anniversary by turning *him* into an idol—a fate he feared, and wished to avoid. Far better, and truer to his philosophical spirit, to treat him as a colleague or companion, as an esteemed fellow-thinker whose diverse efforts we seek to understand and assist and criticize, and from which we seek to benefit—not as a revered figure to be idolized, whose published works are to be regarded as a canon of texts, to be zealously guarded and defended against dilution by any admixture of other material. In dealing with our colleagues, we owe special attention to their finished works; but we also give our attention to their experiments, their tentative suggestions, their drafts and sketches, when we are given access to them. And our understanding of their concerns and projects, and of the contours and drift of their thinking, is based in part on what we come to know of them in all these ways.

We do our colleagues an injustice if we are incautious in our attributions of views to them on the basis of unguarded remarks they make informally rather than in print; but we would be needlessly puritanical to refuse to pay attention to anything they say unless and until they say it in print—especially if they are taken from us abruptly at the height of their powers, in mid-life and mid-stride. Their expressions of things they are thinking about, in conversation or in drafts of work in progress, can and do afford insight into their thinking that is of no little value to us in our attempts to understand them, even if it may be more problematical than what they have gotten around to publishing.

I sometimes refer to myself as a Nietzsche-scholar — and I certainly try to be a responsible one. I get upset when people talk or write about Nietzsche in a way that betrays a lack of good scholarship, whether they are hostile to him or enthusiastic about him. But when I stop to think about my most common relation to him, it seems to me to be most accurate to say that he is like a colleague to me — only a more intimate one than any actual colleague I have ever had. In the language of *Zarathustra,* he is a constant philosophical companion to me, with whom I think about nearly everything in philosophy that interests me. When I read him, and for years now even when I am not actually reading him, it is as though I am in silent conversation with him. I listen to him, respond to him, ask him things, hear him answer, argue with him, and listen again.

It is not only when I read or reflect upon his published and finished writings that this happens. My conversations with him continue by way of other things he wrote as well. I hear my companion Nietzsche in his letters, and in his *Nachlaß* too. I do not stop up my ears when he speaks there, any more than I stop up my ears when one of my living colleagues is talking, trying out some idea he has had. Nothing a colleague says in philosophical conversation is sacred — but then, neither is anything he says in print on some occasion. It all is relevant, contributing to one's understanding of his thinking even if he backs away and tries again. The point of such conversation is not to fix a canon of the person's official pronouncements, but rather to try to come to understand things together, and to understand each other in doing so, even in our areas of disagreement.

I tend to think of everything we have of Nietzsche's writings as part of his extended conversation with any of us who choose to enter into the conversation, as his companions rather than as self-appointed guardians of the sanctity of the texts he published or finished. And I regard it as untrue to his spirit to make so much of certain general standards of scholarship that one falls into a fetishism of the published word, which it is hard to imagine his sharing, and which is likely to impede rather than to promote the understanding and appreciation of his philosophical thinking. When a great deal is made of this matter, I sometimes hear the scornful voice of the Nietzsche of *Schopenhauer as Educator* — and sometimes his equally disdainful laughter.

Suppose that I am writing something about Nietzsche's thinking with respect to human nature — as I have in fact done before, and intend to do again. This is a general topic about which he clearly thought a great deal, for he wrote a great deal about it, turning to it again and again throughout his entire productive life. He says things about it or relating importantly to it in nearly everything he published, from *The Birth of Tragedy* to *The Antichrist.*

But that is not all. He also says things about it or relating importantly to it in "On Truth and Lies," for example, and a great many other such things in his notebooks. This is material most of which he did not publish (though he did draw upon it on many occasions in works he did publish). We will never know which of these things might have found their way into versions he might have gone on to incorporate into published works if his productive life had gone on for another ten or twenty or thirty years, any more than we will ever know what other things he might have eventually come to say on this topic in such a hypothetically extended productive life. But while we can hardly even guess at the latter, we do know at least that it did occur to him to write down the former, and often to rework this material repeatedly, as he reflected on the topic during his actual productive life. And the fact that he had not seen fit to make use of it in any of the things he had published or was intending to publish at the time of collapse does not warrant the conclusion that he rejected it in any larger sense.

What then are we to do with these various written expressions and traces of his thinking on this topic, early and late, published or readied for publication or left in his drawers and notebooks upon his untimely collapse? How should one deal with them, and what use of them is appropriate in one's interpretation of his thinking? There is no single, obvious, correct answer to these questions that would settle them decisively for each and all of us who would write about Nietzsche's thought on such a topic in a manner true to it, true to our intellectual consciences, and true to the standards of sound scholarship. It may be that interpretive priority should be given to things he says in works he published or left ready for publication, and among them to things he says in works written in the latter part of his productive life over those written earlier; but it is by no means obvious that attention ought to be restricted entirely to what he actually said in the finished works of his last productive years.

In fact, it seems to me that this purist approach would be overly abstemious, and would be likely to yield an impoverished interpretation and appreciation of his thinking, inferior in adequacy to that which is attainable, with due scholarly and interpretive care, by availing oneself also of related earlier and unpublished expressions of his thinking relating to the topic. This point is all the more persuasive, in my view, in light of the character of Nietzsche's published writings themselves, none of which gives us a full, final statement of his position on such a topic—one that can be regarded as definitive in relation to the rest. Earlier and later works shed light on each other, as do later works themselves, even if they are not all on a par with each other. And something like this also applies, I suggest, with respect to his finished works and the *Nachlaß*.

The last four years of Nietzsche's productive life are the years that saw the appearance or completion of *Beyond Good and Evil*, *On the Genealogy of Morals*, the fifth book of *The Gay Science*, *Twilight of the Idols*, and *The Antichrist*. In all these works, the issues of how to think about our human nature or "the type man," and of what is to be said about it, figure importantly among the many matters with which he deals. His concern with them underlies and partly motivates his treatment of many of the other issues he discusses. They are problems on which these works show him working, approaching them in different ways and on different levels of generality — as indeed he had been doing earlier. It is hardly surprising to find that he was reflecting upon them extensively and from a variety of angles in his notebooks from this period as well. Some of his thoughts from his notebooks are reflected in these works, as he happened to find places for them or need of them — but only some of them, brought in to address his specific foreground concerns.

What he has to say along these lines in these works is enough to enable one to grasp the outlines of his developing thinking relating to these issues, and a good deal of its elaboration and specific detail as well — and it seems to me that one is well advised to begin with this. But there is more — a great deal more — that also relates to these issues, in a variety of similar and different ways, in the notebooks from this period. What he selected to use in the works he finished is only the tip of the iceberg. One gets a much better and fuller picture of the thinking that led him to say certain of the things he does, and also of the development of his thinking with respect to them, by looking at this larger mass of material and relating it to what he said in these works, than one does by attending to the latter alone.

If one's concern is really to understand as best one can what is going on here, as Nietzsche attempted to come to terms with the problem of "the type man," even in the published works themselves, one *needs* to take into consideration the material in the notebooks. If he had been a different sort of writer, who spelled out his thinking and elaborated his views as completely as he could in systematic treatments of such topics, and who waited to do so until he had his views fully worked out, it would not be so needful to go to his notes and drafts in order to do justice to his thought. But he was not that sort of writer. And so we do best to avail ourselves of the opportunity to explore what lay beneath the tip of the iceberg.

Perhaps I should give a few examples. In *Beyond Good and Evil*

Nietzsche says some very important things about "translating man back into nature" and about the "will to power" as the basic principle of human psychology. In *On the Genealogy of Morals* he says some very important things about the impact of socialization upon our original instinct structure and in the origin of both consciousness and conscience, and about the role played by certain sorts of social practice in the constitution of personal identity. In the fifth book of *The Gay Science* he says some very important things about the origin of self-consciousness and its relation to language and to the social need to be able to communicate, and about the role of consciousness in relation to action. In *Twilight of the Idols* he says some very important things about the nature of "will" and "willing" in relation to action, about reason, and about the phenomenon of sublimation. And in *The Antichrist* he says some very important things about what sets human beings apart from the rest of nature, and about how the notions of enhancement, decline, sickness, health, and human types are to be understood in their applications to our humanity.

In each case, however, and in many other such cases of things he says in these works that are highly relevant to his treatment of our human nature, he does not elaborate upon his points fully enough to make his meaning and thinking entirely clear. What he does say certainly serves to make important points in a vivid and suggestive way; and when these discussions are considered together, the outlines and some of the detail of his developing conception of our nature may be discerned. But when one turns to the notebooks, one finds a wealth of material that fleshes out this conception and reveals the thinking leading to it much more fully and clearly.

I will readily grant that it can always be questioned whether any particular item in the notebooks can be taken to show what Nietzsche really thought on the matter discussed in it—though of course this also applies with respect to any particular passage in *The Gay Science* or *Beyond Good and Evil* or any of his other published works. It may also always be questioned just what he meant in any such case, and whether what he wrote is to be understood with or without qualification of some sort. But it is beyond question that he did write these things; and it may reasonably be assumed that he had something in mind when he wrote them. At the very least, published or not, they are expressions of something he was thinking when he wrote them. And if one takes account of what he says in as many such items and passages relating to a given topic one can lay one's hands upon, bearing in mind what he says in others on related topics, one is in the best possible position to understand what and how he thought about it.

Interpretations of his thinking with respect to such topics may still vary; but it is my contention that they will be better informed, and more likely to do justice to his thinking, if they are based upon a consideration of all available relevant material from both sorts of sources than if they are based upon what he says in the published works alone. One might suppose otherwise if Nietzsche had been a different sort of writer, who put all of his cards on the table in a series of monographs dealing thoroughly and systematically with various general topics, and who had lived long enough to leave no unfinished business. But that is not the way it was in his case.

In passing, I would remark that the campaign to discredit the volume we know as *The Will to Power,* and to show that Nietzsche either never really had or abandoned the idea of publishing such a book, seems to me to be a red herring. Of course it is a "non-book," at least in the sense of something attributable to Nietzsche himself in terms of its selection of material, organization, and publication as a book—though in form it is as much a "book" as many of the things he himself did publish. And I do not dispute the claim that he appears to have abandoned the various plans he sketched for a work with something like that title. But that is neither here nor there with respect to the issue of what to make of the material in the notebooks. If using this material in the manner I have suggested is appropriate, the use of those selections from this material which were assembled in it is appropriate—even though their inclusion in it gives them no privileged status over the rest of the material in the notebooks, of which account should also be taken. Regarded as nothing more than a sample of material from the notebooks, therefore, I see nothing wrong with making use of it—even though care must be taken not to regard it as more than that.

In conclusion: to return to my image of Nietzsche as colleague or companion, my general point is that if one regards him as a more life-sized figure, reflects upon the nature of both his published and his unpublished writings and upon the abrupt early termination of his productive life, and approaches him concerned above all to understand his philosophical thinking as fully as possible, the question of the *Nachlaß* appears in a somewhat different light than it does if one places him beyond such familiar treatment, embraces certain very strict ideas about attribution, and approaches him in a more cautious and scholarly manner.

I have no objection to those who deal with him in the latter spirit. I nearly always benefit from their efforts, and have far more sympathy with them than I do with those who play fast and loose with Nietzsche's writings, seizing upon things that suit their purposes while ignoring others, interpreting them idiosyncratically, and reducing him either to a caricature of himself or to a creature made in their own image. But I prefer to deal with Nietzsche in the more collegial spirit I have described; and I feel able to do so without doing injustice to him, and with my intellectual conscience and scholarly integrity intact. Indeed, I am convinced that it is only in this way that I can do him the greatest justice of which I am capable. And I venture to say that it is in the manner of a colleague and companion that he himself would have most preferred to be treated.

Part Two

APPROACHES

CHAPTER SEVEN

Making Life Worth Living: Nietzsche on Art in *The Birth of Tragedy*

No higher significance could be assigned to art than that which Nietzsche assigns to it in the opening section of *The Birth of Tragedy* (hereafter BT). "The arts generally" are said to "make life possible and worth living" (BT 1). Art was never far from Nietzsche's mind, even when dealing with matters seemingly far removed from it. He includes a number of artists among the "higher" types of human being whom he takes to stand out from the greater part of humankind hitherto, and likens to artists both the "philosophers of the future" he envisages and the "overman" he declares to be "the meaning of the earth." Indeed, he even aspired to art himself, investing much effort and a good deal of himself in poetic and musical composition.

Nietzsche's interest in art was by no means either exclusively academic or merely personal. In his original preface to BT, he speaks disparagingly of readers who may "find it offensive that an aesthetic problem should be taken so seriously," and who are unable to consider art more than a "pleasant sideline, a readily dispensable tinkling of bells that accompanies the 'seriousness of life.'" Against them, he advances the startling contention that "art represents the highest task and the truly metaphysical activity of this life" (BT P). And he goes on to maintain that "the arts generally" serve to "make life possible and worth living" (BT 1). It remains to be seen what he has in mind in saying this, as well as in terming art "the truly metaphysical activity of this life." But these passages provide an ample indication of the centrality of art both in the cluster of issues he deals with in BT and also in his thinking about them.

1

Nietzsche makes no attempt to conceal the influence of Schopenhauer on both his conception of reality and his thinking about the arts. Schopenhauer may fairly be said to have been his primary philosophical inspiration, in a twofold way. On the one hand, Nietzsche was initially convinced of the soundness of much of what Schopenhauer had to say about the world, life and the arts. But on the other, he was deeply unsettled by Schopenhauer's dark conclusions with respect to "the value of existence" and the worth of living. Most of his contemporaries tended to dismiss Schopenhauer as a morbidly pessimistic crank even while being appreciative of his stylistic brilliance. But Nietzsche saw that he had raised profoundly serious questions about life, which could no longer be answered as theologians and philosophers traditionally had answered them, and to which new answers had to be found if those given by Schopenhauer himself were not to prevail. Schopenhauer had concluded that existence is utterly unjustifiable and valueless, except in the negative sense that the inevitable preponderance of suffering endows it with an actual disvalue; and that, for anyone who considers the matter soberly and clearsightedly, oblivion must be acknowledged to be preferable to life.

Schopenhauer's reason for taking this darkly pessimistic position was that in his view existence in general and life in particular are characterized by ceaseless struggle and striving, inevitably resulting in destruction and (among sentient forms of life) involving incessant suffering of one sort or another. The whole affair, as he saw it, is quite pointless, since nothing of any value is thereby attained (the perpetuation of life merely continuing the striving and suffering). No transcendent purposes are thereby served; no pleasure, enjoyments, or satisfactions attainable can suffice to overbalance the sufferings life involves, thus excluding a hedonic justification of living; and so life stands condemned at the bar of evaluative judgment. It is, in a word, absurd. Ceaseless striving, inescapable suffering, inevitable destruction—all pointless, with no meaning and no justification, no redemption or after-worldly restitution, and with the only deliverance being that of death and oblivion: this is Schopenhauer's world as *Wille und Vorstellung*—the pre-Christian apprehension of life attributed by Nietzsche in BT to the Greeks, recurring again in the modern world as Christianity enters its death throes.

Nietzsche does not question the soundness of this picture in BT; and, even though he later rejected the Schopenhauerian metaphysics, he continued to concur with this general account of the circumstances attending life in the world. To live is to struggle, suffer, and die; and, while there may be more to living than that, no amount of "progress" in any field of human enterprise can succeed in altering these basic parameters of individual human existence. Even more significantly, for Nietzsche as well as for Schopenhauer and Nietzsche's Greeks, it is not possible to discern any teleological *justification* of what the individual is thus fated to undergo, either historically or supernaturally. We can look neither to a future utopia nor to a life hereafter that might serve to render our existence endurable and meaningful.

How can one manage to endure life in a world of the sort described by Schopenhauer, once one recognizes it for what it is—endure it, and beyond that *affirm* it as desirable and worth living despite the "terrors and horrors" that are inseparable from it? "Suppose a human being has thus put his ear, as it were, to the heart chamber of the world will," Nietzsche writes, "how could he fail to *break*?" (BT 21). He terms this general recognition of the world's nature and of the fate of the individual within it "Dionysian wisdom"; and he compares the situation of the Greek who attained it to that of Hamlet—and implicitly to that of modern man (with a Schopenhauerian-existentialist world view) as well: "In this sense the Dionysian man resembles Hamlet: both have once looked truly into the essence of things, they have *gained knowledge*, and nausea inhibits action; for their action could not change anything in the external nature of things. . . . Now no comfort avails any more. . . . Conscious of the truth he has once seen, man now sees everywhere only the horror or absurdity of existence. . . . He is nauseated" (BT 7).

Nietzsche desperately wanted to find some sort of solution to this predicament—though he cloaked his longing in the guise of a more detached interest in the question of how it has been possible for "life" to manage to "detain its creatures in existence" even when the erroneous beliefs that commonly shield them are no longer in operation. For this reason his attention was drawn to a people who were already very much on his mind owing to his professional concerns and who constituted a perfect subject for a case study along these lines: the early Greeks. They were no brute savages, mindlessly and insensitively propelled through life by blind instinct; rather, they were highly intelligent, sensitive, and well aware of the ways of the world. Moreover, they were sustained neither by anything like Judeo-Christian religious belief nor by any myth of historical progress and human perfectibility. Yet they did not succumb to Schopenhauerian pessimism; on the contrary, they were perhaps the most vigorous, creative, life-affirming people the world has known. Thus Nietzsche was drawn irresistibly to them, asking of them: how did they do it? What was the secret of their liberation from the action- and affirmation-inhibiting nausea that seemingly ought to have been the result of their own Dionysian wisdom? The answer, he believed, lay in that which was the most striking and glorious achievement of their culture: their art. Thus the passage cited continues: "Here, where the danger to [the] will is greatest, *art* approaches as a saving sorceress, expert at healing. She alone knows how to turn these nauseous thoughts about the horror or absurdity of existence into notions with which one can live" (ibid.).

This is the guiding idea of Nietzsche's whole treatment of art and its significance for human life in BT. The main themes of this work are summarized in the following lines from its concluding section, which expand upon this idea of making reference to the key concepts of the "Dionysian" and "Apollinian" and bring to the fore the most central and crucial notions in Nietzsche's entire philosophy of art—the notions of *overcoming* and *transfiguration:*

> Thus the Dionysian is seen to be, compared to the Apollinian, the eternal and original artistic power that first calls the whole world of phenomena into existence—and it is only in the midst of this world that a new transfiguring illusion becomes necessary in order to keep the animated world of individuation alive.... Of this foundation of all existence—the Dionysian basic ground of the world—not one whit more may enter the consciousness of the human individual than can be overcome again by this Apollinian power of transfiguration. (BT 25)

2

Before turning to a closer consideration of these themes, a fundamental ambivalence in Nietzsche's thinking about the relation between art and life—in BT and also subsequently—must be noted. From first to last, Nietzsche was deeply convinced that art requires to be understood not as a self-contained and self-enclosed sphere of activity and experience detached from the rest of life, but rather as intimately bound up with life and as having the greatest significance in and for it. This is reflected in his later observation (in his "Self Criticism") that art in BT is viewed "in the perspective of life"—a circumstance he regards as one of the signal merits of the work, its many inadequacies not withstanding. And it is one of the most decisive and distinctive features of his general philosophical position that its development is characterized by a kind of dialectic between his understanding of life and the world and his understanding of art—each affecting the other and bringing about changes in the other as the other worked changes upon it.

The underlying unity of the notions of art and life in Nietzsche's thinking is to be seen in BT in his treatment of the basic impulses operative in art—the Dionysian and the Apollinian—as identical with basic tendencies discernable in ourselves and nature alike. And the consequences of his conviction of the existence of this unity are apparent in the subsequent development of two notions that came to figure importantly in his later writings: those of the "overman" and the "will to power." For I would suggest that the latter is to be understood as an outgrowth of the dual notions of the Dionysian and Apollinian "art impulses of nature," in which they are *aufgehoben* in the threefold Hegelian sense of this term: they are at once negated, preserved, and superseded. And I would also suggest that the "overman" is to be construed as a symbol of human life raised to the level of art, in which crude self-assertive struggle is sublimated into creativity that is no longer subject to the demands and limitations associated with the "human, all-too-human."

The overcoming of the initial meaningless and repugnant character of existence, through the creative transformation of the existing, cardinally characterizes both art and life as Nietzsche ultimately came to understand them. And this means for him both that life is essentially artistic and that art is an expression of the fundamental nature of life. "Will to power" is properly understood only if it is conceived as a disposition to effect such creatively transformative overcoming—in nature, human life generally, and art alike. And the overman is the apotheosis of this fundamental disposition, the ultimate incarnation of the basic character of reality generally to which all existence, life, and art are owing.

In BT, of course, neither "will to power" nor "overman" makes an appearance, and the relation between art and life is discussed in other terms. One of the most notable features of the discussion, however, is Nietzsche's readiness to employ the term "art" not only to refer in a conventional manner to sculpture, music, and the other standard "art forms" (kinds of work of art, their production, and their experience), but also in a broader, extended sense. For example, Nietzsche suggests that "every man is truly an artist" to the extent that it is part of the experience of everyone to engage in the "creation" of "the beautiful illusion" of "dream worlds" (BT 1), even though no "works of art" in the usual sense are thereby produced. Furthermore, turning his attention from such (Apollinian) "dreaming" to the experience of what he calls "Dionysian ecstasies," Nietzsche speaks of the Dionysian throng as *being* "works of art" themselves: here "man . . . is no longer an artist, he has become a work of art. . . . The noblest clay, the costliest marble, man, is here kneaded and cut" (ibid.).

Most striking of all, however, Nietzsche refers constantly to "nature herself" as "artistic," and terms both the Apollinian and the Dionysian tendencies "art-impulses" of *nature*. Thus he initially presents them "as artistic energies which burst forth from nature herself, without the mediation of the human artist," and goes on to say, "with reference to these

immediate art-states of nature every artist is an 'imitator' " (BT 2). And
he is not merely suggesting that nature is thus "artistic" as well as
humanity, albeit in different ways; for he contends that these two "art-
states of nature" are "the only two art impulses" (BT 12), and he even
goes so far as to attribute the true authorship of *all* art to "nature" rather
than to human agency considered in its own right. "One thing above all
must be clear to us. The entire comedy of art is neither performed for our
betterment or education, nor are we the true authors of this art world."
The human artist is said to be merely "the medium through which the
one truly existent subject celebrates his release in appearance." Artists
and the rest of us alike are "merely images and artistic projections for the
true author," which is the fundamental principle of reality—the world
will—itself; and we "have our highest dignity in our significance as works
of art," as creations of this ultimate "artist," rather than as producers and
appreciators of art objects (BT 5).

Yet Nietzsche also speaks of art very differently, and in a way that
suggests a much less direct and even contrasting relation between it and
the world. Thus, for example, he writes that "the highest, and indeed the
truly serious task of art" is "to save the eye from gazing into the horrors of
night and to deliver the subject by the healing balm of illusion from the
spasms of the agitations of the will" (BT 19). He repeatedly asserts that
art in all of its forms deals in "illusion" and even "lies." Art spreads a "veil
of beauty" over a harsh reality—and, when he speaks of it as a "transfiguring mirror" (BT 3), the emphasis is on "transfiguring," which pre-
cludes any accurate reflection. Thus he writes that "art is not merely
imitation of the reality of nature but rather a metaphysical supplement of
the reality of nature, placed beside it for its overcoming" (BT 24).

Here the concluding passage of the entire work, cited earlier, should
be recalled, in which Nietzsche returns to this theme of the necessity of
overcoming whatever consciousness of the world's nature is attained by
means of an art of "transfiguration" capable of covering over what has
been glimpsed with a "splendid illusion" (BT 25). It was the "terror and
horror of existence" from which the Greeks needed to be saved; and "it
was in order to be able to live" that they developed their art: "all this was
again and again overcome by the Greeks with the aid of the Olympian
middle world of art; or at any rate it was veiled and withdrawn from
sight" (BT 3). Nor does this apply only to nontragic art forms; for
Nietzsche asserts that "the tragic myth too, insofar as it belongs to art at
all, participates fully in this metaphysical intention of art to transfigure"
(BT 24).

Even while thinking along these lines, however, Nietzsche envisages a
fundamental link between "art" and "life," in that the latter is held to

have been the source of the Greek's salvation from the desperate situation in which it also placed him: "Art saves him, and through art—life" (BT 7). Life thus is cast in a dual role, with the consequence that the relation of art to it is also a dual one. But can the world of art at once be thought of as a world "supplementing the reality of nature, placed beside it for its overcoming," and therefore distinct from it and contrasting to it—and at the same time be understood as the creation of this very nature itself, expressing its own basic "artistic impulses," and therefore fundamentally as homogeneous and even identical with it? In BT, Nietzsche tries to have it both ways, but it is far from clear that it is possible to do so.

3

In any event, it should be clear by now that Nietzsche in BT thinks of what art *is* in terms of *what art does* and *how art does it;* and that for him the answers to these two questions are to be given in terms of the notions of *overcoming* (*Überwindung*) and *transfiguration* (*Verklärung*). These two notions recur repeatedly throughout BT and figure centrally in most of his major pronouncements about art—regardless of what art forms he may be considering, and notwithstanding any basic differences between them.

It should further be evident that this "overcoming" is to be understood in relation to certain human needs that Nietzsche regards as fundamental and profoundly compelling, thereby endowing art with an extraordinary importance transcending that of mere enjoyment or satisfaction derived from entertainment or self-expression. And his interpretation of art in terms of "transfiguration" also clearly involves him in a fundamental break with Schopenhauer and all other cognitivist philosophers of art; for if art is essentially a matter of transfiguration its ministrations to our needs will necessarily proceed otherwise than by heightening our powers of insight and understanding.

Nietzsche's frequent references to "illusions" in a number of contexts make this obvious, but the point applies even where this latter notion does not (notably, in the case of music). Even where some sort of "truth" about reality is purported to come through in art, he takes it to be essential to the artistic character of the expression that a transfiguration of the "true" content has occurred in its artistic treatment—and its artistic character and quality attaches entirely to the element of transfiguration, rather than to this content and its transmission.

It is important to bear in mind the general applicability of the notions of overcoming and transfiguration when turning to Nietzsche's discussion of the art impulses and art forms he is intent upon distinguishing, both to interpret properly what he says about them individually and to avoid the error of supposing that he takes them to be entirely different phenomena united by nothing more than a shared name. He does begin by speaking of "the science of aesthetics" and of "the continuous development of art," thereby implying some degree of unity of both the discipline and its subject. Yet he immediately introduces the notion of the "duality" of "the Apollinian and Dionysian," asserts that "art" is but a "common term" until the two are "coupled with each other" (BT 1), and goes on to analyze them along very different lines—even to the point of maintaining that these notions represent "*two* worlds of art differing in their intrinsic essence and in their highest aims" (BT 16). These "art impulses" and "worlds of art," however, while very different indeed for Nietzsche, are nonetheless both "*art* impulses" and "worlds *of art*." That they have more than merely this same "art" denomination in common is testified to by the fact that their "coupling" had a fruitful artistic issue: tragedy.

Neither in Apollinian nor in Dionysian art, Nietzsche contends, do we encounter unvarnished representations of the world, as it is in itself, as it presents itself to us in experience, or as it might be conceived by a thinker concerned with the natures of the types to which all existing things belong. The impulses to the creation of art for Nietzsche are not cognitive impulses of any sort. If they stand in any relation at all to knowledge, he holds that this relation may best be conceived instead as an *antidotal* one. And it is undoubtedly in part to stress the extent of his departure from any cognitively oriented interpretation of art that Nietzsche introduces his discussion of the Apollinian and the Dionysian by dwelling upon their connection with the phenomena of dreaming and intoxication. Each of these phenomena, he maintains, manifests a deeply rooted and profoundly important aspect of our nature, and each answers to a powerful need. And the strength of the hold art exerts upon us can be understood only if it is recognized that the different art forms have their origins in these basic impulses, and emerge in answer to these strong needs.

Nietzsche's discussion of Apollinian and Dionysian duality in BT is intended to bring out both the radical difference between what he thus takes to be the two basic life-serving and art-generating impulses these names designate, and also the possibility of their interpenetration—and, further, the great importance (for "life" and art alike) of the results when this occurs. At the outset of his discussion of the Apollinian and Dionysian duality he singles out two art forms as paradigms of each—"the Apollinian art of sculpture and the non-imagistic, Dionysian art of music" (BT 1)—but then moves immediately to a consideration of the more fundamental experiential "states" (also termed Apollinian and Dionysian) to which he takes all such art forms to be related: dreaming and intoxication.

Nietzsche contends that human beings are so constituted that they are impelled to each by basic dispositions, and respond to each with powerful but differing positive feelings. Thus he suggests that there is something in "our innermost being" that "experiences dreams with profound delight and joyous necessity" (ibid.), while it is likewise the case that "paroxysms of intoxication" are accompanied by a "blissful ecstasy that wells up from the innermost depths of man, indeed of nature" (ibid.). It is these feelings of "profound delight" on the one hand and of "blissful ecstasy" on the other that are held respectively to characterize the experience of the Apollinian and Dionysian art forms. These forms touch the same deep chords in our nature and so produce the same sort of response. And this is taken to be the key to understanding how it is that they are able to perform their life-sustaining functions (to the extent that they manage to do so).

As Nietzsche views them, dreaming and intoxication are not merely analogs to art, or pre-forms of art, or even experiential sources of artistic activity. There is an important sense in which they themselves *are* artistic phenomena—only the "artist" in these cases is no human being, but rather "nature," working in the medium of human life. In this context, the Dionysian and Apollinian require to be conceived "as artistic energies which burst forth from nature herself, without the mediation of the human artist—energies in which nature's art impulses are satisfied in the most immediate and direct way" (BT 2). Nietzsche does not mean this to be construed merely metaphorically; for it is his contention that human artistic activities are to be regarded as of a piece with these more basic life processes—developments of them, to be sure, but outgrowths sufficiently similar to them to warrant regarding "every artist as an 'imitator'" in relation to "these immediate art-states of nature." Thus he also contends that "only insofar as the genius in the act of artistic creation coalesces with this primordial artist of the world, does he learn anything of the eternal essence of art" (BT 5).

It may be noted in this connection that for Nietzsche it is in this respect—and only in this respect—that art may properly be conceived as involving "the imitation of nature." That is, art imitates nature in that the same sort of thing goes on in the former instance as goes on (among other things) in the latter. But precisely because creative transformation is involved in the former no less than in the latter (as part of the very "imitation" in question), true art no more involves the attempt exactly to represent nature as it confronts us than dreaming and intoxication faithfully record it—nor yet again does true art merely give expression to the contents of experiences had while in these states.

Having said this, it must immediately be granted that Nietzsche does

employ the language of "representation" in speaking of the relation
between both Apollinian and Dionysian art forms and the content of
what might be termed the "visions" characteristic of the associated
experiential states more broadly and fundamentally conceived. It has
already been noted that he is willing to speak with Schopenhauer of
(Dionysian) music as a "copy" of the "primal unity" underlying all
appearances. It has also been observed that he conceives of Dionysian art
as effecting a kind of identification of the individual with this underlying
reality through a captivating revelation of its nature as conveyed by "the
Dionysian artist" who has glimpsed it and "identified himself with" it. To
this it must be added that he also speaks of the employment of "the beat
of rhythm," and tonal architectonics in Apollinian music "for the representation of Apollinian states" (BT 2). And, while it is "mere appearances"
rather than the reality underlying them with which all such states are
held to be concerned, the "beautiful illusions" of Apollinian plastic art
are suggested to be, if not such appearances themselves, at any rate
"appearances of" *those* appearances (BT 4).

In short, Nietzsche holds that there is at least a kind of "mirroring"
relation between what is discerned in Dionysian states and what one
finds in Dionysian art, and also between what is envisioned in Apollinian
states and what one finds in Apollinian art. Indeed, it can even be said
that for him the efforts of artists of both sorts serve at once to share and to
heighten experiences centering upon the contents of the respective sorts
of vision. Were this not so, the "joy in existence" deriving from the
"blissful ecstasy" generated by the one and the "profound delight" arising
from the other (through the generation and intensification of which these
types of art are held to perform their life-sustaining function) could not
be stimulated by art.

The solution to this difficulty is to be found in the fact that for
Nietzsche art transforms even as it thus "represents." It is no simple
faithful mirror of the contents of these states, but rather "a transfiguring
mirror" (BT 3). And it is one of the central points of his discussion of
these two types of art that they not only transfigure even as they mirror,
but moreover transfigure the already dissimilar contents of the visions
associated with the two kinds of state in quite different ways. In view of
this double difference, it is perhaps understandable that Nietzsche could
have been moved to speak of "two worlds of art differing in their intrinsic
essence" (BT 16).

The basic contrast he is concerned with establishing here may be
expressed in terms of the distinction between *images* and *symbols,* and
the double difference just mentioned bears importantly upon it. In the
case of what Nietzsche calls Apollinian art, the chaotic play of crude and

ephemeral appearances associated with such basic Apollinian experiential states as dreaming and imagination undergoes a transformative process, issuing in the creation of enduring, idealized images—"beautiful illusions," as he terms them, illusory because nothing either in the flux of appearance or beyond it corresponds to them, and of greater beauty than the haphazardly constituted contents of this flux. They are transfigurations of appearances—images akin to the stuff of dreams but also contrasting markedly with them.

In the case of Dionysian art, on the other hand, the transformation from which it issues is of the experience of the inexhaustible, dynamic "primal unity" that is "beyond all phenomena and despite all annihilation" associated with such basic Dionysian states as intoxication and orgiastic revelry. What *this* transformation gives rise to is "a new world of symbols," in which "the essence of nature is now . . . expressed symbolically" (BT 2); and it is the resulting *symbolic forms* in which Dionysian art consists. These symbolic forms are transfigurations of ecstatic states—expressions akin to immediate Dionysian ecstasy, but differing markedly from it, no less than from the underlying reality glimpsed in it. Thus Nietzsche holds that "Dionysian art . . . gives expression to the will in its omnipotence, as it were, behind the *principium individuationis*" (ibid.). Yet he insists that even so paradigmatic a case of such art as music is not to be thought of as identical with this will: "music, according to its essence, cannot possibly be will. To be will it would have to be wholly banished from the realm of art" (BT 6). For were it the same as will, it would lack the transfigured character of all art.

Thus it is Nietzsche's contention that there is one sort of art in which the works produced have a symbolically expressive character, and another sort in which the works produced do not, having instead the character of idealized images or "beautiful illusions." And it is one of the seemingly curious but important points of his analysis that the kinds of art generally regarded as most clearly "representational" fall largely into the latter category, while those generally thought of as primarily "nonrepresentational" belong in the former. The idealized images of Apollinian art are not to be thought of as having the function either of faithfully representing or even of symbolically expressing anything at all. They are rather to be thought of as beautiful illusions, to be contemplated simply for what they are in themselves, and to be enjoyed solely on account of their intrinsic beauty. They are, as Nietzsche says, a "supplement of the reality of nature, placed beside it for its overcoming" (BT 24). And, if there is any significant relation between them and this "reality," it does not consist in their genetic link to the experiential phenomena of which they are transfigurations, but rather in their ability to lead us to think better of the world of ordinary experience by regarding it in the "transfiguring mirror" they constitute, "surrounded with a higher glory" (BT 3). Through Apollinian art, the world of ordinary experience is not actually transformed and its harshness eliminated. But to the extent that the idealized images created through the transformative activity of the Apollinian artist admit of association with that which we encounter in this world, our attitude toward the latter benefits from this association, as our delight in these images carries over into our general disposition toward anything resembling them.

Once again, however, it is not knowledge that we thereby attain, but rather only an altered state of mind, brought about by "recourse to the most forceful and pleasurable illusions" and "seducing one to a continuation of life" (BT 3). One may have reservations about the psychological validity of these latter contentions, or about the effectiveness of the process indicated (as indeed Nietzsche himself came to have subsequently). These reservations do not affect Nietzsche's main point here, however, concerning the status of those works of art he terms Apollinian. They are beautiful illusions—idealized images that neither represent nor symbolize, but rather delight precisely by virtue of the beauty they possess as a result of the creative transfiguration accomplished in their production.

In the case of Dionysian art, matters stand quite differently. The Dionysian artist too is creative, and not merely someone with insight and the ability to communicate it—notwithstanding Nietzsche's assertion that, in the paradigm case of such art, "he produces [a] copy of [the] primal unity as music" (BT 5). It may be that there is a kind of "re-echoing" of the nature of this fundamental reality in instances of Dionysian art, as Nietzsche goes on alternately to put the point. In terms of this metaphor, however, such art is no less a "transfiguring echo-chamber" than Apollinian art is a "transfiguring mirror," for the artistic "re-echoing" does not stand in the same near-immediate relation of identity to this "primal unity" as does the more basic Dionysian phenomenon of intoxication, but rather comes back in an altered form, the creative production of which involves "the greatest exaltation of all [human] symbolic faculties."

Thus, Nietzsche goes on to say, "the essence of nature is now to be expressed symbolically; we need a new world of symbols" (BT 2)—and it is this "new world of symbols" that constitutes both the language and the substance of Dionysian art. The issue is somewhat confused by Nietzsche's use of the term Dionysian to refer to the "primal unity" itself ("the Dionysian basic ground of the world," etc.) and also to insight into its nature and the plight of the individual in such a world ("Dionysian wisdom"), as well as to such art, which draws upon our "symbolic powers" and thereby transfigures even while giving expression to the former. But, once again, it must be borne in mind that for Nietzsche, like other art forms, "it belongs to art at all" only insofar as it "participates fully in this metaphysical intention of art to transfigure" (BT 24). For he believes that we could not endure the full glare of an unmediated encounter with the world's essential nature, and that it is only *as transfigured* through its expression in the entrancing symbolic forms of the Dionysian arts that a nondestructive identification with it is possible.

In short, in these arts the world's nature is expressed in a form that attracts rather than repels us—a symbolic form, the attractiveness of which is bound up with the transfiguration involved in this symbolization and made possible by the character of the "new world of symbols" under consideration. Dionysian art does not have the character of a "veil of illusion" radically different from the reality of nature and "placed alongside it for its overcoming," as does Apollinian art for Nietzsche. Yet it does have a somewhat analogous character and function in that it expresses the reality of nature in a manner enabling us to overcome our abhorrence of it and derive "joy in existence" from identification with it, by means of a quasi-"illusory" medium of transfiguring symbolic forms.

The most fundamental and crucial ideas Nietzsche seeks to advance in this connection are that art is essentially not representational (or imitative) with respect to the world either as we perceive it or as it is apprehended in cognition, but rather that it is transfigurative; that, on the other hand, the transfigurations it involves are more than mere pleasing expressions of emotions or fancies in sensuous form; and that they are not all of the same kind. One does not have to subscribe to the version of the appearance/reality distinction that he accepts here (but later rejects), or to his contention that art is the "highest task and truly metaphysical activity of this life," or to his conviction that it has the purpose of performing the kind of "overcoming" function he describes in relation to the "terror and horror of existence" to follow him this far—and farther still.

4

Nietzsche takes the notions of transfiguration and illusion to apply not only to works of Apollinian and Dionysian art conceived as objects of aesthetic experience, but also to the subjects of such experience insofar as they become absorbed in them. The entire significance of art is missed, for him, if one does not recognize that the consciousness of those experiencing these art forms undergoes a transformation analogous to that occurring in their creation—and that, with this transformation, the experiencing subject's very psychological identity is in a sense transfigured, even if only temporarily, and in a way that does not alter the basic reality of one's human nature and existence in the world. The latter circumstance is what renders it appropriate to speak of illusion here—though Nietzsche is no less concerned to indicate the value of such illusion "for life" than he is to point out its illusory character.

The subjective transformation associated with the objective one involved in the creation of the work of art, however, has a very different character in the two general sorts of cases under consideration. Thus Nietzsche contends that they constitute two fundamentally distinct stratagems by means of which "the insatiable will" at the heart of nature conspires to "detain its creatures in life and compel them to live on" (BT 18). He discusses them in terms of what occurs in the case of the "Dionysian man" and in the case of the "Apollinian man," and for the sake of convenience I shall follow him in this—with the understanding, however, that these expressions refer to contrasting types of psychological states rather than to distinct groups of human beings.

The Dionysian does not exchange his physiological and sociocultural identity and situation in the world for another, or escape them altogether, in the course of the "destruction of the *principium individiationis*" of which Nietzsche speaks. As an experiential phenomenon, however, this destruction is very real: the Dionysian is psychologically transformed into one for whom the only reality of which he is aware—and therefore that with which he himself identifies—is that which is expressed in the movements, tonalities, or other symbolic forms in which he is immersed. Thus Nietzsche contends that, through the experience of Dionysian art, "we are really for a brief moment primordial being itself, feeling its raging desire for existence and joy in existence; the struggle, the pain, the destruction of phenomena, now appear necessary for us" (BT 17). As one in a state of intoxication may be said (quite appropriately, even if only psychologically) not to "be oneself," one immersed in the surge and flow of an instance of this type of aesthetic experience "loses oneself" in it. One's consciousness is caught up in it and one's self-consciousness is altered accordingly, whether this transformation manifests itself behaviorally in an enraptured cessation of ordinary activity, in outward inaction making inward tumult, or in entrance into overt participation in the event as well. Such experience is of being blissful, but also in the original and literal sense of the term *ekstasis,* which denotes a standing out from beside or beyond oneself.

To the extent that one's own existence may be conceived as being actually a moment of the reality expressed in Dionysian art and with which one thus comes to feel at one through its mediation, this transformation may be said to have the significance of a dispelling of the illusion involved in one's ordinary consciousness of oneself as something distinct from it and to be characterized in other terms. But, to the extent that such experience leads one to identify oneself so completely with this reality that one feels oneself to enjoy even those of its features that actually characterize it only as a whole, with which one is not truly identical, this transformation may also be said to have the significance of the fostering of another, different illusion. Thus Nietzsche suggests that, here no less than in the case of Apollinian art, we are dealing with a way in which, "by means of an illusion," life conspires "to detain its creatures in existence" despite the harshness of the conditions it imposes upon them—in this instance, through "the metaphysical comfort that beneath the whirl of phenomena eternal life flows on indestructibly" (BT 18).

The illusion in question is not that "life flows on indestructibly" despite the ephemerality of phenomena—for it does. We may be "comforted" (and more) through the transformation of our psychological identity enabling us to achieve a sense of unity with this indestructible and inexhaustible underlying reality, of which we are truly manifestations. But, while such comfort may be termed metaphysical, this transfiguration is not, for it leaves our actual status in the world unchanged and the basic conditions of our human existence unaltered—as we discover that when the moment passes the Dionysian aesthetic experience comes to an end, and we "return to ourselves," our psychological identities transformed back again into their original non-Dionysian state. The only enduring comfort is the recollection of the rapture of the Dionysian experience and the knowledge that it remains available to us. But a profound danger attends this kind of "overcoming," of which Nietzsche is acutely aware: the letdown may be great, the disparity between Dionysian states and ordinary life distressing, the illusion discerned, and its recognition found disconcerting—and thus the long-term effect of such experience may be detrimental rather than conducive to life (BT 7). It is for this reason, more than any other, that Nietzsche has reservations about Dionysian art and experience generally, despite the evident fascination they have for him.

Nietzsche's Apollinian type constitutes a very different case, being the product of quite another kind of psychological transformation. As in the previous case, this transcendence is held to be not only merely temporary but also fundamentally illusory, and the resulting transformation only psychological rather than genuinely ontological. Here, too, Nietzsche sees the cunning hand of nature at work, in this instance "detaining its creatures in life" through rendering the Apollinian "ensnared by art's seductive veil of beauty fluttering before his eyes" (BT 18).

The realm of Apollinian art is a kind of "dream world, an Olympian *middle world* of art" (BT 3) that is neither the everyday world nor the underlying world of will, but rather a created world by means of which the latter is "veiled and withdrawn from sight" and the former is supplanted as the focus of concern. And entrance into this world is possible, Nietzsche holds, only for a kind of dreamer, or Olympian spectator, detached from the kinds of involvements and concerns that both characterize the everyday world and endow us with our ordinary psychological identities. Indeed, it requires that one *become* such a "pure spectator"—or rather, that the images presented are such that they induce a kind of contemplative consciousness through which one's psychological identity is transformed into that of such a subject. They stand outside of time and change, need and strife; and to become absorbed in them is for Nietzsche to have one's consciousness comparably transformed. If, in the experience of Dionysian art, one is enraptured, one may be said here to be entranced. And, in a state of such entrancement, it is as if one had become a part of this world of images—not as one of them, but as a placeless, disembodied center of awareness, a subject fit for such objects and answering to their nature.

While Apollinian art involves "the arousing of delight in beautiful forms," this is not to be construed merely in the sense of providing us with pleasure, but rather in terms of an overcoming of the distress associated with our human condition through what is felt to be a kind of redemption from it. "Here Apollo overcomes the suffering of the individual by the radiant glorification of the *eternity of the phenomenon;* here beauty triumphs over the suffering inherent in life" (BT 16). For the Apollinian "is absorbed in the pure contemplation of images" (BT 5), the beauty of which strongly attracts us and brings us under their spell, causing us to banish all else from our minds and seemingly to become nothing but the delighted awareness of them. Our delight is genuine, and our psychological transformation real—even though on a more fundamental level both the objects of such consciousness and this self-consciousness are merely two aspects of the Apollinian illusion, which is but "one of those illusions which nature so frequently employs to achieve her own ends" (BT 3).

This illusion, however, is by no means as insubstantial as the term might seem to suggest. One indication of this, on Nietzsche's account, is the very fact that it is powerful enough to enable "nature" to achieve its end of "seducing one to a continuation of life" by means of it (BT 3). And if it is the case, as Nietzsche claims in this same sentence, that Apollinian art is thus "called into being, as the complement and consummation of existence," it follows that it is no *mere* illusion that leaves the reality of human life unaffected. It does not fundamentally alter the human condition. But, if it is in some significant sense the "consummation of existence," it may be truly said to effect a significant transformation of "existence"—or at least that portion of it that is the reality of human life. Art is indeed our creation; but we also are (or at least can be) recreated or transfigured by art.

The kind of experience and spirituality that become attainable in relation to the idealized images of Apollinian art may not constitute an elevation of those who attain to them entirely beyond the reach of the entanglements of ordinary life and the deeper harsh realities of existence in this world. Yet they do render the existence of those attaining to them qualitatively different from that of those who remain entirely immersed in the quotidian, or who further succeed only in finding occasional respite through Dionysian experience. It is Nietzsche's appreciation of the magnitude of this qualitative difference that accounts for his celebration of the achievement of the archaic Greeks in their creation of Apollinian art, both plastic and epic.

5

Nietzsche conceives tragic art to be no less Apollinian than Dionysian in origin and nature. At the very outset of the book he advances this contention with respect to the archetype of it, asserting that "by a metaphysical miracle of the Hellenic 'will,'" the "tendencies" associated with each "appear coupled with each other, and through this coupling ultimately generate an equally Dionysian and Apollinian form of art—Attic tragedy" (BT 1). The burden of his entire discussion of tragedy is that its emergence presupposed not only the prior development of the art of Dionysian transfiguration, but also the *retransfiguration* of the latter under the influence of the likewise previously developed art of Apollinian transfiguration.

The birth of tragedy for Nietzsche was an event of the greatest actual and possible future significance. For it did not merely involve the appearance of a qualitatively new art form, thus opening another chapter in the development of art. It also made possible a further qualitative transformation of human life, which he conceives to have been and to be of far greater moment than is generally recognized. The possibility of tragic art did not end with the expiration of Attic (Greek) tragedy, and is not wedded to the dramatic form of the works produced by the classical tragedians. Nor is Nietzsche here thinking in addition merely of Elizabethan tragic drama, together with the tragic opera of his own time, but rather of what he characterizes more generally as *tragic myth*.

Moreover, and even more importantly, he does not conceive of tragic art as a phenomenon the significance of which is confined to but a single sphere of human experience and cultural life. Rather, he views it as the potential foundation and guiding force of an entire form of culture and human existence, which alone is capable of filling the void left by the collapse of "optimistic" life-sustaining myths (both religious and philosophical-scientific). And he looks to it to assume anew the function of "making life possible and worth living," which neither Apollinian nor Dionysian art as such is capable any longer of performing. The former may continue to entrance and delight us, and the latter to enrapture and excite us, and both may continue to transport and transform us in their respective fashions—but the power of the illusions they involve to sustain us has been lost.

In this connection it is both crucial and illuminating to bear in mind the passage cited earlier from the last section of the book, in which Nietzsche contends (clearly with tragic art specifically in mind) that, with respect to the basic character of the world and of existence in it, "not one whit more may enter the consciousness of the human individual than can be overcome again by [the] Apollinian power of transfiguration" (BT 25). To be able to endure the awareness of these stark realities of which we are capable and which cannot in the long run be prevented from emerging, and to be able further to embrace and affirm life despite the attainment of such an awareness, a transformation of this consciousness is necessary. In its starkest, simplest and most vivid form, according to Nietzsche, it would be overwhelmingly horrible, "nauseating," paralyzing and unendurable, save in temporary transports of Dionysian ecstatic self-transcendence that cannot be sustained and so constitute no adequate long-term recourse.

For Nietzsche, tragic art alone is truly equal to this task. As has been seen, he holds that it enables us to experience the terrible not as merely terrible, but rather as sublime; and that it achieves something akin to a Dionysian effect upon us, which however is not identical with it—for it does not take the kind of life-endangering toll that Dionysian intoxication does, inducing an experiential state that differs as significantly from such intoxication as it does from Apollinian dreaming. In the long run it has the character of a tonic rather than a depressant; its aftermath is held to be *exhilaration*, rather than either the overall exhaustion that follows upon Dionysian excitement or the exasperation that Apollinian exaltation leaves in its train. And, considered more immediately, it might be said to *enthrall*, rather than to entrance or enrapture. So to describe what tragic art does is not to give an analysis of it; but Nietzsche's conception of its nature requires to be comprehended in light of this understanding of its effects.

Tragic art too, for Nietzsche, may be said to constitute a kind of "transfiguring mirror." It is a mirror, however, in which we see reflected neither "appearances" idealizingly transfigured nor the character of the reality underlying them symbolically expressed. We are confronted instead with "images of life"—reflections of the human condition (which is also our own) highlighting both the individuation it involves and the fate bound up with the latter in a world in which all individual existence is ephemeral, harsh, and ridden with strife and suffering. What we encounter, however, is not a stark and brutally "realistic" portrayal of this condition as such. We see it in transfigured form—even though this transfiguration of it does not consist in its radical transmutation into a merely imaginary idealized condition *contrasting* to the actual human condition on these counts. And it likewise does not involve the effective obliteration of the salient features of human life through the diversion of attention from the entire domain of individuation to the collective, the impersonal, the merely vital, and the enduring aspects of life underlying it. Rather, the kind of transfiguration occurring here is one that pertains to our perception of individual human existence—*as* existence that is individual rather than merely a part of an inexhaustible and indestructible flow of life, and that is human rather than above and beyond the conditions to which human beings are subject.

This transfiguration pertains first to the character of the dramatic figures with which we are confronted—or, rather, it comes about first in the context of our confrontation with them, but it does not remain confined to this encounter, serving rather to alter our apprehension of the human condition more generally. It is in this sense above all that tragic art may be said to serve as a transfiguring mirror: it works a transformation upon our consciousness of the human reality that is also our own, at the same time as it reflects that reality for us to behold.

Tragic art presents us neither with an ideal to be admired and emulated nor with an avenue by means of which to escape all thought of the hard realities of life. The latter are very much in evidence, and the tragic figure caught up in them is one with whom, as an individual, we empathize—but with whom, as a character, we do not identify. Yet the manner of presentation of such figures, which renders them tragic and not merely pathetic, does much more than merely purge us of our self-directed feelings of fear and pity through an empathic discharge. It can have a powerful positive impact upon the way in which we perceive our human condition and experience the reality of our own lives, by revealing them to us in a very different light from that in which we would otherwise tend to view them. The point might be put by saying that the tragic artist, not through the persona of the tragic figure per se but in the larger structure of the tragic drama, interposes a medium between us and the reality of human existence that does more than simply give expression to the latter; for the medium further shapes and colors our consciousness of reality and is able to help us attain an affirmative attitude toward it precisely by virtue of doing so.

In short, tragic art provides us with a way of apprehending this reality that enables us to come to terms with it—and not only to endure but also to affirm what we thereby see, as we thereby learn to see it. In this way it resembles Dionysian art. And for Nietzsche this similarity of tragic art to the Dionysian arts is by no means merely fortuitous. In tragic myth, as in music and dance, something transcending mere appearances is symbolically expressed—and in being so expressed it is transformed for our consciousness. Here, however, the symbolic forms employed are not primarily those characteristic of these Dionysian art forms, but rather are drawn from the initially nonsymbolic domain of Apollinian art.

Life regarded as tragic is no longer life seen as merely wretched and pathetic; and the "displeasure" associated with "the weight and burden of existence" is overshadowed and forgotten when the latter takes on the aspect of tragic fate rather than mere senseless suffering and annihilation. The fate of tragic figures, when nobly met rather than basely suffered, enhances rather than detracts from their stature, and these figures serve as a symbolic medium through which individual existence more generally is enhanced for us. It is in these terms that the exquisite stimulant distinctively characteristic of tragic art is to be conceived, even though it is strongly supplemented by the presence of that which is characteristic of Dionysian art as well.

The unique achievement of tragic art is thus held to be that it fundamentally alters our apprehension of human existence and the circumstances associated with it, which result in the suffering and destruction of even such extraordinary figures as the central characters of tragic drama and myth. Through it, these circumstances cease to stand as *objections* to human life and its worth and emerge instead as features of it that—as part of the larger whole human lives are and can be—actually contribute to its overall significance and attractiveness. And thus, Nietzsche suggests, it serves to bring it about that existence can "seem justified" *aesthetically* —"only as an aesthetic phenomenon" (BT 24). Nietzsche's use of the term "only" here is highly important, for his general point is that it is *only* in this way, in the last analysis, that it is possible for us to find human life and our own existence endurable and worthwhile without recourse to illusions that radically misrepresent the actual nature of our human reality and the world more generally.

6

As has been observed in connection with Apollinian and Dionysian art, there is for Nietzsche a significant sense in which all images, like appearances more generally, are to be considered illusory. And so, for that matter, are all symbols, for neither may be supposed to correspond even approximately, let alone exactly, to the actual nature of reality. No relation of resemblance obtains between these sorts of experiential phenomena and the constitution of this underlying reality itself; the difference is qualitative, and profound. But it is by no means only in this very basic (and relatively uninteresting) respect that Nietzsche takes tragic art too to involve the generation of illusion.

It has already been observed that this illusion centers on the "image of life" with which we are confronted in the tragic figure. While such figures are not simply "realistically" drawn, or fictitious but true-to-life individuals, or representatives of the elemental characteristics of "Dionysian universality" (as is the chorus), they are not mere Apollinian beautiful illusions either. Like Apollinian idealized images, however, they constitute something on the order of a "supplement of the reality of nature," and of that of ordinary human existence along with it, "placed beside it for its overcoming." The "core of life they contain" is the same as our own, but this core is artistically transformed into images of life expressing possibilities that are more human than mere glorious appearances, and yet that differ markedly from the commonplace, in ways moreover answering to no predetermined human essence or foreordained human ideal. They thus can in no sense be said to confront us with the "truth" of human existence. And, since what they confront us with is something other than truth, they may be said to present us with a kind of illusion. It is in this sense that Nietzsche's remarks to this effect are to be understood.

Yet this illusion is no *mere* illusion, and the transformed consciousness of ourselves that emerges when we view our own lives in the light of the manner of those of these tragic figures is not *merely* illusory, for the creations in which they consist are not distorted or erroneous representations of something that has a fixed and immutable character and cannot be otherwise. And they also are not simply imaginary substitutes temporarily usurping a position in our consciousness that is normally and more properly occupied by our ordinary conception of our own mundane reality. Rather, they are symbols of *human possibility.* And as such they serve to carry us beyond the mere acknowledgment of intractable aspects of the human condition, enabling us to discern ways in which the latter may be confronted and transformed into occasions for the endowment of life with grandeur and dignity.

By means of these symbols, human life thus may come to take on an aesthetic significance sufficing to overcome the distressing character of its harsh basic features. It stands revealed as a potentially aesthetic phenomenon, "justifiable" accordingly in our estimation even in the face of its hardest circumstances. And of paramount importance for Nietzsche is the fact that tragic art works this feat in a non-Apollinian way; it does not confine this perception of the tragic figures themselves, while precluding its application to our lives. These figures stand as symbols serving to facilitate our apprehension of the possibilities they express, together with "the core of life they contain," *as our own* — and so to alter the aspect of our own lives.

To say that this is all illusion, as Nietzsche does, is neither to deny the reality of this alteration nor to downplay its significance. Rather, it is to make the point that our lives thus acquire an experiential character that is no part of their fundamental objective nature, and that this occurs through the transforming mediation of created images enabling us to discern aesthetic significance in human existence—notwithstanding that its basic circumstances warrant the attribution to it of no significance whatsoever.

What is at issue here, once again, is the "aesthetic justification" not simply of the world generally, but also (and more importantly) of human existence, as we do and must live it. And this is something that presupposes the supersession of Dionysian as well as Apollinian (and also ordinary) consciousness. Tragic art is held to be capable of accomplishing this result only by virtue of the "fraternal union of Apollo and Dionysus" occurring in it, not by a victory of the latter over the former. The quasi-Apollinian tragic figure may be "annihilated," but the entire Apollinian element is not. And while "the Dionysian predominates" in "the total effect of the tragedy" (BT 21), it does not emerge in sole possession of the field. If human existence is to be "justified" *despite* its inescapable harsh conditions and fate, it cannot be exhibited in such a way that only the suffering and destruction it involves are made to stand as its final truth, with all aesthetically justifying characteristics being reserved to the "primordial unity" that flows on beneath the surface of individuation and appearance.

The consciousness of human existence and of ourselves that Nietzsche terms "tragic" is neither purely Apollinian nor merely Dionysian, for the tragic myth in accordance with which it is shaped places this existence we share in a new and different light. A new way of seeing it becomes possible, in that our relation to the reality that is at once the ground and the abyss in our existence comes to be regarded as amenable to Apollinian transformation. Here our own existence as individuals is not something to which it is necessary to be oblivious to experience aesthetic enjoyment, as in the cases of Apollinian delight and Dionysian rapture in their separate and more basic aesthetic forms. Rather, human life itself becomes the focus of a kind of aesthetic satisfaction identical with neither but related to both, through its treatment in a way that brings our capacity for responses of both sorts into play in relation to it. To be sure, the underlying character of the world itself and of the human condition is not thereby altered, but the aspect of human existence is, even while it is apprehended against the background of this Dionysian reality.

In a sense, tragic art may thus be said to accomplish the Apollinianization of the Dionysian, in our consciousness of the latter if not also in its actual nature. But it may perhaps more appropriately be said to accomplish a complex and radical transformation of something else, in a less one-sided manner: the aspect of our human existence, at once along partly Apollinian and partly Dionysian lines. What is thus transformed is not tragedy, for the accomplishment of tragic art is not the transformation of tragedy into something else. Tragedy, rather, is the *issue* of this artistic transformation, through which existence comes to be experienced as tragic. This is indeed an artistic accomplishment, since tragedy no less than beauty may be said to exist only in the eye of the beholder, whose sensibility has been formed and cultivated by art. It is no brute fact of human existence, but rather an acquired aspect it may come to bear through the transfiguring agency of the tragic artist.

It is in this way that the tragic myth comes to be endowed with what Nietzsche terms its "intense and convincing metaphysical significance" (BT 21) — and also its most profoundly illusory character, for it leads us to feel something to be the deepest and highest "truth" of human existence — the tragic character it is capable of coming to bear, with all the sublimity and majesty devolving upon it therefrom — which is no part of either its fundamental nature or any intrinsic essence legitimately attributable to it. We are led to view life as though it were a means to the end of actualizing the aesthetic values associated with human existence as it is revealed in the transfiguring mirror of tragic myth.

7

In BT, Nietzsche placed his hope for a revitalization of Western civilization — in the face of the collapse of both otherworldly religiousness and rationalistic-scientific optimism — in a reemergence of a tragic sense of life. But, as he readily acknowledged, such a view of life cannot be sustained in the absence of tragic myth and an acceptance of the understanding of human existence associated with some instance of it. It is for this reason that he devoted so much discussion in this work to the importance of myth and to the need for a new and compelling form of tragic myth in the modern Western world.

Nietzsche obviously thought, when he wrote BT, that Wagner was well on the way to accomplishing the task he thus envisioned. The details of his discussion of this and related matters, however, are of relatively little intrinsic interest—especially since he soon after lost his enthusiasm for Wagner and abandoned his commitment to the ultimacy and indispensability of that form of art he associates here with tragic myth. He further seems to have become convinced that art generally has a significance in relation to life and that it also has a variety of features to which his analysis of it in BT does not do justice. In any event, he subsequently approached the arts somewhat differently, placing less emphasis upon differences between the various art forms and the kinds of experience associated with them and concerning himself more with the phenomenon of artistic creativity generally.

Although Nietzsche devoted at least some (and often considerable) attention to art in nearly all of his later writings, however, he never again subjected it to a comparably comprehensive, intensive, and sustained analysis or treated it with a similar breadth of vision. He subsequently deepened and modified his understanding of art in certain important ways and recast his views with respect to it. Yet he retained most of the fundamental notions in terms of which he interprets it in BT, in one form or another, and continued to give them central roles in his subsequent discussions—not only of art, but also of human life, and of what he came to call its "enhancement"—and the "overcoming of nihilism" along with it. And he not only heralded his *Thus Spoke Zarathustra* at the conclusion of the original edition of *The Gay Science* with the words *"Incipit tragödie"* (GS 342), but also continued to conjoin the motifs of art, tragedy, and the affirmation and enhancement of life to the end. However much his thinking changed, he never abandoned his early conviction of their profound interconnection.

CHAPTER EIGHT

Nietzsche's First Manifesto:
On *Schopenhauer as Educator*

Among Nietzsche's writings, there is perhaps no better intro-duction to his thought than *Schopenhauer as Educator* (1874). Written when he was still a young professor of classical philology at Basel, just beginning to discover his own voice and philosophical calling, it reveals many of the fundamental concerns and convictions that animate his later works. It is a remarkable essay. Though flawed by lack of philosophical sophistication and romantic tendencies of thought and expression that Nietzsche had not yet learned to check, it presents an astute, often eloquent discussion of a broad range of intellectual, cultural, and social issues, and calls powerfully for a reorientation of philosophical and human endeavor. It is also one of the most sustained, vigorous, delightful, and radically discomforting works Nietzsche ever wrote. Subjecting many contemporary practices and institutions to searching and powerful criticism, it offers a perceptive critique of the scholar and of scholarship, and concludes with a violent polemic against academic philosophy. And all of this Nietzsche provides in the context (or in the guise) of an appreciation of "Schopenhauer as educator."

As these remarks suggest, the essay is not really "about" Schopenhauer. Nietzsche made the point himself fourteen years later in *Ecce Homo* in a retrospective comment on his earlier work: "Now that I am looking back from a certain distance upon the conditions to which these essays bear witness, I do not wish to deny that at bottom they speak only of me. . . . In *Schopenhauer as Educator* my innermost history, my *becoming,* is inscribed. Above all, my promise! . . . At bottom it is admittedly not 'Schopenhauer as Educator' that speaks here, but his opposite, 'Nietzsche as Educator.' "[1]

Schopenhauer is certainly honored in this essay, and is frequently mentioned; but his thought is hardly discussed at all—and when Nietzsche does occasionally purport to present certain aspects of it, more often than not he interprets them in ways that will seem strange indeed to those familiar with Schopenhauer's work. Since the title of the essay presumably indicates its subject, its general neglect of the main content of Schopenhauer's world view may at first seem surprising, especially in view of Nietzsche's obvious debt to it in *The Birth of Tragedy* (published only two years earlier), and Schopenhauer's continuing influence upon his thought. (While he came to be very critical of Schopenhauer's understanding of the "will" and his interpretation of our fundamental nature and of life and the world as developed in terms of "will," Nietzsche's own interpretation in terms of "will to power" owes a good deal to it.)[2] But the purpose of this essay is to honor Schopenhauer for the *kind* of thinker and philosopher Nietzsche took him to be, rather than for his doctrines; to declare how much it had meant to him to encounter such an *examplar*; and to argue for the importance of "education" through such teachers and encounters.

The essay is instructive on several counts. It affords considerable insight into Nietzsche's early intellectual development. It also contributes to the understanding of changes in his thinking, as he moved beyond the first major formulation of his views in *The Birth of Tragedy* toward positions elaborated in *The Gay Science* and subsequent writings. But the essay can and should also be read for its interest in its own right. This is perhaps the most rewarding way of reading it, and the one which does greatest justice to its author.

Nietzsche had been appointed associate professor of philology at the University of Basel in 1869 at the astonishingly early age of twenty-four, without even having earned his doctorate, and was promoted to full professor the following year. Great things were expected of him in classical studies; but in his first book (*The Birth of Tragedy*) and in his Basel lectures, he showed himself to be unwilling to conform to the disciplinary norms of classical scholarship, and indeed to be deeply hostile to its limitations and conventional concerns — a critical stance that soon developed into profound discontent with the very character of scholarship and education in the universities of the period. Rather than remaining professionally concerned with classical culture, even in the oblique way of *The Birth of Tragedy*, Nietzsche turned his attention directly to cultural issues of his own day. Over the next three years, he published only the four essays of *Untimely Meditations* (and made notes for a fifth, *We Classicists*, on his own profession), and then until 1878 nothing else.

He never returned to classical philology, but instead focused his attention first on cultural, social, and psychological matters, and later on more overtly philosophical issues. Ill health forced him to resign his Basel post in 1879, but academic life and philology had long ceased to be congenial to him. Indeed, five years earlier in *Schopenhauer as Educator* he had effectively repudiated them. And while he came to see his concerns as fundamentally philosophical and to think of himself as a philosopher during the last decade of his productive life, even in this early essay he distanced himself in no uncertain terms from the academic philosophy of his time. Philosophy as he wanted it understood, as he found it exemplified by Schopenhauer, and as he later practiced it himself, is far removed from what generally passed for it among his contemporaries—and commonly passes for it among us still.

Schopenhauer as Educator is thus, at least on one level, Nietzsche's declaration of intellectual independence—from the academic establishment, from the kind of scholarship practiced and honored by his philological peers, and from the sort of philosophy that had become dominant in the universities. It is also an impassioned appeal for a different kind of intellectual activity, more truly deserving of the title of "education" and "philosophy," and also healthier, more productive, and better suited to the cultivation of our humanity as he conceived it. Owing partly perhaps to his hesitation at this early point to speak directly for himself, but also to his grateful recognition of Schopenhauer's example and its importance for him, he chose to cast his appeal in the form of an appreciation. In so doing, he perhaps gives Schopenhauer more credit than is due, imputing to him intentions and convictions that are clearly Nietzsche's own. But in the end this matters little. What does matter is what Nietzsche had to say about the great cultural issues that concerned him—issues with which we too would do well to concern ourselves.

Something should be said about Schopenhauer himself, to enable those unfamiliar with him to appreciate how remarkable it is that Nietzsche could have regarded him so highly. Arthur Schopenhauer was born in 1788, the son of a successful businessman. He studied philosophy at Göttingen and Berlin, received his doctorate from Jena in 1814, and taught for some years at Berlin. He retired to private life in 1831, after contending in vain with Hegel for influence there, and died in 1860. Both before and after his retirement he was extremely productive, but never received the recognition he felt he deserved. Most of his adult life he lived in isolation, resentful of his neglect, and bitterly hostile to his philosophical rivals, above all Hegel. Greatly influenced by Kant, he conceived himself to be Kant's rightful heir. Taking Kant as his point of departure, he developed certain ideas advanced by Kant into a comprehensive philosophy of his own that, as he saw it, at once completed and superseded Kant's philosophical project.

His most important work, in which he systematically developed his basic views, was *The World as Will and Representation*. First published

in 1818, it was reissued in greatly expanded form in 1844, the year of
Nietzsche's birth. Starting from Kant's distinction between phenomena
and things-in-themselves, he argued that it is possible (contrary to Kant's
denial) to come to know the fundamental nature of things in themselves
and of the world in general, and that their nature is to be conceived in
terms of a dynamic principle that he called "will." The phenomenal
world is its manifestation in experience. The world is thus "will" (in
itself) and "representation" (in its phenomenal manifestation).

But for Schopenhauer the world is also fundamentally irrational and
meaningless, characterized throughout by blind striving, ceaseless conflict,
and pointless suffering. In the belief that there is neither a God nor any
world-historical development in relation to which existence in such a
world might be rendered meaningful, and that there is no prospect of
transforming the conditions of existence to make possible its justification
in terms of the satisfactions it may afford, he considered life and the
world to stand condemned before the bar of evaluative judgment. His
philosophical pessimism thus verged on nihilism; and his counsel was to
withdraw as completely as possible from all worldly activity, either
through detached contemplation or — preferably — through complete asceticism, repudiating all forms of active willing. A better world he deemed
impossible; and so his ultimate ideal was the utter annihilation of the
"world-will" and all of its manifestations: "No will: no idea: no world."[3]

In his assessment of the world's nature and of the meaning and value
of human existence, Schopenhauer thus broke radically with the entire
Western religious and philosophical tradition. His bleak world view and
deep pessimism clashed fundamentally both with the Judeo-Christian
interpretation of the world and human life and with beliefs in the world's
basic rationality, in historical progress, and in the possibility of human
well-being and happiness, by his time widely embraced as secular articles of faith. Dismissed by most of his contemporaries as a morbid crank,
he impressed and disturbed Nietzsche greatly, since in Nietzsche's opinion both the questions he raised and the challenge of his pessimism
needed to be taken very seriously indeed. It might even be said that,
despite Nietzsche's eventual radical opposition to Schopenhauer's conclusions and other criticisms of him, Schopenhauer was his primary inspiration.
In any case, Nietzsche's recognition of the importance of coming to terms
with Schopenhauer and the challenge he posed radically influenced the
direction and development of his own thought from *The Birth of Tragedy*
to his last works.

But Nietzsche's encounter with Schopenhauer was indirect. He was
only sixteen when Schopenhauer died, and they never met. Nietzsche
knew him only through his published work, and made his first acquaint-

ance through *The World as Will and Representation,* discovered quite by accident one day in the late 1860s in a bookstore in Leipzig, where he was studying classical philology. It had a powerful and immediate impact on him. He could not put the book down until he had read it through. It was his introduction to philosophy, to the thinker who became his "educator," and to the basic problems that were to occupy him with increasing urgency for the rest of his productive life, the course of which it altered dramatically and to great effect. For this we too are greatly in Schopenhauer's debt.

Nietzsche's essay bears the title *Schopenhauer as Educator.* But what does Nietzsche mean when he speaks of "educating" and cites Schopenhauer "as educator"? It is of no small importance that the word he employs in his title is *Erzieher.* The kind of educator and education with which he is concerned is not that signified by the words *Lehrer* and *lehren* — the educator as instructor, and education as the imparting of some body of knowledge or doctrine (*Lehre*). Schopenhauer advocated certain doctrines, and sought to persuade others to accept them; but this is not why Nietzsche lauds him as *Erzieher.* He does so rather in recognition of Schopenhauer's significance for his own intellectual development — by challenging, provoking, stimulating, and inspiring, but above all by serving as an *examplar,* by what he sought to do and how he sought to do it. It is in this sense that "educator" is here to be understood. Nietzsche offers his own response to his encounter with Schopenhauer as an example of the way in which one thinker may be educated by another without thereby becoming a mere disciple. And his larger purpose is to suggest, in contrast to all more conventional forms of instruction, learning, and scholarly training, the importance of such education for the realization of one's intellectual and human potential.

The kind of educating Nietzsche has in mind is thus linked to what he calls "the task of making human beings human," by developing their intellectual and creative abilities to the full. For him education has the sense of liberation, self-realization, and the transformation of one's spiritual life. And true "educators" are figures capable of stimulating this development in those who encounter their example, in person or through their work, and who are ripe for such an encounter. In contrast, Nietzsche contends, modern educational practices and institutions fail to provide such educators, and are indeed dangerously stultifying, stunting rather than fostering the development of spiritual life. They enslave rather than liberate, distort rather than cultivate, and restrict rather than stimulate. They also establish norms of intellectual activity that divert those capable of achieving real autonomous and creative spirituality into sterile endeavor, squandering their potential in the pursuit of arid ideals. Thus they not only fail to serve but are actually detrimental to the true end of education, which has to do not with transmission or accumulation of knowledge of various objects of abstruse inquiry, but rather with the enhancement, enrichment, and fulfillment of human life.

Early in the essay, Nietzsche sounds a theme that is at once all too familiar and all too easily misunderstood: *"Sei du selbst! Das bist du alles nicht, was du jetzt tust, meinst, begehrst"* (Be yourself! You are none of those things you now do, think, desire). This appeal can be properly understood only if notice is taken of what sort of "self" he calls upon one to "be" (or "become"). It is one's *"true* self" he has in mind; and this is something other than one's biological, social, and personal identity. "Finding oneself" is a task Nietzsche regards as both difficult and dangerous. It involves restraining, sacrificing, overcoming, and transforming most of what makes up one's initially acquired identity. One's true self, he suggests, transcends this ordinary plane of all-too-human existence and the self as commonly understood. Moreover, it is something that "does not lie hidden deep inside you," already formed and waiting to emerge, but is rather "high above you," to be achieved only through great effort. Nietzsche conceives of it in terms of one's potential for creative activity, and self-realization is construed in terms of the realization of that potential.

True selfhood for Nietzsche is thus not a matter of individuality per se. Individuality is to be desired and given scope only insofar as it is either a precondition or a consequence of such self-realization; and it may assume negative significance if its pursuit interferes with the development of one's creative abilities. As one might expect in view of the importance he attached to the artistic transfiguration of human life in *The Birth of Tragedy,*[4] artistic ability and activity are obviously paradigmatic for Nietzsche here. And in this light we may easily understand how he can accord special significance to "genius" and to exceptional individuals possessed of it, since in them the capacity for "productive uniqueness" (which he is prepared to attribute in some degree to everyone) is present in far greater measure—a fact that renders their self-realization of exceptional importance.

If, as Nietzsche supposes, "the task of making human beings human" has above all to do with the actualization of this potential, it is easy to see why he takes the fullest self-realization of these exceptional human beings to represent the attainment of a higher form of humanity. And since "culture" is the sphere in which such self-realization finds its primary expression and the strongest impetus to its further cultivation, it should also be clear why he associates the enhancement of human life and the emergence of a higher humanity with the flourishing of culture (which he sharply distinguishes from the flourishing of social, political, and economic institutions in response to the more mundane imperatives of human existence). Nietzsche is often thought to have advanced a conception of humanity that reduces it to its natural rudiments. But this essay shows that such a view is mistaken, since great significance is attached to the difference between humanity and mere animality, and to culture as its source (with "genius" as its instrument). Nature and merely natural existence are viewed as devoid of meaning and standing in need of "justification" and "redemption"; and this, Nietzsche contends, can be accomplished only by their transformation through the development of culture.[5]

Culture is the sphere in which, for Nietzsche, human animality is sublimated and transmuted into spirituality. "The task of making human beings human" may thus be conceived as the task of spiritualizing human animals through their introduction to and participation in cultural life. And the exhortation to "become yourself" is to be understood not as a call to return to nature or to intensify one's subjectivity, but rather as an appeal to *ascend* to culture, and to contribute what one can to its enrichment. To be sure, this is possible only by drawing upon energies and cultivating abilities rooted in one's human animality, which is fundamentally but a piece of nature. For Nietzsche, however, everything depends upon what one does with those energies and what one makes of those abilities, and so upon transcending the plane of merely natural existence and the commonplace forms of social existence that in his view still belong essentially to it.

Nietzsche distinguishes a number of general images of humanity that differ from each other as well as from the all-too-human type of social-animal humanity he regards as the human rule. He identifies three images of a more genuine humanity competing for attention and allegiance in his own time (and which bear a strong resemblance to the Dionysian, Apollinian, and tragic types he had depicted in *The Birth of Tragedy*). He designates them with the names of three more recent figures whom he regards as champions and exemplars of the apposite ideals: Rousseau, Goethe, and Schopenhauer (here actually Nietzsche himself)—all Nietzschean "educators" par excellence.

Rousseauean man—for Nietzsche the most problematic of the three—represents naturalized humanity, renewed by emancipation from the shackles of society and restoration to its basic instincts. Goethean man—less dangerous for Nietzsche, but lacking in vitality—is the image of contemplative humanity, cultivated and sophisticated and therefore more truly human owing to its attainment of high spirituality, but essentially withdrawn from active involvement in life. Schopenhauerian (or Nietzschean) man, on the other hand, combines elements of both and also supersedes both. This is the image of a "truly active," creative humanity, at once vital and spiritualized, and that has therefore become most truly itself because most fully human.

The significance of these image-types for Nietzsche is that they have the power to liberate, stimulate, inspire—in short, to *educate*. But because of the different forms of human development that each tends to foster and the shortcomings of the Rousseauean and Goethean models, he regards them as differing not only in kind but also in value. Only the Schopenhauerian (the heir to the tragic type and model of art and spirituality in *The Birth of Tragedy*) holds out the promise of an attainable form of humanity healthy and vital enough to have a real future in this world, and sufficiently creative and spiritualized to justify itself—and human life and the world as well. Rousseauean man neglects human spirituality and the importance of engaging the forces of our natural humanity in its service in such a way that, when tapped, these forces are creative rather than merely destructive. Goethean man neglects to give these forces their due and thereby fails to promote the active expression of human spirituality, without which it necessarily becomes sterile. It is therefore the image and ideal Nietzsche associates with Schopenhauerian man that he commends to us here, and that he subsequently elaborated and celebrated.

A second set of types is intended to anchor this ideal in human reality by singling out certain actually attained exceptions to the human rule in whom, in various respects, this ideal is anticipated. These are the types of the *philosopher*, the *artist*, and the *saint*. Nietzsche here sounds themes developed in later works where he invokes the *Übermensch* as the apotheosis of the enhancement of life, in relation to which a variety of types of "higher humanity" are significant, but are only partial and all-too-human approaches and approximations.[6] In this early essay Nietzsche honors these three types because some significant aspect of the human ideal he envisions has been realized in each of them (albeit in limited and merely provisional form), thereby demonstrating that this ideal is no mere fantasy but one that lies within human reach and legitimate human aspiration.

Having more fully identified the "true man," through whom life may be "redeemed" and "justified," Nietzsche can also identify "the goal of culture": "to foster the production of the true man." Moreover, to the question of how one's life may "be given the highest value and deepest significance," he can now answer: by contributing in whatever way one can to this development. In addition, he considers it possible to "derive a new set of duties" founded upon "the fundamental idea of culture" and its advancement. So he contends that both the advancement of culture and the enhancement of life depend upon the "production" of the philosopher, artist, and saint, because of the emergence and development of certain traits he associates with them. These types are importantly linked to his conception of genius, which is not to be equated with them but embraces and draws upon them.

Thus the figure of the saint is meant to evoke the idea of self-overcoming, of transcending the willful, self-centered individual ego, and attaining unity with all of life and existence. The figure of the philosopher conveys the idea of spiritual liberation, enlightenment with respect to the nature and conditions of human existence generally, and knowledge of the world's basic character. The figure of the artist is employed (rather oddly) to represent the achievement of a fuller knowledge of the various forms of life and existence as well as their creative transfiguration. In each case Nietzsche alludes to both a kind of knowledge and a related kind of transformation. And it is of no small interest that in this essay he considers such special forms of knowledge—as well as the kinds of creative activity mentioned—to be attainable; and, further, that he takes their attainment to be crucial, not only to the enhancement of life and consummation of nature, but also as constituent features of life so enhanced and nature so consummated.

Schopenhauer (whom Nietzsche follows in assigning special importance to the philosopher, artist, and saint) was clearly his model for the philosopher in this trinity of higher types. Nietzsche has much more to say, however, about the kind of philosopher he conceives Schopenhauer to have been; and his remarks in this connection are of particular interest for the light they cast on his emerging conception of the genuine philosopher and on his own later philosophical activity. For Nietzsche, Schopenhauer was no ordinary philosopher or scholar of the types he so severely portrays in the last sections of the essay. His sketches of these types, vividly anticipating his later critiques of their characteristic modes of thought,[7] serve to underscore the contrasting significance he found in Schopenhauer's example. Schopenhauer stands out in bold relief; and the entire discussion plainly demonstrates that Nietzsche considers a different sort of intellectual-philosophical activity to be humanly possible, and that he takes the realization of this possibility to be of immense importance.

Once molded into creatures of their disciplines, the academic philosophers and scholars he describes and criticizes neither are nor can become truly and fully human beings; nor do their labors help others to do so. A philosopher like Nietzsche's Schopenhauer, however, is an exception in both respects. He can hardly be regarded as exemplifying Nietzsche's conception of true humanity completely; but he does represent what Nietzsche means by "genius" in philosophical thinking, and he is viewed by Nietzsche as the kind of philosopher through whom human life might be enhanced.

One of the qualities Nietzsche stresses in his portrait of Schopenhauer as philosopher is *independence* — independence of one's time and of prevailing institutions and interpretations. The philosopher may not be able to escape them entirely — indeed, he cannot and should not ignore them — but a *critical* relation to them is both possible and necessary to genuine philosophical thinking. Philosophy, as Nietzsche would have it understood, presupposes a measure of such independence and also makes possible a fuller liberation from the constraints of conventional thinking, from the strictures and imperatives of existing institutions (social, political, and also academic), and even from the thinker's own biological and historical conditioning. The idea and ideal of the philosopher as pure knowing subject, spectator of all time and existence, may be a Platonizing myth to which Schopenhauer should not have subscribed and which Nietzsche rejects; but there *is* an attainable form of transcendence, exemplified by Schopenhauer, which Nietzsche regards as a crucial distinguishing mark of a truly philosophical thinker. The quest to know nature and one's own time and the human norm and prevailing modes of thought *in order to transcend them* — and, by so doing, not only do justice to them but also criticize and transform them — is for Nietzsche an aspiration that sets Schopenhauer apart, and an essential aspect of what it means to be a genuine philosopher.

The three specific virtues he attributes to Schopenhauer — honesty, cheerfulness, and constancy — add additional detail. All are required in order to persevere and advance in true philosophical endeavor. But these three virtues must be supplemented by the courage to think and live independently and the intellectual ability to *reinterpret* and *revalue* life and existence. Thus, according to Nietzsche, Schopenhauer was not merely a "profane and secularized" thinker no longer under the sway of religious and metaphysical ideas whose time had come and gone, important though Nietzsche believed that to be. He also had a sharp eye for truly fundamental problems — problems that must be freshly and radically reckoned with, such as "the problem of existence itself" and whether life has, or may come to have, meaning and value. He further had the creative originality to develop a new and comprehensive world view, to present "a picture of life as a whole" with significant implications for the meaning of one's own life. Nothing less, Nietzsche suggests, is to be expected of a truly philosophical thinker, in contrast with those who occupy themselves with merely investigating, refining, and applying inherited interpretations and conceptual schemes. And nothing less than this is what he himself subsequently sought to do.

Philosophical thinking, so understood, proceeds through and beyond the analysis, comprehension, and criticism of various matters to their more fundamental and comprehensive interpretation. This in turn makes possible a *re*interpretation and *re*valuation of many specific phenomena of human life. In embracing this conception of philosophy, Nietzsche renounces neither the conception of any sort of truth deserving of the name, nor its pursuit (contrary to the claims of some of his recent interpreters). His emphasis here on the importance of truthfulness and honesty, and on the attainment of knowledge by the philosopher (and by artist and saint as well), makes this abundantly clear. And he has in mind something more than the kinds of truth and knowledge that are abstracted from life and may be pursued only by restricting oneself to problems and methods that depend for their clarity and rigor upon the artificiality of the reasoning patterns and experience in which they are formulated.

A parallel (by no means merely fortuitous) may be discerned between the aims of philosophy and those of education as Nietzsche construes them here. Education of the sort he envisions is associated very revealingly with the attainment of a kind of "truth"; but it is related only incidentally (if at all) to the learning of facts or the mastery of forms of theoretical inquiry. Its focus is rather upon human-spiritual self-realization through the cultivation and employment of one's full intellectual powers. And the measure of "truth" here is the extent to which our lives come to manifest our highest possibilities, we come to be what we have it in us to be, and true humanity is thereby achieved.

The philosophical endeavor Nietzsche champions is likewise concerned above all with the pursuit of a kind of "truth" that is not merely a matter of fidelity of thought and expression to the way things are, even though it presupposes their clear and candid apprehension. More importantly, it also relates to what may become or be made of human life, and therefore of life and the world more generally, as the merely natural is transfigured and higher forms of existence are attained. "Truth" here requires that justice be done to the possibilities inherent in life and the world generally, as well as to their present character. It is this "truth" of existence, at once sobering and promising, and to be grasped through its unflinchingly honest, unmyopic, and imaginative assessment, that Nietzsche suggests may make possible its affirmation, justification, and redemption. It has nothing to do with the illusory forms of metaphysical and religious "comfort" that he earlier (in *The Birth of Tragedy*) had supposed were needed to make life endurable. It differs from most of what does and should count as true, but it still deserves the name of "truth." Indeed, it constitutes a higher form of truth—a truth of the greatest human significance. For it alone may be able to sustain us, whereas truthfulness and honesty in their merely analytical and critical employment only weaken and destroy such illusions without offering anything better in their place.

There are many ways of doing some justice to our developmental possibilities and to life and the world as well. For this reason it is to be expected and even desired that genuine philosophers will be creative in their interpretations, and that these interpretations will differ. Their differences, moreover, should not be taken to mean either that some are wrong or that all are meaningless. If philosophers do what they should be doing, they will think in creatively original as well as analytical and critical ways. They will elaborate a wealth of perspectives diversely illuminating what we and the world are and have it in us to become, thereby summoning us to lives that will further transform the aspect of existence. To serve and pursue the attainment of this highest kind of truth in this way is, for Nietzsche, their fundamental task.

The endowment of human life with meaning and value through its creative transformation is a central theme of Nietzsche's thought. In the earlier *Birth of Tragedy* he first detected this idea at the heart of the ancient Greek response to the problems of rendering life in a harsh and inhuman world endurable and worth living. Subsequently he came to view it as the key to overcoming that nihilistic crisis in which, he believed, this problem had in his own age returned with a vengeance. In *Schopenhauer as Educator* this problem and this conception of its only viable resolution both loom very large. They define the context in which Nietzsche inveighs against what commonly passes for philosophy and education and in which he honors Schopenhauer as a different kind of philosopher and educator—a kind for whom there is now the greatest need. Without such philosophers and educators, he holds, there is little hope that humankind will be able to meet this grave nihilistic challenge and to redeem itself—and nature with it—from meaninglessness. For him the vindication of life depends upon its qualitative enhancement; and that in turn depends upon the emergence of exceptional human beings through whom the potential as well as the reality of our existence and the world are revealed and more fully realized, and by whose examples others are induced to exert themselves in like manner and to still greater effect. In this way humankind may succeed in educating and transforming itself, drawn toward the higher spirituality of which it is capable by a vanguard through whose genius its possibility is envisioned and its realization is furthered. Its attainment may never be widespread; but enough exceptions to the general human rule may occur to justify all.

There is a celebrated image, certainly familiar to Nietzsche, that may well have influenced his conception of the enhancement of life through an educational process of this sort. This is the great image of the "ladder of love" in Plato's *Symposium*. The image is employed by Plato's Socrates to suggest how the soul may, by its attraction to beauty, be liberated and drawn upward toward the highest state of which it is capable. This attraction serves to render the soul responsive to a succession of exemplifications of beauty of progressive refinement. Responding at first only to cruder beauties, it may gradually be educated and elevated as it is drawn to others of a similar but more refined nature. As the process is repeated, the soul may ascend the "ladder of love" to a spirituality far above the rung on which it began, and so become what it ought to be.

For Nietzsche true education may be conceived as involving a comparable ascent and development through one's attraction to a succession of ideas and of exemplary others. Toward the end of the first section of the essay, he even speaks of "love" and employs the image of a "ladder" in this connection. Through such encounters and responses, we may in fact become what we have it in ourselves to be. And by reflecting upon them, we may achieve a better understanding of our true natures, since our attraction to these objects of interest reveals us to ourselves. Our real educators, our liberators and "educers," are all those special influences that have this significance for us, even if certain individuals stand out, as did Schopenhauer for Nietzsche.

It is fitting that, as Nietzsche turned from philology to philosophy, and looked to philosophy liberated from conventional scholarly and social expectations for the resolution of some of the most fundamental problems of human life, he should echo Socrates here. For Socrates engaged in philosophical inquiry in a similar spirit and with similar concerns. He likewise loathed the sterile and servile substitute for it practiced by the sophistic counterparts in his own day of the academic philosophers castigated by Nietzsche. And though he undoubtedly would have been as critical of Nietzsche's interpretation and assessments of many matters as Nietzsche was of his, he surely would have agreed with Nietzsche about the nature and importance of true education and educators.

Given Nietzsche's preference for the pre-Socratics,[8] and his profound ambivalence toward Socrates in *The Birth of Tragedy* and later writings, it is hardly surprising that Socrates is not included along with the pre-Socratics in Schopenhauer's company here. But he could have been, and perhaps even should have been. For Socrates was unmistakably one of Nietzsche's greatest educators, and furthermore one who arguably satisfies Nietzsche's own account of the true educator and the genuine philosopher at least as well as Schopenhauer. And, of all Nietzsche's writings, this essay not only anticipates the literature of existential philosophy most closely, but also is perhaps the most Socratic in spirit. For many this will mean that, early Nietzsche though it may be, it is also Nietzsche at his best.

Notes

1. *Ecce Homo* III:2:3 ("Why I Write Such Good Books: The Untimely Ones," sec. 3).

2. See my *Nietzsche,* chaps. 4 and 5.

3. For fuller discussion of Schopenhauer's thought, see Patrick Gardiner, *Schopenhauer* (Baltimore: Penguin, 1963) and D. W. Hamlyn, *Schopenhauer* (London: Routledge & Kegan Paul, 1980).

4. See my. *Nietzsche,* chap. 8.

5. This echoes his contention in *The Birth of Tragedy* that "it is only as an *aesthetic phenomenon* that existence and the world are eternally justified" (BT 5).

6. See my *Nietzsche,* chap. 5.

7. See ibid., chaps. 1 and 2.

8. See Nietzsche's early essay (which he did not publish or even finish, but which is of considerable interest in connection with the present essay) *Philosophy in the Tragic Age of the Greeks.*

CHAPTER NINE

The Nietzsche-Spinoza Problem: Spinoza as Precursor?

I am utterly amazed, utterly enchanted! I have a *precursor,* and what a precursor! I hardly knew Spinoza. . . . Not only is his over-all tendency like mine—namely, to make knowledge the *most powerful* affect—but in five main points of his doctrine I recognize myself . . . : he denies the freedom of the will, teleology, the moral world-order, the unegoistic, and evil. Even though the divergences are admittedly tremendous, they are due more to differences in time, culture, and science.
—Nietzsche to Overbeck, July 30, 1881

Nietzsche's relation to Spinoza is of great interest, not only because it is highly complex and richly ambivalent, but also because it is very illuminating with respect to both of them. And we need all of the help we can get, as we seek to reckon vitally as well as responsibly with them, for there is much about each of them that makes this very difficult indeed. I hope here to be able to contribute something to the understanding of them by looking at them in relation to each other. Along the way I will try to say something useful about their theories of the "affects" and about the problem of Spinoza's famous *conatus* and Nietzsche's equally famous "will to power," its apparent counterpart and rival.

1

Modern Western philosophy has had two fundamental tasks with respect to what may at least loosely be called our human nature, as this tradition has struggled to emancipate itself from the dominance of Christianity: as Nietzsche put it, "to translate man back into nature" (BGE 230)—and then to read ourselves out of it again, this time more tenably, as a natural and yet also more than merely natural form of existence. To these two tasks, moreover, a third has been added, by at least some philosophers in this modern tradition: to articulate a secular version of the difference between the kind of humanity human beings commonly exhibit and that which they have it in them to attain (but can and do attain only under special conditions), which in Christianity is expressed in terms of fallenness and salvation.

These tasks and themes are often and very properly associated with Nietzsche, in whose writings they are addressed with exceptional vividness. The second and third of them distinguish him very importantly from the host of those before and after him who have been so preoccupied with the first that they settled for and advocated reductionist interpretations of our nature. For them, we are nothing more than a peculiar piece of the de-deified world of material substances, matter in motion, or forces in interplay and combination. For Nietzsche (as I understand him), on the other hand, all such interpretations are as unsatisfactory as those that construe our nature in terms altogether different from those applicable to the rest of mundane existence. There long have been and continue to be many religious and philosophical thinkers, however, who have been all too ready to lump together all those who (like Nietzsche) reject extra-naturalistic religious or metaphysical interpretations of our nature with those who restrict themselves reductionistically to the first of these tasks and themes.

This tendency has distorted the understanding of Nietzsche for much of the past century; and it likewise plagued the reception of Spinoza for a century and more after his demise. In both cases, however, the result was a failure to appreciate what they actually were driving at and attempting to put in place of the religious and metaphysical interpretations of our nature they opposed. Both were fundamentally naturalistic in their construal of our nature—but naturalistic in a nonreductionist sense.

Paul Tillich, who first inspired my interest in Spinoza as well as Nietzsche, used to like to say that they both were "ecstatic naturalists" (as indeed he conceived himself to be). By this he meant that for them the nature of which we are a part amounts to something more than merely natural and material existence, and that our emergent and attainable humanity reflects and expresses something inherent in the basic character of reality itself that is the real meaning of the idea of the divine. To speak with Nietzsche, both the emergence and the enhancement of the form of life humanity represents are nothing more or less than expressions of the fundamental character and impetus of the natural and only world and reality there is, distinctively configured and transfigured. Spinoza's naturalism likewise is of no mere prosaic kind, the manner of its presentation notwithstanding.

Despite his many critical remarks about Spinoza, Nietzsche clearly recognized in him a kindred spirit—and quite rightly. He did so for many reasons, prominent among which were his appreciation of the attempt made by Spinoza to read our humanity back into nature, and to propose a psychology and anthropology that linked the mental with the physical and physiological in a fundamental way. But no less appealing to him, I suspect, was Spinoza's attempt at the same time to do justice to our capacity to transcend our merely natural existence by way of its transformation.

In some obvious ways Spinoza and Nietzsche could not be more different. In other important respects, however, these two of the greatest philosophical psychologists are closer to each other than either of them may be to anyone else in the history of modern philosophy. And their similarities make their differences all the more interesting.

Both Spinoza and Nietzsche were deemed profoundly dangerous and insidious thinkers for a long while after the untimely early ends of their productive lives (at almost exactly the same age). This was owing not only to their shared reputation as atheists, but also to the dismayed perception of them as advocates of interpretations of life and the world shorn of those transcendentally grounded and guaranteed qualities and values upon which their significance and worth long have been supposed to depend. In retrospect this seems to at least some of us today to be ironic, since this preoccupation with what they denied has obscured the fact that both sought to work out interpretations that held greater promise *in these very respects* than those they were intended to replace.

Both Spinoza and Nietzsche were profoundly *affirmative* thinkers, seeking to show the way to a deeper affirmation and more just assessment of our existence and world than could be attained and upheld on traditional and commonplace ways of thinking. Both were obsessed with the question of what we have it in us to become, and of the higher humanity that at least some among us might attain, beyond the rather sorry all-too-human manner of existence that is the general human rule. And both took this to be a matter of our capitalizing upon certain of our general human resources, transforming and giving altered expression to powers that are merely natural to begin with, and are not essentially different from those characteristic of all forms of life and existence.

This meant, for both, that something like psychology is the path not only to the understanding of our human nature and possibilities, but also to the reassessment of whatever sort of significance and worth may properly be accorded to human existence. When Nietzsche asks rhetorically "Who among philosophers was a *psychologist* at all before me?" (EH IV:6), implying that none were, he should have added, "apart from Spinoza," whom he very well knew had been an exception.

A difficulty we face in dealing with them, however, is that each links his psychology to a comprehensive interpretation of life and the world that most contemporary philosophers find it difficult to take seriously. Spinoza's "God or nature," conceived as an essentially rational single substance embracing all existence, informs and colors his psychology and account of our nature — as does Nietzsche's "will to power," construed as an essentially *non*rational disposition accounting for the manner in which everything in this world comes to be and passes away. These interpretations cannot be reconciled; and they also are stumbling blocks to most of us today. Eventually, however, they must be reckoned with; and that is not easy. A full reckoning with them is beyond the scope of this chapter; but some of what I shall have to say may contribute to it, taking my cue from the way in which Nietzsche himself responded to Spinoza.

2

While Nietzsche offers a number of criticisms of Spinoza, none of them has to do with what might seem to be the most obvious and fundamental point of difference between them: Spinoza's retention and ubiquitous use of the term "God." Nietzsche would seem to write this off as one of those "divergences" owing to "differences in time, culture, and science," and to regard it as nothing more than a terminological bow to traditional discourse that is to be glossed in terms of a "nature" no longer distinguished from and understood in relation to a deity transcending it. His Spinoza has essentially abandoned the "God-hypothesis," even if not "God-language," and conceived of nature and human reality in what for Nietzsche is a fundamentally "de-deified" manner — even if, in his supposition of the basic rationality of this all-encompassing "nature," Spinoza still clings to a major remnant of the metaphysical faith from which Nietzsche contends we must free ourselves.

I consider Nietzsche to be quite right not to be distracted by this apparent difference between them. For Spinoza, as for him, what he calls "the old god" of traditional Judeo-Christianity is "dead." For both, the idea of such a transcendent being is no longer worthy of being taken seriously, and is to be abandoned. Indeed, all of his talk of "God" notwithstanding, Spinoza surely deserves to be regarded as Nietzsche's "precursor" in this matter — the first of the great modern philosophers to take this recognition as his point of departure, and to make a serious and comprehensive attempt to work out the consequences.

Yet this is not the whole story for either of them. Suitably reconceived, the term "God" — like the term "soul" — may be reintroduced, to good effect. As Nietzsche has Zarathustra say, "the soul is only a word for something about the body" (Z I:4) — but it is a word that has its uses in working out a richer and more profound understanding of "the body" than can be given in terms of either mere matter in motion or the dynamic successor of this model. And so also with "God" where the world is concerned, Nietzsche allows, to the same purpose. Spinoza may be thought of as making the same sort of point, in speaking of both "mind" and "God." For him, as for Nietzsche, neither term properly refers to entities or substances transcending our bodies and the world. Rather, both are words for something about ourselves and the world that needs to be added in order to guard against their underestimation and reductionistic misconstrual.

In any event, both Spinoza and Nietzsche seek not only to enhance our respect for what the body is capable of, but also to rehabilitate the notions of mind and soul as meaningful characterizations of significant dimensions of our existence that must be understood in nonphysiological terms. Both insist that we are part of nature through and through, and of no altogether different extranatural kind. But their "nature" is not a nature that is—and remains even in us—nothing more than what may be described entirely in the language of the natural sciences.

Both are commonly abhorred as fatalistic determinists, whose rejection of "free will" and ideas of necessity make a mockery of the notions of human freedom and dignity. Yet beyond the amor fati that both advocate as the highest state to which a philosopher can attain, both also seek to shift the terms in which human freedom and dignity are conceived, with the result that an enhanced form of life becomes discernible as a real if exceptional human possibility, in which these notions become newly meaningful after all—precisely by way of the obtaining of a configuration of our dispositions that transforms the manner of our existence. And for both, the attainment of a kind of knowledge of ourselves—and of a form of self-mastery that it makes possible—is within our power, and plays a crucial role in any such "higher humanity's" realization.

For both Spinoza and Nietzsche the "theory of the affects" is the key to understanding all human psychological phenomena. Both are often derided for their contention that our basic nature is to be conceived in terms of a single ultimate disposition, which gives rise to all other affects of a more specific nature as it plays out in different contexts of interaction and relation. Yet both get a great deal of mileage out of the hypotheses along these lines they advance, and give accounts of how this elaboration of our affective life occurs that makes sense of a very wide range of phenomena. For both, moreover, this basic disposition has to do with our endeavor to increase our "power of activity" (in Spinoza's phrase); and both impute the same Ur-disposition to all else that exists as well. They at least appear to differ, however, about precisely how this disposition is to be more completely characterized.

The fact that Spinoza makes much use of the notions of "God" and "mind," moreover, while Nietzsche shies away from them, is not as important as it may appear to be. They *do* differ radically with respect to the question of whether all of reality is or is not a fundamentally *rational* affair, eternally ordered in accordance with immutable laws constituting a rational unity. But that is not the difference that separates them when it comes to their accounts of human nature and psychology—or at any rate, there are other differences of much greater interest and moment in the context. Set it aside—imagine Spinoza coming to be convinced of Nietzsche's basic picture of the fundamentally nonrational character of this world— and then these other differences become importantly discernible.

It would be disingenuous of me to pretend otherwise than that I side with Nietzsche here. However, I do not do so dogmatically; and my esteem for Spinoza, while exceeded by my regard for Nietzsche in these matters, is nonetheless greater than my esteem for almost any other thinker in the history of philosophy. Reflecting upon their differences, for me, is one of the best ways of posing some of the truly critical questions and alternatives in this crucial area of inquiry.

3

One important difference between them pertains to the methodological issue of how to best go about working out a philosophical psychology and theory of the affects. Spinoza, with the example of geometry guiding him, is content to construct definitions of certain basic concepts that he believes can be mapped on to phenomena with which we are familiar from experience. Nietzsche, on the other hand, in the spirit of his conception of scientific method, seeks first to acquaint himself with a wealth of phenomena encountered in human life and then to frame hypotheses enabling one to make interpretive and explanatory sense of them.

In doing so, Nietzsche makes use of his famous "perspectival" procedure, seeking to view various phenomena "with many different eyes" on the way to an integrating understanding availing itself of what thereby comes to light (GM III:12). For Spinoza, on the other hand, it suffices to have found a place in his unfolding scheme for the varieties of affects for which we have ordinary names and of which we have experience. He is indeed mindful of the latter as he proceeds, looking for places for them and ways of accommodating them; but Nietzsche is much more prepared to be guided by his perspectival analyses of them, and to reshape his construal of their general nature accordingly—even though he further seeks to relate them to an emerging comprehensive conception of their underlying unity. This is a difference of which Nietzsche makes less than one might expect; but it is an important one, to which I shall return.

Nietzsche quite remarkably seems prepared—at least in his 1881 communication to Overbeck—to write off many of his differences with Spinoza to mere "differences in time, culture, and science," as though they were but the form and not the matter of the thought. Yet in the mid-1880s, some five years later, he makes much of certain points that would seem intended to underscore other differences to which he had become acutely sensitive, notwithstanding his many areas of continuing agreement and admiration. Curiously enough, it was as a "psychologist of philosophers" that Nietzsche became particularly critical of Spinoza— and *of Spinoza as psychologist,* on several counts that seem at first to be quite unrelated, but turn out on Nietzsche's analysis to be deeply connected.

Prior to his real discovery of Spinoza in 1881, Nietzsche had referred to him only occasionally, usually in a respectful but rather distant way— for example, as "the perfect sage" and "prototype of genius" (HH I:475, 477). In the first edition of *The Gay Science,* published in 1881, in several passages of no little importance in view of his comment about their shared concern "to make knowledge the *most powerful* affect," he chides Spinoza for being naive about the origin and motivation of the impulse to knowledge. So, for example, he accuses him of an "error" in supposing that "in science one possessed and loved something unselfish, harmless, self-sufficient, in which man's evil impulses had no part whatsoever" (GS 37). More explicitly, he writes: "*The meaning of knowing.* —*Non ridere, non lugere, neque detestari, sed intelligere,* says Spinoza, as simply and sublimely as is his wont. Yet in the last analysis, what else is this *intelligere* than the form in which we come to feel all three at once?" (GS 333).

Nietzsche's basic point here is that, although Spinoza most laudably had in effect undertaken to "translate man back into nature" (as Nietzsche characterizes his own task), he was not thorough enough about it, and did not realize that the same treatment must be given to human knowing that he proposed to give at the outset of part 3 of the *Ethics* to the emotions. Nietzsche means to deny neither the possibility nor the importance of knowledge, as his reference to his "over-all tendency" and many passages in this same work clearly indicate. But he does insist upon the necessity of recognizing our capacity for knowledge to be the product of a complex development of a very mundane sort, like everything else that is now a part of our psychological makeup. And his complaint about Spinoza here is thus that he did not carry his psychology far enough, either in the scope or in its "naturalistic" reinterpretation.

Half a dozen years later, this complaint is made again—but this time it is made against something much more fundamental than Spinoza's treatment of knowledge. Yet it does not prevent Nietzsche from continuing to embrace Spinoza as an ally with respect to the "five main points" he mentions to Overbeck, and with respect also to a variety of more specific points as well. So, for example, in *On the Genealogy of Morals* (1887), all of his references to Spinoza are favorable, on such matters as his low estimation of pity (GM P:5), his recognition of the naturalness in certain circumstances of such phenomena as hatred and cruelty (GM II:6), and his reduction of the *morsus conscientiae* to the mere feeling of something having "unexpectedly gone wrong" (GM II:15). All of this is of a piece with his more general appreciation of Spinoza's having anticipated his own naturalistic approach to the analysis and reinterpretation of human psychological phenomena—and of Spinoza's related critique of teleology.

But Nietzsche also takes Spinoza severely to task in this same final period of his productive life, in several fundamental respects, both in *Beyond Good and Evil* and subsequently. It is as though he were saying to Spinoza: "Psychologist, analyze thyself!" What makes his charges especially interesting is that they not only raise important questions about Spinoza, but also might conceivably be leveled against Nietzsche himself—as he may well have been uncomfortably aware. My thought here is that it may have been precisely because he felt such a kinship with Spinoza that he was so hard on this "alter ego," in an attempt to warn himself—and us too, if we are kin to them—of things to beware of in proceeding to attempt to plumb the depths of our human reality as philosopher-psychologists.

4

Early in *Beyond Good and Evil* Spinoza is singled out (along with Kant) by Nietzsche as providing an example of how often philosophers "are not honest enough in their work," and "pose as if they had discovered and reached their real opinions through the self-development of a cold, pure, divinely unconcerned dialectic," even though actually "at bottom it is . . . most often a desire of the heart that has been followed and made abstract . . . that they defend with reasons they have sought after the fact." He writes:

> Or consider the hocus-pocus of mathematical form with which Spinoza clad his philosophy—really "the love of *his* wisdom," to render that word fairly and squarely—in mask and mail, to strike terror at the very outset into the heart of any assailant who should dare to glance at that invincible maiden and Pallas Athena: how much personal timidity and vulnerability this masquerade of a sick hermit betrays! (BGE 5)

Perhaps so—or at least, this raises a legitimate kind of suspicion that, while by no means decisive, should put us on our guard against being overly impressed by the form in which Spinoza presents his thinking in the *Ethics*. But if so, it is a sword that cuts both ways— especially since it is *another* "sick hermit" speaking here, who employed a different but no less problematic style in presenting *his* views. I refer to Nietzsche himself and his fiery rhetoric, which may well have—and may even at bottom have been *intended* to have—the same cowing effect upon the reader that Nietzsche here describes. One might with equal justice or injustice say: "how much personal timidity and vulnerability *this* masquerade of a sick hermit" may likewise perhaps betray. Spinoza and Nietzsche are no identical twins, but they may well be brothers in this respect. I suspect that Nietzsche at some level knew it, and worried about it.

The "masquerade" theme and criticism recur not long thereafter, in a further and more pointed way, expressing a deeper worry and criticism: that the sickness Nietzsche called *ressentiment* may be at work beneath the surface of Spinoza's thought, in that special variant of *ressentiment* he discerns in a great many philosophers who have been profoundly distressed by their lot in this world. He writes:

> These outcasts of society, these long-persecuted, wickedly perse-cuted ones—also the compulsory recluses, the Spinozas or Giordano Brunos—always become in the end, even under the most spiritual masquerade, and perhaps without being themselves aware of it, sophisticated vengeance-seekers and poison-brewers (let someone lay bare the foundations of Spinoza's ethics and theology!). (BGE 25)

This too is perhaps a legitimate worry for one like Nietzsche who recognizes that what he calls a "psychology of philosophers" is needed as one approaches and attempts to assess their thinking—but if so, it is a worry that may be felt in the case of Nietzsche himself as well. For he too was something of a case in point; and one may reasonably wonder whether his diatribes against the "herd," and his celebration of those who stand out from and against it, are likewise tainted by such "all-too-human" tendencies. This passage likewise thus may well reflect an uneasi-ness on his part not only with respect to Spinoza, but also with respect to himself.

Later in the same work, Nietzsche cites Spinoza as one of those whose thinking represents a response to an *internal* danger as well as to exter-nal adversity. This internal danger is the threat posed by an incipient anarchy of the passions, to which the response is made of attempting to achieve self-control by way of a misguided desperation strategy of suppressing them. He writes:

> All those moralities that address themselves to the individual, for the sake of his "happiness," as one says—what are they but counsels for behavior in relation to the degree of *dangerousness* in which the individual lives within himself; recipes against his passions. . . . All of it is, measured intellectually, worth very little and not by a long shot "science," much less "wisdom," but rather, to say it once more, three times more, prudence, prudence, prudence, mixed with stupidity, stupidity, stupidity. . . . [E.g.,] that laughing-no-more and weeping-no-more of Spinoza, his so naively advocated destruction of the affects through their analysis and vivisection. . . . (BGE 198)

Coming from one who knew this "dangerous" condition very well, and even took it to be one of the preconditions of both human and philosophical greatness, this passage has a special poignancy. Spinoza is here thus recognized as a kindred type, but faulted for having failed to appreciate the futility of attempting to deal with the passions in this manner and to discern how they might more effectively and constructively be dealt with (by learning to sublimate and control them).

This failure is related by Nietzsche to what he takes to have been the fundamental mistake enshrined in Spinoza's basic and central doctrine of *self-preservation* as the fundamental aim of the *conatus* that he takes to be the very essence of everything that exists, ourselves included. Nietzsche attacks this doctrine on several levels, one of which is more straightforwardly philosophical rather than psychological. In one such criticism he invokes Spinoza against himself, contending that Spinoza's advocacy of it is inconsistent with his avowed repudiation of teleology—on which point Nietzsche is in complete accord with him. "Physiologists," he writes, and philosophers too,

> should think twice before putting down the instinct of self-preservation as the cardinal instinct of an organic being. A living thing seeks above all to *discharge* its strength—life itself is will to power; self-preservation is only one of the indirect and most frequent *results*.
>
> In short, here as elsewhere, let us beware of *superfluous* teleological principles—one of which is the instinct of self-preservation (we owe it to Spinoza's inconsistency). Thus method, which must be essentially economy of principles, demands it. (BGE 13)

Yet here Nietzsche is very close indeed to Spinoza; and it may at least be wondered whether his "will to power" is any less teleological than

Spinoza's *conatus* to self-preservation. If they turn out to be more or less on a par with each other in this respect, the purported difference between them would seem to have to be cashed out in terms of the suggestion that Spinoza's principle is a *"superfluous* teleological principle," whereas Nietzsche's is not in the same way superfluous. And indeed Nietzsche does elsewhere argue that the latter is the case. But the very heat of his critique of Spinoza on this point may well be owing to his recognition that the hypothesis he advances in place of Spinoza's is uncomfortably close to it in this respect.

A second level of Nietzsche's attack would seem to be intended to provide a different and perhaps more telling reason for having doubts about Spinoza's alternative to Nietzsche's own position. Here Nietzsche again brings his "psychology of philosophers" into play, in a manner intended to undermine Spinoza's doctrine. His point is that it may be regarded as symptomatic of the physiologically "distressed" condition both of Spinoza and of those who are attracted to his position. He writes, a year after *Beyond Good and Evil,* in the fifth book of *The Gay Science* that he added to its second edition in 1887: "It should be considered symptomatic when some philosophers—for example, Spinoza, who was consumptive—considered the instinct of self-preservation decisive and *had* to see it in that way; for they were individuals in distress" (GS 349).

This may well strike one not only as unfair—since Spinoza undoubtedly arrived at his position on this matter well before his health deteriorated—but also as quite evidently false, at least as Nietzsche puts it. For Nietzsche himself was a living counterexample: an "individual in distress" owing to poor health if there ever was one, who nonetheless obviously did *not* "have to" consider the "instinct of self-preservation" primary and "decisive"—since he did not do so. What he might more plausibly have said was that the adoption of this view should perhaps be regarded as symptomatic of a "distressed" condition, but only in the sense of being *one way* of responding to this condition—with his own alternative position likewise perhaps being symptomatic of the same condition, as *another* way of responding to it. In that event, however, he surely would need to observe that this in neither case actually settles the question of the soundness of the position taken, but rather only places a large question mark beside it, to be either removed or confirmed by considerations of other kinds.

Before leaving this passage, it should be noted that it continues in a similar vein, but with a somewhat different specific thrust, as follows: "That our modern natural science has become so thoroughly entangled in this Spinozistic doctrine (most recently and worst of all, Darwinism, with its incomprehensibly onesided doctrine of the 'struggle for existence') is probably due to the origins of most natural scientists . . . [among] the 'common people' " (GS 349).

The basic idea and diagnosis remain the same—that what motivates the acceptance of the doctrine of the primacy of the endeavor to seek self-preservation is a condition of distress on the part of those accepting it. Here, however, the kind of distress Nietzsche has in mind is not that of serious ill-health, but rather is the less acute and more general kind of want of strength and vitality that he supposes to be characteristic of the common run of humanity, for whom anything more than self-preservation is not a real possibility. Nietzsche is in effect suggesting that an attraction to such a doctrine is just what one might expect of those for whom, by virtue either of ill-health or an otherwise impoverished constitution, self-preservation is the limit of their aspiration and their primary preoccupation.

Nietzsche's basic critical response to Spinoza in this final period thus focuses upon the central doctrine of his philosophical psychology—the doctrine that the *conatus* to secure self-preservation is the fundamental principle of our nature and the nature of all things. His critique proceeds by way of an attempt to call this doctrine into question and to undermine it by subjecting it to psychological scrutiny. This scrutiny extends both to its content and to the manner in which Spinoza presents it. In this way, Nietzsche believes, we may get further in the necessary attempt to decide what to make of the kind of psychology Spinoza offers us than we otherwise might, if we merely take it at face value.

The psychological approach to our nature that Spinoza pioneered warrants treating it too as a psychological phenomenon—at least in its genesis—that is not to be spared the knife and microscope of psychological analysis. Yet if this is so, the same applies to Nietzsche's own analysis of it and proposed alternative to it; and as I have been suggesting, his recognized deep kinship with Spinoza is also accompanied by an uneasy recognition that he has his work cut out for him if he is to avoid being tarred with the same brush.

5

Nietzsche's response to Spinoza is suggestive of his own sensitivities; but its interest is not restricted to what it shows about him. For many of us today, it is hard to decide what to make of Spinoza. It is all too easy both to be awed and to be put off by both the form and the apparent content of his system; and both reactions are not very conducive to reckoning seriously with him as a philosopher. Here Nietzsche may be helpful to us; for he cuts through both the form and the apparent content of Spinoza's thought to its general tendency and fundamental interpretive core, find-ing at once much to esteem and something crucial with which he takes issue.

Neither Spinoza's religious-metaphysical language nor his formalistic manner of presentation are of much concern to Nietzsche; for he regards them as but the surface and skin of Spinoza's thought and as warranting neither its acceptance nor its rejection. Either to admire or to reject Spinoza for his language or his manner of presentation is for Nietzsche to miss the mark. What matters in Spinoza is his determination to interpret our humanity in the same terms as the rest of the "nature" of which we are a part; his repudiation of teleology in doing so (even if he slips in this respect); the insightfulness of his treatment of specific psychological phenomena—and his conviction that self-preservation is the general object of all more specific dispositions and forms of striving.

It is on this last point that Nietzsche parts company with Spinoza; and virtually all of his critical remarks are addressed to the problem of what to make of that conviction. He does not fault Spinoza for supposing that our entire affective life is the outgrowth, manifestation, and elaboration of a single basic impulse; for Nietzsche himself does so as well, and regards psychology as the key to dealing appropriately with it and the development of our entire spiritual, more-than-merely-natural human existence. In this he takes Spinoza to be a great ally and precursor of his own way of thinking. But he contends that Spinoza went fundamentally and seriously wrong in framing his entire interpretation of ourselves—along with the world in which we find and become ourselves—in terms of mere self-preservation.

Rather than attacking this view head on, Nietzsche attempts to show that this interpretation is misguided and ill-motivated, by the way of a consideration of what might have prompted Spinoza to take such a position—for all-too-human reasons. His aim in doing so is to prepare the way for a more favorable reception of his alternative interpretation, which he casts in terms of what he contrastingly calls "will to power." Interpretations such as Spinoza's cannot be refuted by direct counter-argument, any more than an interpretation like his own (or Spinoza's) can be vindicated by comparably direct argumentation. But as his treatment of Spinoza suggests, he believes that they can be *subverted* by bringing forward the kinds of considerations he raises with respect to Spinoza, *if* they cannot be vindicated by independently adduced considerations. And he would appear to believe that such vindication *is* possible in the instance of his alternative interpretation, which initially may well seem to be vulnerable to the same sort of psychological-genealogical subversion.

But how different actually are Nietzsche's and Spinoza's interpretations?

Is Spinoza's *conatus* to self-preservation all that different from Nietzsche's "will to power"? To listen to Nietzsche, one would think that they are very different indeed. But they may turn out to be a good deal more similar than he would have us suppose, their apparent radical divergence notwithstanding. Both notions conjure up the same general idea of a fundamental disposition, even if the thrust of the disposition in the two cases would seem to be different. Both likewise are deemed to be the most primitive and fundamental form of affect, giving rise to the entirety of our more specific affective repertoire.

The psychologies of both Spinoza and Nietzsche are explicitly characterized as theories of the "affects," taking the affects to be the central phenomena of our psychological life, and seeking to comprehend their "origin and nature," as Spinoza puts it in the heading of the third part of the *Ethics*. Both further attempt to exhibit our entire affective repertoire as "the development and ramification" of *one* basic form of disposition, as Nietzsche puts it (BGE 36). Whether Spinoza really goes as far as Nietzsche does in including our entire mental life within this single domain, as a special development of it rather than a kind of activity autonomous in relation to it and proceeding in accordance with its own principles, is not clear. Nietzsche at least would appear to think that this is not a significant point of difference between them, however, for he does not have anything critical of Spinoza to say on this point, as he surely would have otherwise. This is a point that deserves consideration; but I shall defer it, in order to attend more closely to the relation between their two basic principles.

6

The notion of "power" figures in Spinoza's conception of his *conatus,* as well as in Nietzsche's conception of "will to power." In the latter case, however, it would appear to stand as the object of this fundamental disposition and impulse; whereas for Spinoza it is introduced in a seemingly different way, as the "power of activity in the body" (*Corporis agendi potentiam*), and as the "power of thought in the mind" (*Mentis cogitandi potentiam*) that subserves that power of bodily activity (Props. XI and XII). The enhancement of these powers is indeed held to be something always sought, but only derivatively and in a limited way — namely, with a view to self-preservation, or (more precisely) the "persevering" of a thing "in its own being" (*in suo esse perseverare*). That, and not the extension or wider expression of the power of a thing in relation to other things, is for Spinoza the actual object of the fundamental *conatus* of which he speaks.

It is on this point that Nietzsche accuses Spinoza of an inconsistency, by introducing a piece of teleology that is incompatible with his rejection of all teleology. If it is eliminated, one is left with just the "power of activity" itself, the expression of which may or may not have "perseverence" as a consequence. But this is very close indeed to Nietzsche's own conception. And the similarity becomes even closer with the recognition that the "power of activity" of a body among other bodies is essentially a *relational* affair, realized not within the sphere of the body's simple existence *an sich,* but rather in the context of its relations to other such "power of activity" loci.

So understood, however, it is hard to see any remaining significant difference between Nietzsche's conception of "will to power" and Spinoza's de-teleologized *conatus.* And indeed I would suggest that Nietzsche's conception is *precisely what one gets* if one modifies Spinoza's in this way—as Nietzsche contends Spinoza himself ought to have done to be consistent. This would help account both for Nietzsche's fundamental resonance to Spinoza, and for his sharp criticism of Spinoza for making so much of self-preservation. It is as if Nietzsche were saying: he ought to have known better.

But is not Nietzsche's own conception likewise teleological? Not, I believe, if it is properly understood. The phrase "will to power" itself *can* be used to refer to an intention to bring about the attainment of a particular sort of result—for example, the possession of power conceived as control over some domain of objects or creatures. But that is not how Nietzsche would have it most generally and fundamentally understood, even if something of the kind may be no less common a *result* than he acknowledges self-preservation of systems emerging in the course of events to be.

The primordial disposition this notion is ultimately meant to designate, for Nietzsche, is simply the disposition of all dynamic quanta to *assert* themselves (as it were) in relation to other dynamic quanta, *expending* their force in ways that may result either in their replenishment or their exhaustion. This gives rise to power relationships everywhere, and to configurations that may have the *appearance* of exhibiting a teleology of power-as-control. But this appearance is actually only the expression of the play and interplay of power-as-assertion on the part of dynamic quanta, the very "actual essence" of which (to speak with Spinoza) is neither more nor less than just such assertion.

Nietzsche's basic complaint against Spinoza is that this is exactly what *he ought to have held*—and that he instead imposed a teleology of self-preservation upon this picture for reasons (or motives) of an all-too-human sort. The diagnosis of this ulterior motivation is what the critical

observations cited above are intended to suggest. And before one objects
to this treatment of Spinoza, one ought at least acknowledge it to be a
problem that Spinoza gives no real argument at all for his famous and
critical Proposition VI ("Everything, in so far as it is itself, endeavors
[*conatur*] to persist in its own being"). He does indeed supply a proof for
it; but it comes down to nothing more than the question-begging assertion that every thing "is opposed to all that could take away its existence"
(Prop. VI, Proof).

This pretense of a "proof" leaves one wondering about what might
have led him to take the position he does on this matter. Nietzsche's
contention is that if no persuasive case for it is discernible, either in
Spinoza or elsewhere, his proposed psychological *diagnosis* of Spinoza
and others who subscribe to it is a plausible *explanation* that deprives it
of its credibility. But no such case for it *is* discernible. And so, as Spinoza
would say, Q.E.D. This has the consequence for Nietzsche that Spinoza's
philosophical psychology must be revised accordingly—along the lines
Nietzsche himself proposes, if one would stay as close to it as one can.
Once this move is made, however, the way is open for him to draw upon
Spinoza's thinking with respect to a good many specific matters, as well
as to follow him in the general approach he takes to the affects in part 3 of
the *Ethics,* beginning with the remarks with which it opens.

7

But let us now return to a glaring profound difference in the ways in
which Spinoza and Nietzsche approach and work out their philosophical
psychologies. Both begin by proposing to construe our affects in a manner
consonant with the rest of nature; and both interpret them one and all as
deriving from the development and elaboration of a single basic impulse
that is itself at one with the fundamental impetus animating all forms
of natural existence. But the ways in which they do so differ form the
outset; and this difference divides not only Nietzsche but also most of the
rest of us from Spinoza. It poses a serious problem for both Nietzsche and
ourselves, with respect to Spinoza's entire psychological project. Nietzsche's
way of dealing with it may not be the only one possible; but it may be the
best we can do, in the interest of salvaging as much as possible of this
project.

The difference I have in mind is signaled in the final sentence of
Spinoza's remarkable introduction to part 3. Having just suggested that
"there should be one and the same method of understanding the nature
of all things whatsoever, namely, through universal laws and rules," he
then concludes by saying: "I shall consider human actions and desires in

exactly the same manner, *as though I were concerned with lines, planes, and solids"* (emphasis added). Spinoza's interpretation and treatment of nature in general, and therefore of "human actions and desires" as a part of it, are not only modeled upon geometry, but also presuppose that the kind of logic appropriate to geometry may be relied upon to ascertain the specific natures of all particular sorts of phenomena, deducing them by means of appropriate definitions and postulates. His rationalistic method is thus at one with and a consequence of his embrace of a geometric model of all existence.

For Nietzsche, on the other hand, and for most of the rest of us, this will not do. Geometry and its logic may have their uses, but they can no longer be supposed tenably and fundamentally to model the world of nature as he and we have come to understand it, as a dynamic world consisting of configurations and interplays of forces, constrained by no such logic and consisting of no such geometric forms. As Nietzsche likes to observe, we now realize (or should) that we have merely read these abstract forms and this artificial logic into the world; and we are therefore obliged to cease to do so if we are to have any hope of comprehending what transpires in it—and in ourselves. Our affects thus must be approached in an entirely different and much more empirical manner, taking the wealth of observable phenomena as our untidily diverse points of departure, even if our interpretation of them is still best guided by the heuristic idea of the economy of basic principles. We must work back from multiplicity and variety to the interpretive discernment of whatever underlying unity there may be, rather than proceeding from the aprioristic postulation of some such unitary fundamental principle to the deductive elaboration of a scheme into which the diversity of observable phenomena may be fit (or forced, with Procrustian insensitivity).

Nietzsche is surely right about this. Spinoza's method is radically ill-suited to his subject here; and even if he may be forgiven for adopting it, it would seem to deprive his entire psychological enterprise of viability. Yet this for Nietzsche is not the end of the matter, for he gives Spinoza credit for a good many psychological insights and fruitful suggestions, which Spinoza found ways within his system of including and expressing. So it could well have been with Spinoza among others in mind that he wrote: *"Error of philosophers* — the philosopher believes that the value of his philosophy lies in the whole, in the building: posterity discovers it in the bricks with which he built and which are then often used again for better building: in the fact, that is to say, that the building can be destroyed and *nonetheless* possess value as material" (HH II:201).

The way to appreciate Spinoza as a psychologist, for Nietzsche, is not to dwell upon his geometrical model and method, and upon whether the "proofs" he offers of various propositions he advances are sound. It is rather to attend to the ideas encased in them that he advances with respect to various psychological phenomena, which often are insightful. Spinoza is to be honored as a philosophical psychologist, Nietzsche is in effect suggesting, *despite* rather than *because of* his system and method, and instead for the many insights he hit upon that are scattered throughout his exposition. He may have arrived at some of them by way of his systematic reasonings—for such reasonings may be fruitful in psychology as elsewhere—and at others by observations or reflections for which he subsequently found places and "proofs" to satisfy his systematic requirements. But for Nietzsche it matters less how Spinoza hit upon them than that he did. And had he not been as *insightful* as he was, his system would have little interest for anyone other than historians of philosophy, even if his reasonings were as perfect in their logic as it is humanly possible for any such reasonings to be.

If we follow Nietzsche's lead here—as I am inclined to believe we are well advised to do—we will do no little violence to Spinoza's intentions. But that, for me as for Nietzsche, will enable greater justice to be done to him than approaching him in an all-or-nothing way, determined either to accept him whole on his own terms or to dismiss him because we find we cannot do so. The living rather than dead Spinoza emerging from such a selective appropriation and recasting reinterpretation of him may look— and be—quite different from the Spinoza we encounter in the pages of the *Ethics*. And the kinds of cases that can and will have to be made out for the views that are salvaged from the scheme he offers us will be of a quite different kind from those he puts forward to substantiate them— perhaps looking much more like the sorts of reflections one finds in Nietzsche than like Spinoza's "proofs." But I am convinced, as Nietzsche was, that this way of dealing with him will render him an even more interesting and important figure in the history of modern philosophy than the most respectful and faithful scholarly treatment of him can.

8

What I have been suggesting—unwelcome though this suggestion may be to some—is that Nietzsche was fundamentally right in regarding Spinoza as his "precursor," and that in many respects Nietzsche's thought may be regarded as a latter-day recasting of Spinoza's, along lines that a nineteenth-century Spinoza might well have found congenial. It is hard to imagine a Spinoza two centuries after the original who would have employed either the theological-metaphysical idiom or the aprioristic approach and geometrical model and mode of argumentation and presentation of the original. Such a latter-day Spinoza, however, might well have pursued the lines of thought with which part 3 of the *Ethics* begins, and which are suggested in such remarkable passages as the Note to Proposition III, in ways like those we find Nietzsche pursuing two centuries later, in the aftermath of Hume, Kant, Hegel, and the biological revolution of the nineteenth century. Indeed, the response of Nietzsche to Spinoza may very usefully provoke a consideration of just what Spinoza's thought might look like if his basic ideas were recast and worked out within the context of a post-theological/metaphysical/Kantian/Hegelian naturalistic philosophical framework. My conjecture is that what one would come up with would bear at least a strong and striking resemblance to Nietzsche's.

But the Nietzsche I have in mind in making this suggestion is not the post-structuralist Nietzsche. Rather, it is the Nietzsche I take to be determined to hold on to a revisionist but nonetheless significant conception of the possibility of a "philosophy of the future," aiming at a deeper, more insightful, and fruitful comprehension of our human reality and its attainable enhancement than philosophy and other forms of inquiry hitherto have been capable of achieving. This is the Nietzsche who wrote to Overbeck of Spinoza that "his over-all tendency [is] the same as mine—namely, to make knowledge the *most powerful* affect." It is further the Nietzsche who like Spinoza conceived of the possibility of an "enhanced" form of human life, in which such a heightened capacity and drive for "knowledge" has a crucial role to play.

Here Nietzsche's appreciation of Spinoza may serve importantly to support my way of interpreting Nietzsche, as well as to guide the effort to recast Spinoza's thought in more contemporary terms. The testimony of Nietzsche in his communication to Overbeck—as well as in many passages to be found in his later writings—shows quite clearly that he does *not* suppose either the meaningfulness of the very notion of knowledge nor the human possibility of its attainment to be a casualty of the "death of God" and the "translation of man back into nature." On the contrary, as he vividly proclaims in the opening section of the 1887 fifth book of *The Gay Science* (which he begins by restating the theme of "the death of God"): "all the daring of the lover of knowledge is permitted again; the sea, *our* sea, lies open again; perhaps there has never yet been such an 'open sea'" (GS 343).

To be sure, this is also the Nietzsche who in the very next section of *The Gay Science* goes on to recognize that the "will to truth" is not only an affective rather than purely rational phenomenon, but a derivative one as well, bound up in its genealogy with "our most enduring lie": "even we seekers after knowledge today, we godless anti-metaphysicians still take our fire, too, from the flame lit by a faith that is thousands of years old, that Christian faith which was also the faith of Plato [and likewise of Spinoza, he might well have added], that God is the truth, that truth is divine" (GS 344).

But this recognition does not prompt Nietzsche to *renounce* the "will to truth" and the search for "knowledge." On the contrary, he affirms them anew, taking them to admit of affirmation as expressions of the "will to power," and championing them against those others of its expressions that run counter to it. Spinoza had sought to point the way to a reordering of our affective lives that would permit the love of knowledge to emerge above our other passions and become the supreme disposition within us. And Nietzsche likewise seeks to show how knowledge and its pursuit might be made a real and dominating feature of our affective constitution, establishing the human possibility of "philosophers of the future," and of an enhanced form of human life characterized by "knowledge as the most powerful affect."

It is helpful in the interpretation of Spinoza to see him as a precursor of Nietzsche, whose thought tended in the direction of Nietzsche's despite his very un-Nietzschean idiom, manner, and rationalism. But it is also helpful in the interpretation of Nietzsche to see him as a successor of Spinoza—not only in the basic tendency of his thought, but also in his determination to make provision for knowledge as a paramount human possibility, and indeed to make its refined pursuit a cardinal virtue and salient feature of the higher humanity we have it in us to attain. There may be more than this to Nietzsche's conception of such a higher humanity and the enhancement of life; for the Romantic Revolution left its mark upon him, prompting him to celebrate the creativity associated paradigmatically with art, as well as the knowledge that we are capable of pursuing and attaining as philosophers of the kind he envisioned and sought to be. But he did not abandon the latter for the former; and to that extent at least he remained true to the spirit of the Spinoza he so admired. And it is my deep conviction that we today will do well to do likewise.

CHAPTER TEN

How to Naturalize Cheerfully: Nietzsche's *Fröhliche Wissenschaft*

When will all these shadows of God cease to darken our minds? When will we complete our de-deification of nature? When may we begin to *"naturalize"* humanity in terms of a pure, newly discovered, newly redeemed nature? (GS 109)

For one interested in Nietzsche as philosopher, *Die fröhliche Wissenschaft* (*The Gay Science*) is without question one of his finest, most illuminating, and most important published works. In the four "books" in which this work originally consisted, and the fifth added five years later, continuing the project begun in the first four, we have much more than the disjointed collection of reflections and aphorisms that it may at first glance appear to be. In this work Nietzsche the philosopher emerges with greater clarity than in any of his previous works, revealing a great deal about the issues in which he was interested, and how and what he thought about them. In style and format it is similar to the series of volumes of such collections preceding it, to which he stated in the original edition that it belongs.[1] Yet it goes well beyond the other volumes in this series, in both coherence and content. Indeed, I shall argue that it constitutes a sustained attempt to sketch the outlines of the kind of reinterpretation of nature and humanity he calls for in the passage cited above, and to indicate how they are to be filled in.

1

The Gay Science is Nietzsche's first and perhaps his most complete attempt to take seriously the proposition "God is dead" and to reckon with its many consequences: "And we—we still have to vanquish his shadow, too" (GS 108). The "death of God"—the demise of the God-hypothesis (in any of its guises) as an idea worthy of acceptance—is the theme with which he explicitly begins both the third and the fifth books of the volume, and that hovers over the others. It implicitly sets the context of the opening of the first book, and again the fourth, and it animates the second, as well as the rhymes and songs with which the volume is framed. The pathos of the "madman" section (GS 125) is a pathos Nietzsche may have experienced; but it is one that—like the "nihilistic rebound" he suggests elsewhere is "pathologically" linked to it (WP 13)—he himself has overcome and left behind.

In tone and in content, the volume deserves its title. After having struggled through a period of some years of intellectual crisis, its author has attained a new philosophical and spiritual health, of the sort he describes at the fifth book's end (GS 382). He has become profoundly and joyfully affirmative of life and the world and has discovered that "all the daring of the lover of knowledge is permitted again" (GS 343). He is in love with knowledge and with life and the world, and with the humanity emerging out of them; for, having earlier become hard and disillusioned by them, he has now become newly appreciative of them. Thus he cheerfully and confidently sets out to explore them as they stand revealed in the "new dawn" that has broken in the aftermath of "the news that 'the old god is dead'" (GS 343). While he recognizes that there is more to life and living than knowledge and its pursuit, he goes so far as to say that with the idea of *"Life as a means to knowledge"* in one's heart, "one can live not only boldly but even gaily, and laugh gaily, too" (GS 324). He is intent upon attaining a new and better knowledge of our world and ourselves, and he also is fascinated by the human and philosophical problem he calls *"incorporating* knowledge and making it instinctive" (GS 11). What he calls "the ultimate question about the conditions of life" has come to have a new and great interest for him: "To what extent can truth endure incorporation? That is the question; that is the experiment" (GS 110).

To be sure, the truth and knowledge of which Nietzsche here speaks— the possibility of which he evidently is persuaded—must be squared with his contention that "How far the perspective character of existence extends or indeed whether existence has any other character than this" is a question that "cannot be decided," and that we therefore "cannot reject the possibility" that the world may admit of "infinite interpretations," or limitless "possibilities of interpretation" (GS 374). The force of the entire volume, however, is that this reflection does not doom the "lover of knowledge" to despair, but rather should serve to redirect his or her quest: away from the impossible dream of absolute knowledge and toward the comprehension of our own human reality and possibility in the world with which we find ourselves confronted.

Here, as so often elsewhere, Nietzsche deals with many large problems and issues in succession, usually relatively briefly. Near the end of the fifth book, he confronts and rejects the idea that his brevity is ill-suited to the treatment of such problems in an insightful way:

> For I approach deep problems like cold baths: quickly into them and quickly out again. That one does not get to the depths that way, not deep enough down, is the superstition of those afraid of the water, enemies of cold water. . . .

> Does a matter necessarily remain ununderstood and unfathomed merely because it has been touched only in flight, glanced at, at a flash? . . . At least there are truths that are singularly shy and ticklish and cannot be caught except suddenly—that must be *surprised* or left alone. (GS 381)

It is Nietzsche's clear aim in the five books of this volume to touch upon, surprise, fathom, and understand many of the matters that require being considered anew in the aftermath of the collapse of the "God-hypothesis" and associated modes of interpretation. To cover as much ground as he attempts to cover, brevity was in any event a necessity; and his manner of covering it also has the advantage of enabling one to discern more readily the general shape of the comprehensive interpretation he is working out, and the connections between its various particular features.

Nietzsche moreover is far from being altogether unfaithful to the association of the term *Wissenschaft* he employs in his title with the idea of a systematic cognitive endeavor. The surface disorderliness of the volume only lightly masks the rather remarkable thoroughness of his reexamination of the philosophical and intellectual landscape, and the fundamental coherence of his treatment of its various features. This coherence is all the more noteworthy in view of the passage of the time between the publication of the first four books (in 1882) and the addition of the fifth (in the "new edition" of 1887).

The continuation of the task begun in the first four books in the fifth also entitles one to considerable confidence in taking them to be indicative of the contours of Nietzsche's thought during the period they span, and in all likelihood beyond it into the final year of his productive life. It therefore is something of a mystery why this volume does not receive more attention and figure more centrally in interpretations of his philosophical concerns and thought. If there is any one of his published works in which "the essential philosophical Nietzsche" is to be found, it would seem to me to be this one. And Nietzsche the philosopher is nowhere more accessible, persuasive, and impressive in any single thing he wrote, in my opinion, than he is in the fifth book in particular (the date of which further warrants regarding it as an expression of his mature thought).

Indeed, I would suggest that the cause of understanding and appreciating Nietzsche's philosophical thought would be markedly advanced if the rest of his writings were read in relation to it, and construed in the light of what he does and says in it.

2

Very broadly speaking, what Nietzsche undertakes to do in *The Gay Science* is to show how he proposes to carry out the task of "naturalizing" our conception of humanity and redirecting our thinking about human possibility. This is held to involve first reading humanity back into a post-Christian and postmetaphysical, "newly discovered and newly redeemed" nature—and then reading it out again, as something no longer *merely* natural in consequence of its transformation. Through a variety of sorts of reflections, all of which shed light on these matters in different but important complementary ways, he seeks to arrive at an understanding and appreciation of the kind of creature we fundamentally are, the basic features of our existence, our all-too-human tendencies and the kinds of development of which they admit, and the ways in which human life may be enhanced.

One of Nietzsche's main themes here is thus *what we are;* and another, equally important to him, is *what we may become.* These twin themes—of the generally human, naturalistically reconsidered, and of the genuinely or more-than-merely human, reconceived accordingly—are the point and counterpoint that give the volume its underlying structure and unity, with the "death of God" as pedal-tone. Along the way, Nietzsche finds it needful and appropriate to say something about nearly every major domain of philosophical inquiry, in order both to shed further light upon our nature and possibilities and to suggest what light his emerging view of the latter sheds upon the former. His concern with what we are and may become, however, is accorded centrality in relation to his thinking with respect to other philosophical and related matters, at once drawing upon them and providing inquiry into them with a new organizational and interpretive orientation.

Rather like Marx, but (it seems to me) with greater sophistication and power, Nietzsche thus advocates and exemplifies what might be called an *anthropological shift* in philosophy. By this I mean a general reorientation of philosophical thinking, involving the attainment of what might be called an *anthropological optic* whereby to carry out the program of a de-deification and reinterpretation of ourselves and our world. It thus in effect involves the replacement of epistomology and metaphysics by a kind of *philosophical anthropology* as the fundamental and central philosophical endeavor. Philosophy for Nietzsche does not reduce to philosophical anthropology in *The Gay Science;* but it revolves around and finds its way by means of the project of comprehending our nature and possibilities.

His "gay science," as this volume shows, is a comprehensive philosophical enterprise that extends to the consideration of truth and knowledge, science and logic, religion and art, social and cultural phenomena, morality and value, and even life and the world more generally. Its point of departure and constant return, however, is *human life and possibility.* To come to know ourselves—our fundamental nature, what we have become, and what we may have it in us to be—is for the author of this volume something at once difficult and possible, and of the greatest importance. And he is further convinced that in the course of coming to do so a great many other matters with which philosophers have long concerned themselves may be better comprehended and more appropriately dealt with as well.

These, for Nietzsche, are philosophical tasks, even if the kind of thinking required to pursue them departs in various ways from those favored by most philosophers before and since. He calls it "gay science" as well as "philosophy," as he understands and practices it; and its manner reflects what he takes to be the basic requirements of pursuing these tasks as unproblematically and successfully as is humanly possible. It is avowedly experimental, multiperspectival, and interpretive; but it also is without question cognitive in intent. It has the attainment of sound and penetrating comprehension as a central aim (even if not its only one); and it has as its primary focus a domain in which Nietzsche considers this attainment to be a genuine possibility—both because there is something there to be known, and because it is within our power to come to know it.

That domain, once again, is the domain of the human. Nietzsche does reject the notion of "man" as a being possessed of some sort of immutable metaphysical essence; but he is very differently disposed toward the notion of "man" reconceived along the lines of the " 'naturalized' humanity" to which he seeks to direct our attention in *The Gay Science.* It is his main topic in this work; and the elaboration of a philosophical anthropology, in the sense of a comprehensive understanding of the nature and prospects of this remarkable and peculiar creature that is at once animal and no longer merely animal, is his general task. Indeed, with this volume Nietzsche may be said to have launched the project of such a philosophical anthropology, the importance of which has yet to be adequately appreciated, and the example of which has all too rarely been followed.

This lamentable situation may at long last be changing; and I venture to hope that it will soon come to have the high place on the agenda of philosophical inquiry it deserves. I doubt, however, that we are likely to see anyone surpass Nietzsche's wealth of contributions to it. Wrong or unsatisfactory though some of his conjectures and analyses may have been, the richness and suggestiveness of his reflections along these lines in *The Gay Science* and subsequent writings render them an invaluable and virtually inexhaustible source and stimulus for anyone who chooses to work in this area. And anyone who does so should come to terms with him.

3

While I shall for the most part focus on the fifth book of the volume, the structure and content of the first four books warrant some comment. The point and counterpoint mentioned above are sounded at the very outset, in the opening sections of the first book. In the first section we are immediately confronted with an example of how Nietzsche would have us go about reading man back into nature, and thinking about man as a piece of nature in whom fundamental natural principles are powerfully at work, even in dispositions that might seem to be of a loftier nature. In the next two sections he shifts his attention abruptly to a consideration of certain marks of a higher humanity that set some human beings above and apart from the common run of humankind. Then, in the fourth, he just as abruptly returns to another reflection of the former sort.

This point and counterpoint continues throughout the first book, with many variations. Nietzsche considers a wide variety of human phenomena, reflecting upon basic human traits and their common manifestations, and also upon the more uncommon and exceptional transformations and developments of which they admit. He is at pains both to show how the latter are linked to the former and to stress how they differ from them, thereby to counter our tendency to become so preoccupied with the one that we lose sight of the other, and thus fail to attain a due appreciation of each. It is through such reflections, he appears to think, and only through many of them, that one can make significant headway with the project he describes in the passage from the beginning of the third book cited at the outset (in which he has been engaged all along, and continues to pursue throughout the volume). Our affects, morality, science, knowledge more generally, art, and religion are among the many matters that come under consideration in the first book, and to which he subsequently returns — at greatest length in the third book, and again in the fifth. And the controlling perspective in which they are examined, interpreted, and assessed is what he elsewhere calls "the perspective of life" (BT P:2).

In the second book, and again toward the end of the third, one

encounters a large number of reflections and aphorisms of several kinds
that at first glance seem to have little relevance to this general project.
Upon further consideration, however, they may be seen to have a good
deal to do with it, and to be very instructive with respect to the way in
which Nietzsche conceives of it and seeks to carry it out. Some are
psychological and social-psychological, and their fundamental significance,
beyond the astuteness and interest of the particular insights they often
express, lies in their collective indication of how he proposes to understand the kinds of tendencies that inform most of what goes on in
ordinary human life. In this way he seeks to take account of the commonplace surface features of our lives, in a manner enabling him to tie them
in with the broader "naturalized" interpretation of our humanity he is
developing, while at the same time attending to their fine texture and so
demonstrating that his interpretation is not simplistically and objec-
tionably oblivious to them.

Other sections in these books have a very different focus but serve the
same general purpose. In them he deals with a broad range of social,
cultural, artistic, and intellectual phenomena. On one level they can be
taken and appreciated simply as the penetrating and often barbed observations of a critic of this scene. On another, however, they too serve at
once to marshal further evidence for the "naturalizing" account of human
life he is advancing, and to show that such phenomena do not count
against it, by revealing them to admit of inclusion in it. Remarkable
though these phenomena may be, it is as remarkably wrought transformations and expressions of very human dispositions and fundamental human
capacities that they are so. On the other hand, Nietzsche would be the
first to insist that the transmutation of our human animality into a
spirituality that takes such forms is one of the most interesting and
important features of our humanity, which is all the more deserving of
appreciation once man has been translated back into nature.

With this observation, however, we are brought back to the counterpoint of Nietzsche's concern with the possibility of a higher humanity,
repeatedly touched upon in the first books of the volume, heralded with
considerable fanfare at the conclusion of the third, and made the main
topic of the fourth. If, as Nietzsche announced in the original edition, his
volume "marks the conclusion of a series . . . whose common goal is to
erect *a new image and ideal of the free spirit,*"[2] this final book of the
series is certainly the culmination of that endeavor. And in it he shows
very clearly how concerned he is to counter the nihilistic tendency to
devalue our humanity, which he fears may all too readily be prompted by
its "naturalization" and the broader "de-deification" of our thinking
about ourselves and the world.

In one sense his efforts along these lines may be regarded as supplementary to his "naturalized" interpretation of our human nature. His investigation into our general human nature serves to prepare the ground for the development of a new approach to the question of human worth, constituting the centerpiece of a naturalistic theory of value complementing his philosophical anthropology. In another sense, however, what Nietzsche has to say along these lines may be understood as belonging importantly to his anthropology, which he would regard as incomplete without account being thus taken of the possibility of the sort of higher humanity he has in mind and of the significance of the enhancement of life it represents. Its exploration too is part of his "gay science"; for he considers it to require being extended in this way if justice is to be done to our human nature, the developmental potential of which is no less important to its comprehension and assessment than its basic character and commonplace manifestations.

Disillusioned inquiry into our fundamental nature and what we have come to be, for Nietzsche, must be accompanied by a consideration of what we have it in us further to become. Otherwise our understanding of our humanity will be incomplete and perhaps fatally short-sighted, leading to an underestimation of ourselves that may have lamentable consequences. Our human animality and past, and the varieties of the all-too-human and the general features of human life, may easily absorb the attention of philosophers who have made "de-deification" and "naturalization" their first orders of business. A preoccupation with them, however, is likely to result in an impoverished picture of ourselves, which leaves out something Nietzsche regards as essential. In his notion of "becoming those we are," which is one of his main themes in this fourth book, he underscores the point that *what we are* embraces not only what we *have* become but also what we *have it in us to* become. In this way, he seeks to establish a basis for deriving a kind of normative force from his philosophical anthropology, privileging the attainment of the higher humanity to which he directs attention in relation to more commonplace forms of human life.

To summarize my discussion to this point: the concerns and issues to which Nietzsche addresses himself in *The Gay Science,* and his manner of doing so, are indicative of the nature and tasks of the sort of thing philosophy is for him, which he considers it appropriate to characterize as *fröhliche Wissenschaft.* His philosophical *Wissenschaft* aims at a comprehensive reinterpretation of a broad range of matters centering upon our nature and possibilities in the aftermath of the "death of God." Its intent is both cognitive and evocative; for it is animated by a hard-won confidence that it may at once issue in an enhancement of understanding, and also point the way to an enhancement of human life. And its point of departure for Nietzsche is "completing our de-deification of nature" and proceeding "to 'naturalize' humanity" accordingly.

4

I now shall turn to the fifth book of this volume. I consider it to be of particular significance because it confirms and continues the general project begun considerably earlier in the first four books; because it shows what kinds of questions and issues the mature Nietzsche took to require being dealt with in the course of carrying it out; and because it provides further indications of how he proposes to deal with them and what he is prepared to say about them. He is much more straightforward about these matters here than he frequently is in other writings. This fifth book thus is also of considerable value as a guide to the interpretation of what he elsewhere does and says. More specifically, I would suggest that it is of particular value to the task of deciding what to make of the contents of his notebooks from the crucial period spanned by the writing and publication of the first and last books of the volume. Material from the notebooks that is consonant with things he shows himself here to be prepared to say may be taken with some confidence to likewise reflect his thinking with respect to the matters discussed.[3]

On the other hand, one feature of the fifth book, which virtually impels one to look at Nietzsche's notebooks as well as to other things he published, is that for the most part he here simply says what he thinks, stating his views on various issues without indicating at all clearly and completely what considerations may have led him to hold them. He sketches the outlines and main features of a rather comprehensive reinterpretation of human life and related matters; but he does relatively little in his book to elaborate his case for it. Here and there lines of argument and supporting considerations are suggested. On the whole, however, he is content merely to present it in quick and vivid strokes, as though concerned to ensure that the forest will not be lost sight of for the trees.

Consider now the structure and content of this remarkable set of forty sections and an epilogue. It begins (GS 343) by "cheerfully" sounding the theme of the "death of God" and its consequences, and stressing the resulting liberation of "the lover of knowledge" for new ventures. It ends (GS 382) with a celebration of the conception of a new "great health" and of a higher humanity, contrasting markedly with those of "present-day man," and superseding the transitional stage on the way to them described a few sections earlier (GS 377). Immediately preceding this conclusion there is a retrospective section (GS 381), noted above, in which Nietzsche remarks that he considers his reflections to be compromised neither by his style and brevity nor by the admitted limitations of his own knowledge of many matters with which scientists concern themselves. Thus, in the latter connection, he observes that "we need more, we also need less" than scientific inquiry, in dealing with "such questions as concern me."

The nature, limits, and value of science and scientific knowledge are among the issues with which he deals, beginning with his critical consideration of the "will to truth" in scientific inquiry in the second section (GS 344), and continuing in a number of later sections.[4] In a related series of reflections he discusses the limitations of the kind of thinking characteristic of "scholarly" types;[5] and in others he extends his analysis and critique to the ways of thinking associated with religion.[6] As might be expected, he likewise subjects morality to scrutiny,[7] and art as well.[8]

The context in which he examines and assesses these various human types and phenomena, and in which these reflections take on their larger significance, is further set by what Nietzsche has to say in a number of other very important sections, in which he indicates his general view of the kind of world this is (GS 346), the basic character of life (GS 349), and certain salient features of our human nature (GS 354-61). Our humanity—as it has come to be and as it may become—is Nietzsche's fundamental concern, here as in the four earlier books; and his way of bringing it into focus is by alternating between these complementary kinds of analysis, each of which is intended to illuminate the other.[9]

It is of no little importance to the understanding of Nietzsche's chosen task and thinking, at least as they are here to be seen, that his remarks about "the perspective character of existence" and "the possibility that it may contain infinite interpretations" (GS 374) are offered as unanswerable questions, rather than as propositions he is prepared to assert. They certainly would not seem to be considerations he supposes to be fatal to the kind of knowledge he concedes to science. And he likewise does not appear to take them to preclude the more penetrating comprehension of ourselves and the world to which he suggests philosophical "lovers of knowledge" may newly aspire. He has a number of things to say about "the way of this world," for example, in one of the early sections of the fifth book that sets the stage for what follows; and they are said confidently, with no suggestion that they are subject to qualification along these lines. "We know it well," he says; "the world in which we live is ungodly, immoral, 'inhuman'; we have interpreted it far too long in a false and mendacious way . . . according to our *needs*" (GS 346).

As these remarks suggest, Nietzsche supposes himself to be doing otherwise, and to be doing so more truthfully—notwithstanding the fact that, in the preceding section, he has cautioned against supposing the "will to truth" to be unproblematical with respect to both its underlying motivation and its value for life (GS 345). A few sections later he further ventures to state what he takes "the really fundamental instinct of life" to be, saying that it "aims at *the expansion of power*" and asserting against the popular version of Darwinism: "The struggle for existence is only an *exception,* a temporary restriction of the will to life. The great and small struggle always revolves around superiority, around growth and expansion, around power—in accordance with the will to power which is the will of life" (GS 349).

This is not the manner of speaking of one who believes that our comprehension can extend no further than a recognition of the structure and contents of the world as we have arranged it for ourselves in a perspective determined by our needs. And even in the remainder of his discussion, most of which has to do with our human existence rather than with life and the world more generally, our existence is discussed from a standpoint Nietzsche considers himself to have attained that transcends ordinary human perspectives, and enables him to arrive at a more adequate and insightful interpretation and assessment of it. The attainment of such a standpoint, he grants, in a section near the end in which he is speaking specifically of morality, is difficult and cannot be supposed to yield knowledge that is absolute; but it is clear that he takes it to be possible. He writes:

> "Thoughts about moral prejudices," if they are not meant to be prejudices about prejudices, presuppose a position *outside* morality, some point beyond good and evil to which one has to rise, climb or fly. . . . That one *wants* to go precisely out there, up there, may be a minor madness, a peculiar and unreasonable "you must"—for we seekers for knowledge also have our idiosyncracies of "unfree will" —the question is whether one really *can* get up there.
>
> This may depend on manifold conditions. In the main the question is how light or heavy we are. . . . One has to be *very light* to drive one's will to knowledge into such a distance and, as it were, beyond one's time, to create for oneself eyes to survey millennia and, moreover, clear skies in those eyes. (GS 380)

This is something Nietzsche seeks to do not only in the case of morality, but with respect to the other human phenomena with which he specifically deals in the course of the book and to the broader contours of our humanity more generally. In his treatment of these matters too, he conceives of himself and proceeds as a "seeker for knowledge," impelled—

perhaps "peculiarly and unreasonably" but nonetheless strongly—to "drive" his "will to knowledge" far enough to enable him to bring them into focus and achieve a just comprehension and assessment of them. So, for example, beyond what he has to say about the basic character of life and the world, he offers several sustained discussions relating directly and importantly to the understanding of human thought and action generally, and so to the comprehension of what he elsewhere frequently refers to as "the type 'man' [*Mensch*]." In one such section (GS 354) he develops a general account of the fundamental relation between our consciousness (conscious thought and self-consciousness), language, and the need for communication associated with our social manner of existence. In another, he sketches what he takes to be one of his "most essential steps and advances" along these lines: learning "to distinguish the cause of acting" —which he characterizes as "a quantum of dammed-up energy that is waiting to be used up somehow"—"from the cause of acting in a particular way, in a particular direction, with a particular goal" (GS 360).

Moreover, in many of the sections in which he directs his attention to such phenomena as art or morality. Nietzsche is concerned to draw upon his observations concerning them to shed light upon our nature, as well as to make particular points about them; for he considers them among the richest sources of insight into our nature.[10] In this respect Nietzsche shows himself to be an heir of Hegel, for whom *"Wesen ist was gewesen ist,"* and the "phenomenology of spirit" is the path to the comprehension of our fundamental and attained spiritual nature (in which connection such phenomena are taken to be particularly revealing). And one may even discern an echo of Kant here, for whom reflection upon the nature and conditions of the possibility of certain types of our experience can afford us otherwise unattainable insight into our fundamental mental constitution; although profound changes accompanied Nietzsche's naturalized and historicized revision of Kant's understanding of what we are.

Thus Nietzsche's strategy of looking at various forms of human experience and activity "in the perspective of life," while in some respects importantly different from that of Kant as well as Hegel, in another is interestingly similar. It is intended both to enhance our understanding of these phenomena by bringing out their relation to our fundamental nature and its modifications and to shed light upon the latter by reflecting upon what they reveal about the kind of creature capable of them and disposed to them. In some cases Nietzsche interprets such phenomena as expressing and revealing something characteristic of particular types of human beings. In others he takes them to be indicative of something more comprehensive—sometimes about "present-day man," and sometimes about our humanity more generally.

All of this, of course, is "interpretation," rather than argument of a rigor that would yield conclusions of such certainty and finality that they would preclude the possibility of error or improvement. Moreover, the object of investigation is no fixed and immutable substance and has no timeless essence, but rather is a form of life that has come to be what it is, exhibits considerable diversity, and may be supposed to be capable of further transformation. Thus the kind of knowledge of which this object of inquiry admits must be recognized to be nothing absolute for yet other reasons. But neither of these considerations serves to deter Nietzsche. The fact that he did not complete his project, and indeed that it cannot ever *be* completed, likewise does not tell against it. One can get somewhere with it, just as one may go astray, and even though one's attained understanding may always admit of being improved upon.

Nietzsche is prepared to allow, and indeed to insist, that the *value* of the knowledge of ourselves that may thereby be attainable is problematical. He also holds that in any event there is more to the enhanced sort of life he associates with the higher humanity he envisions than the pursuit and attainment of such knowledge. Nonetheless, his conviction of its possibility and his own commitment to its attainment are clear. As he wrote in *Beyond Good and Evil,* a year earlier:

> To translate man back into nature; to become master over the many vain and overly enthusiastic interpretations and connotations that have so far been scrawled and painted over that eternal basic text of *homo natura;* to see to it that man henceforth stands before man even as today, hardened in the discipline of science, he stands before the *rest* of nature, with intrepid Oedipus eyes and sealed Odysseus ears . . . —that may be a strange and insane task, but it is a *task* —who would deny that? (BGE 230)

It is also significant that he goes on here to observe that, while one may well ask "Why did we choose this insane task?" this question, "put differently," is the question "Why have knowledge at all?" For this implies that, whatever the answer to these questions may turn out to be (and even if the last question should turn out to have no answer at all, or an answer cast ultimately in terms of the "will to power" rather than in terms of the intrinsic value of truth), Nietzsche is nonetheless persuaded that something deserving of the name of knowledge is possible and attainable here. It is to be distinguished from interpretations of the sort to which he refers, as the outcome of persisting in the "task" of which he speaks. And our nature is its central object.

In this connection, I would stress a point that comes through nicely and clearly in the fifth book of *The Gay Science,* as it also does in the earlier books, and elsewhere as well. The common view of Nietzsche's general conception of our nature, seemingly supported by passages of this sort, imputes to him strongly reductionist and biologistic tendencies. This view, however, is importantly distorted and misguided, misrepresenting his actual approach to it and understanding of it quite seriously. He may suggest, as he has Zarathustra say, that "the soul is only a word for something about the body" (Z I:4), and that "perhaps the entire evolution of the spirit is a question of the body," as "the history of the development of a higher body that emerges into our sensibility" (WP 676). But he also considers human life to have been fundamentally, pervasively, and fatefully transformed—or rather, to have *become* human life in the first place—with the advent of *society*.

Nietzsche contends that this development "sundered" mankind from its "animal past." It is held to have established "new surroundings and conditions of existence" for the human animal, which resulted in its becoming "something so new, profound, unheard of, contradictory, *and pregnant with a future* that the aspect of the earth was essentially altered" (GM II:16). And the greater part of his philosophical-anthropological investigations—which in effect began in *The Birth of Tragedy*, and continued to the end of his productive life—proceed by way of reflections upon phenomena associated with human social and cultural life. As has been observed, he does insist upon the importance of bearing in mind that "the entire evolution of the spirit" along these lines is ultimately to be referred back to "the body" and our physiological constitution and interpreted accordingly. However, he considers it equally important to be instructed with respect to the way in which human life has come to be reconstituted and shaped in the course of its development by attending to the social and cultural phenomena in which its emergent nature is manifested, and through which the conditions of the possibility of its further enhancement have been established.

In his reflections upon these matters, therefore, far from setting his philosophical-anthropological concerns aside, Nietzsche actually is pursuing them in the manner he considers to be most illuminating and fruitful and indeed to be called for by the sort of thing our humanity has become. A kind of "higher body" our spirituality may fundamentally be; but it must be approached with eyes attentive to its attained features and subtleties if it is to afford us insight into the kind of creature we are, and if neither our emergent nature nor our potential higher humanity is to be too simplistically conceived and so misunderstood.

Nietzsche was ultimately more interested in what we as human beings have it in us to become—that "future" with which he says we are "pregnant"—than he is in what we already are. He was hard-headed enough to recognize, however, that any "new image and ideal" of a higher humanity that might be "erected," to be more than idle speculation and fantasy, must be grounded in and derived from a sober and clear-sighted assessment of our humanity as it is, taking account of both the general rule and exceptions to it. Moreover, he was astute enough to recognize that, to investigate and do anything approaching justice to something so complex, one must learn "how to employ a *variety* of perspectives" upon it "in the service of knowledge." For, as he goes on to observe, "the more eyes, different eyes, we can use to observe one thing, the more complete our 'concept' of this thing, our 'objectivity,' will be" (GM III:12). And what this means and implies for him, in the case of our own reality, is that one must approach it by attending to the many different phenomena that have emerged in the course of human events, in ways that are appropriate and sensitive to their emergent features as well as that lend themselves to a more comprehensive integration and interpretation.

In this light, good and important sense can be made of Nietzsche's excursion through many forms of human cultural and social life in the course of the fifth book of *The Gay Science*. It constitutes a kind of reckoning up of what humanity has made of itself in the course of its development to this point of a nature and "higher body" that is spiritual as well as physiological, and of the resources and capacities this schooling and transformation of the "basic text of *homo natura*" have placed at its disposal, to be drawn upon in effecting its further enhancement. So, when he in conclusion evokes "the ideal of a spirit" that, "from overflowing power and abundance," is able to "play" freely with "all that was hitherto called holy, good, untouchable, divine" (GS 382), he has in mind a higher humanity that is heir to all that he has surveyed, while also overcoming the all-too-human limitations and defects upon which he remarks in doing so. These phenomena together flesh out the portrait of the sort of creature we have come to be, and in doing so also enable one to discern what we have to work with and build upon in becoming what we have it in us to be. Their examination is essential to the assembling of the materials required to elaborate the sort of philosophical anthropology Nietzsche has in mind and seeks to inaugurate, in this and subsequent works.

6

The Gay Science is thus a very revealing work. It exemplifies Nietzsche's philosophical "gay science," revealing both his conception of its main tasks and problems and his manner of approaching and dealing with them that he considers such inquiry to call for and involve. If one has some preconceived idea of what a philosophical anthropology would be and what it means to talk about human nature, it might well turn out that it would be inappropriate to characterize his concerns in such terms. But one may instead choose—as I do—to allow oneself to be instructed by what he does and says in this and related works in speaking of "man" and our "humanity" (as he so often does), and thus of the sort of nature he takes it to be appropriate to ascribe to ourselves. And one may further choose (as I do) to take what he does and says along these lines as constituting his version of a philosophical anthropology, conceived as philosophical inquiry into these matters.

There can be no doubt that Nietzsche does inquire into our nature so conceived, very extensively, here and elsewhere; and that his interest in it underlies and motivates many of his reflections on diverse particular human social, cultural, and psychological phenomena. It may seem that little is gained by calling all of this his version of a philosophical anthropology. My reason for doing so, however, is that I find it a very helpful way of bringing much of his discussion into focus. And I would further suggest that, when his efforts are viewed in this light, good and important sense can be made of them, not only piecemeal, but as a whole.

Nietzsche may have linked his proclamation of the "death of God" with an attack upon the "soul-hypothesis"; but he did not proceed to an announcement of what Foucault has called "the death of man"[11] as well, contrary to the efforts of Foucault and his kindred spirits to make Nietzsche out to be the herald of this sequel they themselves proclaim.[12] If one attends at all closely to what he says and undertakes to do in *The Gay Science* and subsequent writings, it should be clear that he instead supposes the "death of God" and the demise of the clutch of metaphysical hypotheses associated with the God-hypothesis (in particular the soul- and being-hypotheses) to serve rather to prepare the way for what might be called "the *birth* of man" as a newly significant philosophical notion.

Nietzsche did indeed repudiate the notion of "man" as a kind of "eternal truth," very early on (HH I:2). But it is of no little significance that he did so very early—and that, having made this point, he then went on to *recast* this notion, devoting a great deal of effort to the investigation of our nature thus reconceived. He evidently was convinced that this notion can and should be rehabilitated—liberated from metaphysical and theological interpretations, and also from its status (made much of by Foucault[13]) as a conceptual correlate of certain disciplines originating earlier in his century—and made the focus of enlightened philosophical inquiry of the sort he commended to his "new philosophers" and sought himself to undertake.

For Nietzsche, such inquiry should serve not (as Foucault would have it) to bring to an end the "anthropological sleep" of the nineteenth century,[14] but rather to bring about what might be contrastingly termed a more sophisticated "anthropological awakening." Far from thinking that the end of metaphysics and the critique of the disciplines Foucault scrutinizes preclude anything like a philosophical anthropology,[15] Nietzsche writes as though they open the way for such inquiry to assume stage front and center in philosophy — along with the revaluation of values and the development of a new theory of value, the genealogy of morals, and the naturalization of morality.

Nietzsche did not think that the only questions that can meaningfully be asked and answered about our human nature are best handed over to the life sciences, and that beyond that level of discourse human nature dissolves into myriad forms of social and cultural life best left to cultural anthropologists, sociologists, and historians. He also did not think that conceptual, linguistic, and phenomenological analyses are the only available and proper alternatives to human-scientific inquiry to which a philosopher has recourse. And he did not suppose that the end of metaphysics spells the end of philosophy. He called for "new philosophers," convinced that philosophy has a future — and not merely as the handmaiden either of the sciences or of the literati. And the kind of philosophy he advocated and practiced had a reconsideration of our nature as one of its main items of business; for he was persuaded that it makes good and important sense to talk about "the type 'man,'" and believed that the kind of thinking and inquiry in which he understood genuine philosophizing to consist has a crucial role to play in doing so.

In styling himself a psychologist, and in saying that from now on the other disciplines are to serve psychology, which is the path to the resolution of the most fundamental problems (BGE 23), Nietzsche is giving expression to these convictions and this program — meaning a *philosophical* psychology and psychologically sensitive philosophy, rather than the particular behavioral-scientific discipline psychology has become in this century. So also when he calls for translating men back into nature — and then complements this call by directing attention to what our "dis-animalization" has involved and accomplished — *our* "genealogy." And when he seeks to develop a "theory of affects," and reflects upon language, consciousness and self-consciousness, reason and knowledge as matters of *our* manner of existence.

It is thus no objection or fatal obstacle to the enterprise of a philosophical anthropology, for Nietzsche, that our humanity has a history and a genealogy, and that it remains capable of further transformation. In both cases, the moral he draws is not that the concept of humanity and notion of "the type 'man'" are ruled out, or that they are matters with which philosophy is incapable of dealing. Rather, it is that philosophy must and can adjust to the character of these objects of inquiry, in aspiration and method, as it proceeds to deal with them.

Why is this of interest? It is not merely because this is part of Nietzsche's thought, which has come to be of interest to growing numbers of us recently. More important, it is of interest because it should be instructive to us as philosophers, and relevant to a number of ongoing debates (about human nature and about philosophy itself, among others). It has significant implications for the setting of an agenda for philosophy today and tomorrow—the posing and framing of questions and issues with which we would do well to concern ourselves, and the decisions to be made about how we are to deal with them. And to my mind, it is further of interest because what Nietzsche had to say along these lines, when he got down to cases, warrants serious consideration, and richly rewards it.[16]

Notes

1. Not in the text itself, but on the back cover of this edition (see GS 30).
2. Again, not in the text itself, but on the back cover of this edition (see GS 30).
3. In interpreting Nietzsche, it is undeniable that interpretive priority should be given to what he actually published over the *Nachlaß*. One should also be prepared to grant, however, that use of material from the *Nachlaß* may be warranted by the appearance of comparable lines of thought in his published work. See chapter 6.
4. For example, GS 355 and 373.
5. For example, GS 348, 349, 366.
6. For example, GS 347, 350, 351, 353, 358.
7. For example, GS 345, 352, 359, 380.
8. For example, GS 367, 368, 370.
9. Nietzsche thus anticipates Sartre's advocacy and practice of what Sartre calls the "progressive-regressive method" in his *Search for a Method* (New York: Vintage, 1968), in which he too is concerned to work out a way of arriving at an appropriate and fruitful way of conceiving and comprehending human existence and possibility.
10. In doing so, Nietzsche proceeds in a manner not unlike that of his near-contemporary Wilhelm Dilthey (with whose *Lebensphilosophie* his own enterprise is often associated). For Dilthey too took the key to the comprehension of human life to be its various expressions in the form of such social and cultural phenomena. See H. P. Rickman, ed., *Meaning in History: Dilthey's Thought on History and Society* (New York: Harper, 1962).
11. Michel Foucault, *The Order of Things* (New York: Vintage, 1973), 342.
12. Ibid., 385.

13. Ibid., chap. 10.

14. Ibid., 340–43.

15. As Foucault argues in chap. 10 of *The Order of Things* and indeed throughout the book.

16. For a more extended discussion of Nietzsche's thinking with respect to human nature and related matters, see my *Nietzsche* (London: Routledge and Kegan Paul, 1983), chap. 5.

CHAPTER ELEVEN

Of Morals and *Menschen:*
Nietzsche's *Genealogy*
and Anthropology

Sitting in moral judgment should offend our taste. Let us leave such chatter and such bad taste to those who have nothing else to do but drag the past a few steps further through time and who never live in the present—which is to say the many, the great majority. We, however, *want to become those we are* —human beings who are new, unique, incomparable, who give themselves laws, who create themselves. To that end we must become the best learners and discoverers of everything that is lawful and necessary the world: we must become *physicists* in order to be able to be *creators* in this sense— while hitherto all valuations and ideals have been based on *ignorance* of physics or were constructed so as to *contradict* it. Therefore: long live physics! And even more so that which *compels* us to turn to physics—our honesty! (GS 335)

Thus spoke the Nietzsche of the first edition of *The Gay Science* in 1882. As the subtitle of *Ecce Homo* ("How One Becomes What One Is") shows, Nietzsche held on to the idea of "becoming those we are" to the end. By the time he published the second edition of *The Gay Science* and *On the Genealogy of Morals,* however, he had come to realize that something more than "physics" was also necessary in this connection, and indeed even more crucial. A knowledge of something the natural sciences do not suffice to enable us to comprehend is indispensable if we are to position ourselves for this sort of "becoming"—namely, our already attained "no longer merely animal" humanity. It too is something that has "become"; and as this passage of 1882 shows. Nietzsche was convinced even at that time that we must comprehend what we already are, and how we came to be that way, in order to discern what we might yet become, and to take stock of what we have to work with as we set about to realize this possibility.

But to this end a kind of inquiry appropriate to the manner of the historical transformation of our initial merely natural existence into our present humanity—our "dis-animalization," as he had earlier put it—is

needed. Five years after writing these lines,[1] Nietzsche had a new name
for it: "genealogy." And he also had come to recognize that, while such
inquiry is quite different from "sitting in moral judgment," attention to
"morals" was an important part of it, owing to their role in the emergence
and shaping of our humanity. More than "genealogical" inquiry focusing
upon morals is also necessary in this connection. So Nietzsche reaffirmed
his earlier characterization of his larger endeavor as *"fröhliche Wissenschaft"*[2] by publishing an expanded edition of his book bearing that title
at this time, in the newly added fifth book of which he addresses a
variety of other matters from other perspectives, to the same end.[3] But
the importance he attached to such a "genealogical" effort is clear from
his devotion of an entire book to it — *On the Genealogy of Morals*
— published in the same year (1887).

The same "honesty" that had earlier prompted Nietzsche to extol
"physics" now led him to turn to genealogy. While he had earlier held
that "we must become physicists" in order to come to know ourselves well
enough to go on to "become those we are," he became convinced that we
must become "genealogists" as well. He did not thereby abandon the idea
that "to that end we must become the best learners and discoverers of
everything that is lawful and necessary in the world," but rather extended
it, with appropriate modifications, to take account of the historical as well
as natural character of our humanity. We must also "become the best
learners and discoverers" of everything that has contributed significantly
to its historical development, and so of how we have come to be "those
we are," actually as well as potentially.

It is in this spirit, I would suggest, that Nietzsche engaged in the
project that issued in *Genealogy,* as well as in its companion work, the
fifth book of *The Gay Science.* His larger task, of positioning ourselves to
"become those we are" in the sense indicated, requires "genealogy" — and
more. For it involves an assessment of the various possibilities that our
attained humanity opens up to us — and this requires not only interpretation but also evaluation. So we find Nietzsche from this time onward (in
his prefaces of 1886 and after, as well as in his subsequent books) making
much of "the problem of value," and of the need for a "revaluation" and
"rank-ordering" of values. Such value inquiry goes beyond anything that
can be "learned" about how we have come to be what we are, and about
how prevailing modes of valuations have come about. Nietzsche's recognition of this point is reflected in his repeated insistence that the value of
something is by no means settled by a knowledge of how it originated, as
well as by his frequent reiteration of the point that the task to which his
other inquiries have led him is to take up the problem of value and the
"revaluation of values." At the same time, however, he recognized that

these tasks require to be pursued in conjunction with inquiry into the nature of our fundamental and attained humanity, which must be reinterpreted by drawing upon a variety of perspectival investigations of aspects of our humanity and the conditions under which they have taken shape.

1

Nietzsche's preface to *Genealogy* consists not only in a discussion of how his thinking in it relates to his earlier concerns and efforts, but also in a reflection upon these very points. Observing that he had long been interested in "the *origin* of our moral prejudices," he then remarks that this interest eventually gave rise and gave way to other questions, both interpretive and evaluative: "*what value do they themselves possess?* Have they hitherto hindered or furthered human prosperity? Are they a sign of distress, of impoverishment, of the degeneration of life? Or is there revealed in them, on the contrary, the plenitude, force, and will of life, its courage, certainty, future?" (GM P:2).

As Nietzsche immediately goes on to observe, his concerns further extended to evaluation as well as interpretation. He summarizes the relation between these sorts of inquiry—all encompassed within and characterizing his kind of philosophy—as follows: "Let us articulate this *new demand:* we need a *critique* of moral values, *the value of these values themselves must first be called in question* —and for that there is needed a knowledge of the conditions and circumstances under which they grew, under which they evolved and changed . . . a knowledge of a kind that has never yet existed or even been desired" (GM P:6).

Nietzsche's "genealogical" inquiries are often taken to have a kind of reductionist intent, as though he believed that the manner in which something originated *settled* the questions of its nature and of what is to be made of it. In fact, however, while he does believe (and here tells us) that one does well to *begin* by considering how something may have originated, he is equally insistent that this settles nothing on either score. For what is of decisive importance in both respects, he repeatedly insists, is what thereby has emerged and become possible. It is above all *by their fruits* —and not merely *by their roots* —that he would have us "know them," whether it is morals or "the type 'man'" or ourselves as "men of knowledge" that is at issue.[4] And to this end, he suggests that a variety of kinds of questions must be posed and investigated, from a variety of different perspectives.

It seems evident to me from Nietzsche's remarks in this preface that he considers not only the interpretive but also the evaluative parts of his discussion in the *Genealogy* (as elsewhere) to be concerned with matters that admit of *comprehension,* and to lay claim to characterization of them in terms of "knowledge," as well as to be proper concerns of philosophy. This is the clear implication, for example, of the following passage:

> *That* I still cleave to [the ideas that I take up again in the present treatises] today . . . that they have become in the meantime more and more firmly attached to one another, strengthens my joyful assurance that they might have arisen in me from the first not as isolated, capricious, or sporadic things but from a common root, from a *fundamental will* of knowledge, pointing imperiously into the depths, speaking more and more precisely, demanding greater and greater precision. For this alone is fitting for a philosopher. (GM P:2)

The fact that Nietzsche begins this preface by observing that "We are unknown to ourselves, we men of knowledge" (GM P:1) does not detract from the significance of his approving references to "knowledge" in such other passages as this one. He clearly does mean to shed light upon himself and ourselves as "men of knowledge" in the course of his discussion of the ways in which morals (and in particular "ascetic ideals") have influenced our development as such a peculiar human type. But he also distinguishes fruits from roots, and allows for the possibility (which he explores in the very first section of the first essay) that very "human, all-too-human" dispositions and motivations *may* issue in the attainment of genuine comprehension—if they come to be configured and transformed in a certain manner—*despite* the fact that none of them may constitute anything like a "will to knowledge" to begin with. So he conceives of the possibility of "investigators and microscopists of the soul" emerging from a particular development of this sort with the capacity as well as the determination to come to understand much about it that most people do not know, and would rather not know—"brave, proud, magnanimous animals, who know how to keep their hearts as well as their sufferings in bounds and have trained themselves to sacrifice all desirability to truth, *every* truth, even plain, harsh, repellent, unchristian, immoral truth. —For such truths do exist" (GM I:1).

An interesting and significant parallel may thus be observed between the outcome of his genealogical and other reflections on morals and morality, on the one hand, and of his related genealogical and other reflections on ourselves as "knowers" and on the knowledge we may attain. As he observes at the end of the first essay, he trusts that it should be "abundantly clear what my *aim* is," and more specifically "what the aim of that dangerous slogan is that is inscribed at the head of my last book *Beyond Good and Evil.* — At least this does *not* mean 'Beyond Good and Bad' " (GM I:17). This aim is a double one: both to take us to the point that we understand and are emancipated from the all-too-human "herd" and "slave" morality of "good and evil," and to awaken us to the possibility and preferability of a different mode of valuation and "higher morality" along the lines of his contrasting polarity of "good and bad."

Similarly, I would suggest, the aim of his reflections on "knowers" and knowledge is likewise a double one, and their outcome is positive as well as negative. One might take some of his pronouncements to be variants of a like "dangerous slogan," along the lines of "Beyond True and False." But to this it must be added that his larger aim should be "abundantly clear" to readers of this same book — and that "at least this does *not* mean 'Beyond Truths and Lies, Errors and Illusions.' " For his double aim is both to enable us to comprehend and free ourselves from all-too-naive and all-too-metaphysical ideas and ideals of truth and knowledge, and to show us *that* and *how* a different sort of thinking is humanly possible, for which there is more to be said than there is for others, in terms of honesty and insightfulness. His investigations in *Genealogy* serve both of these purposes.

In the next few opening sections of the first essay Nietzsche goes on to indicate a number of the sorts of sophistication and sensitivity that he considers to be needful if such "investigators of the soul" are to be equal to their task and subject. Their eyes and thinking must be sharpened and attuned to historical, psychological, linguistic, sociological, and cultural phenomena and developments (GM I:2-5); for all of these perspectives are held to yield insights into aspects of what "the soul" has come to be in the course of human events.

All of this is stage-setting for the particular investigations with respect to "morals" that Nietzsche proceeds to undertake, beginning shortly thereafter. Yet these opening remarks obviously have a considerably broader applicability — to the investigation of other such phenomena that also are encountered when one turns one's attention to the varieties of human experience, and to our attained humanity in which they figure along with them. Genealogical inquiry, of the sort Nietzsche here undertakes with respect to "morals," and involving their exploration by bringing the various sorts of sensitivity indicated above to bear upon them, is here advocated — and not only with respect to them. It is commended with respect to "the soul" more generally as well — that is, to "the type 'man'," the "no-longer-merely-animal animal" that has acquired what came to be called a "soul," both as a general "type" and in its considerable diversity. It is thus commended (and practiced) not only for the purposes of Nietzsche's kind of moral philosophy, but also in connection with what may correspondingly be called his kind of philosophical anthropology.

2

Nietzsche's *Genealogy* is therefore more than an elaboration of what he (in his preface) calls "my ideas on the *origin* of our moral prejudices," even though he goes on to say that "this is the subject of this polemic" (GM P:2). As has been observed above, he is also and just as deeply concerned to inquire into *our* origin and genealogy as "men of knowledge." But this is not all. The *Genealogy* is further a companion piece to the fifth book of *The Gay Science* (published, as has been noted, in the same year). It is an extension of his *fröhliche Wissenschaft,* and has the same fundamental focus. In *The Gay Science* Nietzsche deals with many topics and issues; but his fundamental concern is to carry out the project of what he calls " 'naturalizing' our humanity, in terms of a newly redeemed ['de-deified'] nature" (GS 109).[5]

That is a project he pursues in the *Genealogy* as well. His general and underlying concern, in both works, is with *our human* nature and possibilities. And in the *Genealogy* he is offering us further suggestions pertaining not only to the genealogy of morals and of knowers, but also to the genealogy of the humanity we exemplify, as it has become to be and may yet become. He obviously seeks to shed light on the origin of our "moral prejudices" and of our commonplace ways of "knowing," with a view to attaining a perspective upon them by means of which we might go beyond them. But he further is concerned to shed light on the origins of our humanity, in general and also in some of its more remarkable forms, with a view to attaining a more comprehensive perspective upon them by means of which we might at once arrive at a better understanding of what he calls "the type 'man'," and also discern "what might yet be made of man."

I shall not deal here with what Nietzsche has to say in the *Genealogy* about the "moral prejudices" he discusses, "slave" and "master" moralities, the "bad conscience" and "ascetic ideals," and about the relation of these phenomena to scholarly ideals and related ways of construing and esteeming truth and knowledge—important and central to this work though his discussion of these matters certainly are. I shall instead be concerned with the *Genealogy* as a contribution to Nietzsche's development of his philosophical anthropology, and with the ideas he seeks to advance and substantiate in it with respect to our emergent human nature.

My general claims are these: that Nietzsche's enterprise in this work requires to be understood in the context of his philosophical anthropology, which it also helps to illuminate; that the inquiries he here pursues are intended fundamentally to contribute to this larger enterprise, no less than to an assessment of the particular phenomena with which he deals; that part of what he is concerned to do in this work is to advance certain important claims specifically addressed to the issue of how our human nature is to be understood; and that what he has to say sheds important light both on how he conceives of our nature (what sort of nature he believes it to be appropriate to attribute to ourselves as human beings), and also on how he believes it is best approached and dealt with.

It is no objection to my attribution to Nietzsche of the idea that we *have* a nature with which it is the task of his *fröhliche Wissenschaft* to deal (in part through his genealogical inquiries), to observe that he rejects the idea of "man" as an "eternal truth" possessed of a timeless and ahistorical essence. This observation is certainly correct; but it leaves open the possibility that he proposes to replace *this* conception of our nature with one of another sort, which nonetheless is (at least to his way of thinking) still deserving of the name. And it is likewise no objection to observe that he makes much of contingencies that have influenced our development, and have given rise to differences among various types of human beings. For while this observation too is correct, it is entirely consistent with the view that he intends all of this to contribute to our understanding of the *sort* of nature we as human beings have, and does not rule out the idea that we *have* any such nature of which it is meaningful to speak.

Nietzsche makes it clear at the outset, in his preface, that his concern with "the type *Mensch*" underlies his more immediate investigations in the three essays of which the *Genealogy* consists. So he frames them by expressing his motivating suspicion that "precisely morality would be to blame if the *highest power and splendor* actually possible to the type man was never in fact attained" (GM P:6). And it may further be observed that, in order to be able to carry out a critique and revaluation of "morality" in the terms suggested here, the attainability of a comprehension of "the type 'man'" (taking account of this "type" both as it has come to be and as it has the potential to become) is presupposed.

This is something of which Nietzsche shows himself to be well aware. As I read him, he is attentive—in *Genealogy* as well as elsewhere—to the fact that it is thus incumbent upon him to supply the anthropological foundation or context for the assessment of morality to which his "genealogy of morals" is intended to contribute. So, on numerous occasions along the way, he pauses to indicate and sketch relevant features of the conception of the nature of "the type 'man'" with which he is working, upon which he is drawing, and to which he also means his examination of the moral phenomena he considers to contribute. My picture of Nietzsche's procedure is thus that of a double movement, drawing upon general anthropological considerations to illuminate various moral phenomena, while at the same time availing himself of the insights thus attained into these phenomena to refine the interpretation of our nature he seeks to develop and substantiate.

This procedure has its dangers, and invites the charge of circularity; but I believe that Nietzsche would respond (as would Heidegger, and with equal justice) that one can do no better—and that any circularity here is not vicious but hermeneutical. Further: interpreters we are, and cannot but be, in dealing with both "morals" and "the type 'man'"; but this does not mean that we therefore are not and cannot be "knowers." It only means that it is in the manner and spirit of conscientious interpreters and would-be "good philologists" that we must proceed, if we are to have any prospect of doing something approaching justice to our "text." As I read him, Nietzsche does not repudiate this hope as a vain and impossible dream, but rather embraces it as a coherent and legitimate aspiration. Nothing less is worthy of his "new philosophers" who are to be "men of knowledge" and "lovers of knowledge" as well as "legislators of values," on that newly open sea of which he speaks so evocatively at the conclusion of the fifth book of *The Gay Science*.

3

Let us look briefly at each of the three essays in the *Genealogy* in turn, to see what Nietzsche does and has to say along these lines in this work. At the outset of the first essay, he insists upon the importance of "the *historical spirit*" in any such undertaking (GM I:2), if moral phenomena and our nature more generally are to be properly understood. Each may be *better* understood if approached in a manner attentive to its historical development. A little further on, after having introduced his conceptions of the different modes of valuation "good and bad" versus "good and evil," and linking the latter to the influence of "priestly" activity, he remarks: "it was on the sort of this *essentially dangerous* form of human existence, the priestly form, that man first became *an interesting* animal, that only here did the human soul in a higher sense acquire *depth* and become *evil*—and these are the two basic respects in which man has hitherto been superior to other beasts!" (GM I:6).

Nietzsche goes on to observe: "Human history would be altogether too stupid a thing without the spirit that the impotent have introduced into it" (GM I:7). Much of what he has to say in the following sections is intended to elaborate his account of how this came about, and what occurred as the immediate result of this process. He sums it up in the suggestion that "the *meaning of all culture,*" at least to date and broadly speaking, "is the reduction of the beast of prey 'man' to a tame and civilized animal, a *domestic animal*" (GM I:11).

Nietzsche next proceeds to advance a sketch of a part of a psychological theory—a *general* theory, clearly intended not only to apply to the understanding of the origin of the phenomenon of *ressentiment* (his immediate topic), but also to pertain to the understanding of our nature more generally. It is cast in the terms of a general model of events, treating human actions as a class of such events. Here I merely draw attention to it, as an illustration of my general thesis. It is at this juncture that he contends that "a quantum of force is equivalent to a quantum of drive, will, effect—more, it is nothing other than this very driving, willing, effecting," rather than something "caused" to occur by some sort of underlying "subject" entity—for "there is no substratum; there is no 'being' behind doing, affecting, becoming; 'the doer' is merely a fiction added to the deed" (GM I:13). Nietzsche then goes on to apply this sketch of a part of a picture of our nature to the interpretation and understanding of the phenomenon of *ressentiment* and the associated moral ideals—at the same time deriving support for his generalized hypothesis from the plausibility of the account it enables him to give of them.

Finally, it is of no little interest and relevance that he concludes this first essay with a "Note" in which he calls not only for attention to be given to the light linguistics and etymology may "throw on the history of the evolution of moral concepts," but also for an "amicable and fruitful exchange" between "philosophy, physiology and medicine," in order that questions relating to "the problem of value" and "the determination of the order of rank among values" may be approached and dealt with in their proper general and fundamental context. For this context is clearly implied by these suggestions and his other remarks to be that of human life more generally, and of our human nature and possibilities, both in their general outlines and in what might be called their "human type-specificity."

Nietzsche opens the second essay by posing a question about our human nature in the very opening lines of the first section: "To breed an animal *with the right to make promises* —is this not the paradoxical task that nature has set itself in the case of man? Is it not the real problem regarding man?" And he concludes this section, which goes on to deal with the general usefulness of "forgetting" in healthy animal life (thus generating this "paradox"), with the observation that "man must first of all have become *calculable, regular, necessary,* even in his own image of himself, if he is to be able to stand security for *his own future,* which is what one who promises does!" (GM II:1).

In the next section Nietzsche goes on to spell out the general significance of this "tremendous process" for the understanding not only of moral phenomena such as "guilt" and "bad conscience" but also of our attained humanity—and further, of a higher humanity that it has made possible, of which account must likewise be taken in an adequate interpretation of our humanity. So he remarks that "society and the morality of custom at last reveal *what* they have simply been the means to: . . . the *sovereign individual*" (GM II:2). By what he terms "the labor performed by man upon himself during the greater part of the existence of the human race, his entire *prehistoric* labor," we have made ourselves into the type of creature we now are, with this prospect of further enhancement. It is this above all that Nietzsche seeks here to comprehend and elaborate, with the specific topics of the moral phenomena he discusses serving chiefly as points of departure and clues, evidence, and means of confirmation.

So also, in the next section, his guiding question is the more general one: "How can one create a memory for the human animal?" (GM II:3). In the same vein, when he returns to the genealogy of morals in the following section, his remarks are couched in terms of his more general concern with our attained humanity, as when he writes that "a *high* degree of humanity had to be attained before the animal 'man' began to make the sorts of distinctions" attributions of guilt and responsibility involve (GM II:4). In subsequent sections Nietzsche has a great deal to say about how all of this may have come to pass, which is as much material for a "genealogy of humanity" as it is elaboration of a "genealogy of morals." Along the way, he even brings in his "theory that in all events a *will to power* is operating" (GM II:12). He does so, once again, because he is concerned to relate his genealogy of morals to its larger interpretive context, and to his larger interpretive enterprise.

Nietzsche's whole discussion in this second essay culminates in his famous "provisional statement" of his "hypothesis concerning the origin of the 'bad conscience,' " which is actually a much more comprehensive hypothesis concerning the way in which "man first developed what was later called his 'soul'." It involves his contention that "All instincts that do not discharge themselves outwardly turn inward—this is what I call the *internalization* of man," and that this "fundamental change . . . which occurred when he found himself finally enclosed within the walls of society" transformed the "semi-animals" we once were into the "humanity" we now are (GM II:16). This for Nietzsche was the crucial step in what might be called "the birth of man." The *Genealogy* is in effect his attempt to make a case for the decisive importance of this development, and for the associated interpretation of our nature it suggests. The remainder of the second essay is devoted chiefly to working out an account of the "moral" phenomena of "guilt" and the "bad conscience" that both draws upon this interpretation and supports it by demonstrating its explanatory power and sense-making usefulness.

In the third essay, on the question "What is the Meaning of Ascetic Ideals?" Nietzsche carries his inquiry a step further, seeking not only to answer this question but to make use of his investigation of this topic to add further detail to his portrait of our nature. Thus, in the first section, he states: "*That* the ascetic ideal has meant so many things to man . . . is an expression of the basic fact of the human will, its *horror vacui: it needs a goal—and it will rather will nothingness* than *not* will" (GM III:1). And it is with this same reflection that he concludes this essay, with the observation: "Apart from the ascetic ideal, man, the human *animal,* had no meaning so far" (GM III:28).

Nietzsche's basic question in this essay is: How is the phenomenon of the ascetic ideal possible, and what light does it shed upon our nature? And he clearly takes this light to be considerable. In the course of his discussion he draws upon his general view that "every animal," ourselves included, "instinctively strives for an optimum of favorable conditions under which it can expend all its strength and achieve its maximal feeling of power" (GM III:7); and he employs the phenomenon of "ascetic ideals" to show how this general disposition has taken on particular form in our own case, which the developments discussed previously have greatly complicated. Thus he likens the ascetic priest and kindred types to a "caterpillar" form, and contemplates the extent to which "that many-colored and dangerous winged creature, the 'spirit' which this caterpillar concealed," has begun to be "unfettered at last"; and he looks to the further realization of this salient possibility our attained humanity harbors within it (GM III:10).

Throughout this essay, Nietzsche repeatedly asks: What does all this *mean?* And his attempts to answer this question are conducted in the spirit of his reflections on the possibility and conditions of attaining "knowledge" here, of the sort of creature we ourselves are, in one of the most notable passages in the entire book. "Precisely because we seek knowledge," he contends, we must avail ourselves of many perspectives; and so, he goes on to observe, "the *more* affects we allow to speak about one thing, the *more* eyes, different eyes, we can use to observe one thing, the more complete will our 'concept' of this thing, our 'objectivity,' be" (GM III:12).

In the course of his discussion, Nietzsche dwells upon the point that "man is more sick, uncertain, changeable, indeterminate than any other animal . . . he is *the* sick animal," and upon the questions of "how that has come about" and where it all may lead (GM III:13). His ideas concerning this "sickness" that has come to characterize us, and upon the possibility of a new and greater "health," beyond it as well as beyond mere animal vitality, both require and are intended to help elucidate a conception of the sort of nature we have that now admits of both possibilities. And much of what he has to say about the shortcomings of various remedies to which human beings have resorted presupposes the possibility of a comprehension of our nature, in relation to which it makes sense to assess them and find them wanting. Here again, his examination of moral phenomena and his elaboration of a philosophical anthropology thus go hand in hand, each serving to contribute to the other.

4

Perhaps the best way to make my case, and at the same time to convey more clearly some of the central features of Nietzsche's thinking with respect to our nature, is to look more closely at one of these three essays, to see what he has to say along these lines in it.[6] I shall focus upon the second essay here; for he develops several ideas in it that are of the greatest importance not only to his understanding of the attained humanity of "the type 'man' " as it has come to be, but also to his conception of the sort of humanity that has thereby come to be humanly attainable. Both of these interrelated concerns had long preoccupied him—they are arguably the twin basic themes of *The Gay Science*, for example—and quite clearly do so here as well; and in this second essay in particular, his developing thinking about them is deepened and extended.

Nietzsche addresses himself to these matters at some length twice in this essay: in the opening sections, and then again shortly after its midpoint. I shall consider the latter discussion first, because it is the more fundamental of the two, and deals with a development he considers to have set the stage for that with which he begins.

It is Nietzsche's general view that, while the eventual outcome is still very much in doubt, nature is making a unique experiment in us. In our social and conscious life, a complex alternative to the general kind of instinct structure operative in other forms of life has emerged. Indeed, he considers certain aspects of the conditions imposed upon us by our social life to have played an important role in the breaking down of our former instinct structure, as well as in the filling of the resulting void. This may be seen in his discussion relating to the emergence of "the bad conscience" in the *Genealogy.* He takes this phenomenon to be a "serious illness" marking the onset of a larger "sickness," that

> man was bound to contract under the stress of the most fundamental change he ever experienced — that change which occurred when he found himself finally enclosed within the walls of society and of peace. The situation that faced sea animals when they were compelled to become land animals or perish was the same as that which faced these semi-animals, well adapted to their wilderness, to war, to prowling, to adventure: suddenly all their instincts were disvalued and "suspended." From now on they had to walk on their feet and "bear themselves" whereas hitherto they had been borne by the water: a dreadful heaviness lay upon them. . . . In this new world they no longer possessed their former guides, their regulating, unconscious and infallible drives: they were reduced to thinking, inferring, reckoning, co-ordinating cause and effect, these unfortunate creatures; they were reduced to their "consciousness," their weakest and most fallible organ! (GM II:16)

Nietzsche goes on to refer to this departure from our instinctive "former guides," in favor of conscious processes better attuned to the different and variable circumstances of social life, as "a forcible sundering from [man's] past, as it were a leap and plunge into new surroundings and conditions of existence," involving a "declaration of war against the old instincts upon which his strength, joy and terribleness had rested hitherto." At the same time, however, he is quick to draw attention to the potentiality and promise implicit in this development. Thus he considers it important to "add at once" that this spectacle of "an animal soul turned against itself," departing from the life its old instincts marked out for it, and having to oppose and disengage them by means of and in favor of a very different sort of life-regulating and guiding process, "was something so new profound, unheard of, enigmatic, contradictory, *and pregnant with a future* that the aspect of the earth was essentially altered" (ibid.).

As these remarks indicate, it is not Nietzsche's intention to suggest that, either at this point in human development or subsequently, our old instincts simply vanished altogether and without residue, leaving the field entirely to the socially conditioned conscious processes that thus came to the fore. On the contrary, he contends that in the circumstances described, even while no longer possessing their former sovereignty, "the old instincts had not suddenly ceased to make their usual demands!" And although with the breaking of their hold upon the course of life their structure too is suggested gradually to have broken down, he holds that the basic drives once finely articulated in this structure can by no means be supposed to have disappeared. They may in a sense be said to have been "reduced" from the highly differentiated and specialized state characteristic of other complex forms of life, and presumably also of that which was ancestral to our own. The drive reduction presumed thus to have occurred here, however, is suggested to be qualitative rather than quantitative.

Moreover, on Nietzsche's view, this drive reduction has not been carried to completion in the interval. Strong residues of our old instinct structure are held to have survived the "fundamental change" he describes in the passage cited above, and to survive to some extent still. And their survival is purported to have played a profoundly important role in the specific direction taken in the development of major portions of our spiritual life, as well as serving (together with the more generalized forces released through drive reduction) to fuel and inform the whole range of our conscious processes and activities. Thus in this same context he advances one of his central ideas touched upon briefly above: "All instincts that do not discharge themselves outwardly *turn inward* — this is what I call the *internalization* of man: thus it was that man first developed what was later called his 'soul.' The entire inner world, originally as thin as if it were stretched between two membranes, expanded and extended itself, acquired depth, breadth, and height, in the same measure as outward discharge was *inhibited*" (GM II:16).

Instincts so inhibited by the pressure of circumstances from discharging themselves "naturally" do not (as Freud was also to observe) simply dissipate. Rather, Nietzsche suggests, they "seek new and, as it were, subterranean gratifications." When they take such modified and sublimated forms as "the bad conscience" or that broader class of phenomena with which he deals later in the same work under the rubric of "ascetic ideals," their impact upon human life tends to be negative and even self-destructive. But this phenomenon can also take a very different turn. Thus Nietzsche regards this process of "internalization" and sublimation as the key to the emergence of all the life-enriching and life-enhancing phenomena of human spiritual life as well, from the political to the emotional, artistic, and intellectual. If he considers it appropriate to term this too a form of "sickness" in relation to the "healthy animality" of a kind of life governed by an undisrupted, smoothly functioning, and comprehensive instinct structure, he is far from supposing that the latter is inherently preferable to it. Thus he remarks elsewhere that we would do well to consider whether "the will to health alone is not a prejudice, cowardice, and perhaps a bit of very subtle barbarism and backwardness" (GS 120).

Nietzsche further contends that a great many of the major constituent features of our mental life are *social* rather than either purely intellectual or merely biological phenomena, owing their very origins to circumstances associated with our social existence. He is particularly concerned to establish that this is so with respect to those that have long been regarded as operations of special faculties of "the mind"—of which, after "reason," two of the most prominent examples are memory and conscience. He identifies the context in which their development received the most powerful stimulus as the practical one of action. Thus he links the phenomenon of memory to that of *promising;* and his answer to the question "How can one create a memory for the human animal?" is developed with reference to this social practice (GM II:3). He approaches the matter by rhetorically asking: "To breed an animal *with the right to make promises* —is not this the paradoxical task that nature has set for itself in the case of man?" (GM II:2). The thought he expresses here is deserving of attention in its own right, owing to its implications for the issue of our human nature.

Nietzsche contends that this ability required the development of a kind of memory going beyond the (basically animal) capacity to absorb and retain things experienced. Where the latter alone is operative, such experience "enters our consciousness as little while we are digesting it . . . as does the thousandfold process involved in physical nourishment" (GM II:1). For promising to be possible, a further sort of more explicit memory had to be developed, involving the partial abrogation of what he terms the overt "forgetfulness" characteristic of this basic retentive capacity. "A real *memory of the will*" had to be attained. And "it was only with the aid of this kind of memory," he suggests, "that one came at last" to be capable of "reason, seriousness, mastery over the affects, the whole somber thing called reflection, all those prerogatives and showpieces of man." He goes on to observe, moreover, that "they have been dearly bought," at the price of "much blood and cruelty" (GM II:3).

The account Nietzsche goes on to provide of how this came about—in terms of debt, punishment, and cruelty—is highly speculative, and its details may certainly be questioned. All he requires for his larger purposes, however, is that the phenomenon of overt remembering may plausibly be accounted for in an entirely naturalistic manner, in terms of *some such* social-psychological etiology—and thereby, along with it, the various forms of spirituality and conscious activity of which it is the precondition, and for which it prepares the way. The only essential point of the story he tells here is that it was the social necessity of rendering human beings reliable that was the original and primary impetus to its development. Without this necessity there would and could never have emerged the phenomenon of a "long chain of will" sufficing to override our natural condition of being "attuned only to the passing moment."

Nietzsche takes the consequences of this development to have been (and to continue to be) of the greatest importance, both for our manner of relating to our environing world and for our own identity. With regard to the former, our immersion in and preoccupation with the "passing moment" is thereby at least partially broken; we are impelled to learn to "see and anticipate distant eventualities," to operate in terms of ends and means, to "think causally," and "in general to be able to calculate and compute." And with regard to the latter, Nietzsche observes that something of profound significance had to occur: "Man himself must first of all have become *calculable, regular, necessary,* even in his own image of himself, if he is to be able to stand security for *his own future,* which is what one who promises does!" (GM II:1).

This socially induced development has important implications for the nature of human action. The behavior of a mere creature of the moment, doing what it does in accordance with whatever impulses and dispositions happen to be dominant on any given occasion, may no more appropriately be considered *action* than such a creature may be ascribed personal identity. And the same sorts of social impositions that engender the latter also serve to establish the context in which the former emerges, through the disruption of this immediacy that occurs when one learns and is compelled to take the past and the future into account. Human action involves at least a minimal degree of what Nietzsche terms "mastery over the affects" (GM II:3), even if it never occurs in their absence or without their influence; and it is by means of the "social straitjacket" that a degree of such mastery is first achieved.

A fundamental distinction between human action and animal behavior is therefore clearly implied, and is held to be bound up with the development of this cluster of social practices and with the transformation of one's manner of comporting oneself through initiation into them. The acquisition of language is only the first step in this process, albeit an important and indispensable one. The decisive step is a matter of coming further to be able to operate in terms of promises, agreements, rules, values, and in general, to frame and act pursuant to *intentions.* The social character of the conditions of human action by no means implies that all such intentions are but the internalization of general social influences. This should be clear from Nietzsche's remarks about the possibility of "the sovereign individual" (GM II:2). But even the very "autonomy" and "independent protracted will" of which he speaks in characterizing an individual of this sort are represented as outgrowths of what is basically a social phenomenon, rather than attributes assignable to some special non-natural and extrasocial faculty of the individual as such. He does not consider all human action to be completely determined by prevailing social institutions together with our general human and particular individual biological endowments, let alone by these latter endowments exclusively. But he does hold that it is grounded in the social transformation of our fundamental biological nature; and he takes the more exceptional forms of action to which autonomy and independence may legitimately be ascribed to be a matter of the individual transformation of a previously established social nature.

5

I certainly would not maintain that this way of reading the *Genealogy* is the only appropriate way of doing so, or that Nietzsche is doing nothing more in it than what I have been talking about. But I *would* maintain that he is doing *nothing less* than this in it, and that reading him as doing this in it is not being unfaithful either to his text or to his intentions—or at least, to some of them. To my way of thinking, this work, along with *The Gay Science* and a good many others, provides clear evidence that he considers it appropriate and philosophically important to think about "the type 'man'" as well as about various particular human types—and further, that he believes there to be a good deal to be said along these lines, which he is intent upon saying, toward the development of what I have been calling a philosophical anthropology.

I further would not maintain that his thinking on this topic is set out whole and complete in the *Genealogy*. On the contrary, in it he approaches this topic only from certain angles. He approaches it from others elsewhere, to equally good effect. But I *would* maintain that Nietzsche's *Genealogy* constitutes a good example of the kind of investigation he believes to be called for in order to make progress in this larger project of comprehending our nature, in terms of its development, attained general character, variability, and prospects. As *some* might conceive of the ideas of human nature and of the project of a philosophical anthropology, he clearly will have no part of them. *He* conceives of them differently, however; and his *Genealogy* is a significant contribution to his attempt (and ours) to deal with them. I consider it important to the understanding of what he sought to do to read him, and this work, with these eyes, if also with others as well.

In *The Gay Science* Nietzsche makes the interesting remark that, while his scientific knowledge is lacking in a good many respects, this does not greatly matter for his purposes, since "we need more, we also need less" than science, for the questions that concern him (GS 381). He calls what he is doing *fröhliche Wissenschaft*, and what he is after "knowledge"; but his point is that something other than natural- and social-scientific inquiry is involved and required in order to deal best with the main issues with which he is concerned. And one of my points is that, in works like *The Gay Science* and the *Genealogy,* he shows us what he has in mind. For Nietzsche, they enable one to get further with these matters than one can get in other ways, shedding more light upon them than the kinds of inquiries pursued by scientists and different types of philosophers can and do.

This is an important and interesting suggestion about philosophical *method,* in certain areas at least, which we would do well to take seriously ourselves, as well as reckon with in interpreting Nietzsche. But what are the kinds of issues and questions that Nietzsche says "concern *him,*" to which this suggestion is meant to apply?

Clearly "the origin of our moral prejudices" is one of them—as is his analysis and revaluation of moral "values" and other "values" more generally. Clearly what he calls his "psychology of philosophers"—and also of scientists, scholars, priestly types, "herd" and "master" types and the like—are others. So also is the status of the various forms of what commonly passes for "truth" and "knowledge." But so too, and more fundamentally, is what he calls "the type 'man',' " and therewith also both the "all-too-human" and the possibility of exceptions to the human rule.

Even if this point is granted, however, and even if it is further agreed (as I would hope) that this too is an important and interesting suggestion about the *agenda* of philosophy, which we also would do well to take seriously ourselves,. as well as reckon with in interpreting Nietzsche— even then, it may still be asked: why call this *philosophical anthropology?*

For some reason, this label seems to make many people feel uncomfortable. Labels like philosophical psychology, theology, biology, and even cosmology seem unobjectionable to most. Why not "philosophical anthropology" too? What better could one call inquiry into "the type 'man' " of the sort Nietzsche undertakes in these and other works? As his remark about needing less and also more than science suggests, it is clearly a philosophical rather than a merely biological- or social-scientific endeavor. As his repeated references to "the type 'man' " and our "humanity" make clear, its focus is upon *anthropos* rather than upon some otherwise delineated object of inquiry. "Anthropology" is the least artificial and most commonplace coinage to designate such inquiry. It may have associations with ways of thinking we and Nietzsche do not embrace and wish to disavow; but so does "psychology," which he and we nonetheless are ready enough to appropriate and retain. Why balk at "anthropology," then, and at "philosophical anthropology"?

This expression does a better job than any other of conveying what is under investigation here, and that its investigation is to be understood as "needing less and also more" than human-scientific inquiry (even if perhaps some of that as well) to be carried out at all adequately. In the end, of course, the important thing is not what this endeavor is called, but rather that its possibility and importance are recognized, and that it is pursued. I would suggest, however, that appropriate labels have their uses in the directions and focusing of attention and effort, and that no other label at hand does the job better than "philosophical anthropology."[7] In any event, this is an important part of the task Nietzsche sets for himself and his type of philosopher, whatever it may be called; and I believe it to be an important part of the agenda of philosophy today, thanks in no small measure to Nietzsche.

Notes

1. By 1887, when *On the Genealogy of Morals* was published.
2. The German title of (*The*) *Gay Science.*
3. The second (expanded) edition of *The Gay Science,* in which Nietzsche added a fifth book and preface to the four "books" making up the original edition, was completed in 1886 and published in 1887, just prior to *On the Genealogy of Morals.*
4. The use of the term "man" to render Nietzsche's term *Mensch* is virtually unavoidable. Nietzsche may well be deserving of criticism for at least some of his views with respect to men and women; but it is not his use of the term *Mensch* that invites such criticism. Whether it is objectionable on other grounds (e.g., that there is no such thing as human nature or "the type *Mensch*") is a different matter, that must be differently addressed and settled. It is Nietzsche's commitment to notions of the latter sort and his thinking with respect to them that are the issues in this essay; and they neither stand nor fall with his ideas about "men and women." (Indeed some of the latter may even be inconsistent with them, and so may be subject to internal criticism and correction; but that is a topic for another occasion.)
5. See the previous chapter.
6. This section is derived in part from chapter 5 of my *Nietzsche.* Interested readers may find it helpful to consult this entire chapter.
7. See my "Philosophical Anthropology: What, Why and How," in *Philosophy and Phenomenological Research,* vol. 50, Supplement (Fall 1990), 155–76.

CHAPTER TWELVE

How to Revalue a Value:
Art and Life Reconsidered

Nietzsche's enthusiasm for art in *The Birth of Tragedy* (henceforth BT) was so great that further reflection could only have tempered it—as it in fact did. The Nietzsche of the subsequently attached "Attempt at a Self-Criticism" is no longer the ardent "art-deifier" he sees himself as having been in BT. And as he indicates in an entry in his notebooks from the same period as this "Self-Criticism," he had long since ceased to subscribe to the gospel of "Art and nothing but art!" according to which art is "the only superior counterforce to all will to denial of life" (WP 853). Moreover, obviously thinking of this early work, he writes in the contemporaneous fifth book of *The Gay Science* that "initially I approached the modern world with a few crude errors and overestimations"—among which, he goes on to make clear, he numbers certain of his views with respect to art (GS 370).

While Nietzsche's thinking on this matter did change, he also continued to adhere to a good deal of what he had initially maintained, at least in a rather general way. He remained persuaded, among other things, of the validity and usefulness (albeit with some restrictions and modifications) of "the conceptual opposites which I have introduced into aesthetics, *Apollinian* and *Dionysian*," making use of the notions on a number of occasions, as shall be seen (TI IX:10). He also continued to view art, as he observes in his "Self-Criticism" he had in BT, "in the perspective of life." Thus in his subsequent writings he devotes considerable attention to the sources of art in human nature, and to certain general human tendencies that frequently manifest themselves in it; and he likewise is very much concerned with the various functions art can and does perform in human life, and with the light it sheds upon our human nature and possibilities. And many of his later views on these matters are at least connected with points he had made earlier.

When, for example, he argues that, in dealing with art, "one must examine the artist himself, and his psychology," and must consider not only the products of his efforts but also "what drives he sublimates" (WP

677), one can see the continuation of a form of investigation begun in BT. The difference here is largely a matter of his deepening this investigation, in the course of which he seeks to demythologize, and to some extent modifies, certain of his initial suggestions. And when he insists (as he often does in his later writings) that "art for art's sake" is a "dangerous principle," and that art should rather be viewed as a "means" serving "the aim of enhancing life" (WP 298), he is obviously thinking in a way not very far removed from the conception of art as "the great means of making life possible, the great seduction to life, the great stimulant of life" that he retrospectively sees himself as having advanced in that first book (WP 853). The former is no mere reiteration of the latter, as shall be seen; but there is an evident relation between them.

Nietzsche further continued to adhere to the noncognitivism in his interpretation of art that finds expression in BT in his emphasis upon the centrality of "illusion" in the various forms art takes. Indeed, in his later writings this theme becomes if anything even more strongly pronounced, most notably in his frequent association of art with "lying." Thus in a relatively early aphorism with the heading *"The Muses as Liars"* he states: "If one for once conceives of the artist as deceiver, this leads to fundamental discoveries" (HH II:188). His employment of such language invites misunderstanding, however, and care must be taken in interpreting his meaning. This is an instance of something one encounters time and again in Nietzsche's discussions of many different matters—his provisional adoption of language used by philosophers with whom he is in radical disagreement, as he takes up the gauntlet they have thrown down. In the present case he elects to concur with Plato's characterization of the poets as "liars," and of art as a kind of "lying," but with an intent that runs directly counter to Plato's. For while he is prepared to insist, with Plato, that art stands at a considerable remove from "truth," he urges against Plato that this is by no means a telling objection against it.

The burden of what Nietzsche has to say along these lines is twofold. First, he argues that art is *not* to be thought of as having to do basically with the revelation of fundamental truths about reality. And second, he maintains that this is to its credit rather than discredit, since what it *does* involve is not only to be conceived in other terms altogether, but also is of the utmost importance. He concedes that it is commonly supposed, both by many artists and by others who hold art in high esteem, that in artistic vision "the true essence of the world" is approached; but he denies that this is actually the case. The arts, he writes, "are to be sure flowers of the world, but are certainly not *closer to the root of the world* than the stalk: one can by no means understand the nature of things better through them, although this is believed by almost everyone. *Error* has made man so deep, sensitive and inventive that he has produced such flowers as religions and arts" (HH I:29).

It is necessary to rid ourselves of the idea that art can and does have major cognitive significance, and that both its nature and its importance are to be conceived accordingly, he argues, if we are to be able to proceed to a reconsideration of it that will do justice to it. And for the later as well as for the early Nietzsche, this does not mean shifting attention merely to the pleasure art is capable of affording to those possessing a sensibility attuned to it. Rather, it involves recognizing the *transfiguring* character of artistic creativity, and the role it is thereby capable of performing in the service of human life. In BT, in which he later observed he took the position that "man must be a liar by nature, he must above all be an *artist,*" since "*we have need of lies*" in order to conquer this reality, this 'truth,' that is, in order to live" (WP 853), he had achieved this recognition, but in a form he subsequently found to be too narrow.

What Nietzsche here and elsewhere calls the "lying" in which art traffics is actually only the aspect borne by artistic creations when they are viewed in terms of their cognitive import. They cease to bear this aspect when that perspective of assessment is abandoned and art comes to be construed in terms of the creativity it involves, rather than the (failing) attempt to apprehend the nature of reality and the way things actually (and merely) happen to be. The cognitivist interpretation of art seemed to him to be so deeply entrenched, however, that it could not simply be ignored in favor of an immediate modification of the terms in which it is conceived along these extracognitive lines. And so he employs the language of a defiant anticognitivism on many occasions, even though the entire preoccupation with the issue of the cognitive status of art is something he is ultimately concerned to lay to rest.

Perhaps the most glaring departure of the later Nietzsche from the Nietzsche of BT (at least where artistic matters are concerned) is in his complete turnabout in his assessment of Wagner, culminating in the scathing denunciation of him, his art, and his effect upon art in *The Case of Wagner.* This change of heart is of no little interest; but what is of greater general importance is the modification of his view of the relation of art to life that underlies it, and the attendant new distinctions he is led to make. Its basic character is suggested by his emphatic repudiation, in the "Self-Criticism" he attached to BT, of the desirability of anything on the order of an "art of metaphysical comfort," and his advocacy instead of an "art of *this-worldly* comfort," which might enable one "some day [to] dispatch all metaphysical comforts to the devil" (BT S-C:7).

The true "sense of art," for the later Nietzsche, is "life." "Art is the great stimulus to life" (TI IX:24). It is fundamentally not merely a "means of easing life" (HH I:148), but rather (as has been observed above) a "means" with "the aim of enhancing life" (WP 298). And he contends that it is not limited to serving this aim simply by rendering existence endurable through various sorts of "illusions" that console, divert, or protect us. For it further—and in the long run more importantly— does so by teaching us to "love the things of 'this' world," and to discover "the great conception of man, that man becomes the transfigurer of existence when he learns to transfigure himself" (WP 820). He recognizes that art *may* be "a consequence of dissatisfaction with reality," and perhaps often has been. But he holds that it may also be "an expression of gratitude for happiness enjoyed" (WP 845). And it further can establish the conditions sufficing to elicit that gratitude and occasion that happiness, through the transformation of the aspect of the reality that concerns us. "What is essential in art remains its perfection of existence, its production of perfection and plenitude; art is essentially *affirmation, blessing, deification of existence*" (WP 821). Existence so transformed ceases to be something the "truth" of which is so unendurable that we would perish of its apprehension. *Its* "truth" can be affirmed, and "art affirms"—affirms its "perfection and plenitude," and therewith also the life of which it is the issue. Its role in the "enhancement of life" thus extends beyond the preservation of life's endangered human children, to the alteration of the character of their existence.

This leads to one of the aforementioned distinctions that figures importantly in Nietzsche's later thought. "Every art," he writes, "may be viewed as a remedy and an aid in the service of growing and struggling life." But it performs different services in the case of "those who suffer from the *over-fullness* of life." So he goes on to say: "Regarding all aesthetic values I now avail myself of this main distinction: I ask in every instance, 'is it hunger or super-abundance that has here become creative?' " (GS 370). And he considers this distinction to be crucial to the understanding and assessment of certain artistic phenomena that can be and often are confused and mistakenly identified. Indeed, this would appear to be one of the "crude errors" of which he here speaks of himself as having initially been guilty. It might be thought that the basic distinction to be drawn is that between cases in which "the desire for *being* prompted creation" (leading to the attempt "to fix, to immortalize"), and those in which the desire for "*becoming*" (embracing "destruction" and "change") is predominant. In fact, however, Nietzsche argues that "both of these kinds of desire are seen to be ambiguous when one considers them more closely," and views them in the light of the former and more fundamental distinction.

Thus he contends that the latter desire *may* be "an expression of an overflowing energy that is pregnant with a future"; but it may instead be merely an expression of "hatred" on the part of "the ill-constituted," who seek to "destroy, because what exists, indeed all existence . . . outrages and provokes them." And similarly, he observes, the former desire "can be prompted . . . by gratitude and love; art with this origin will always be an art of apotheosis." But it may on the other hand be only an expression of "the tyrannic will" of one who is "tormented" and seeks to turn "the idiosyncrasy of his suffering into a binding law and compulsion" (ibid.). In this way Nietzsche gives what he regards as a more discriminating and penetrating answer to the question "What is romanticism?" than it commonly receives; and he also draws attention to an ambiguity he sees in art more generally, owing to which his later discussions of it are marked by an ambivalence not to be found in BT. Like human life itself, art often has been and is a good deal less than it might be. And what he has to say about it in his subsequent writings sometimes applies to the former and sometimes pertains to the latter. This is something it is imperative to bear in mind in considering the scope and implications of his assertions with respect to it, which often seem strikingly at variance with one another.

It should be observed in this connection that, as the above passage itself suggests, the distinction upon which Nietzsche there insists does not obliterate the differentiation of those basic artistic tendencies he initially baptized and on occasion continued to refer to as "Apollinian" and "Dionysian." And it would be an error to suppose that he means to identify the latter alone with "super-abundance that has become creative," and to relegate the former to the status of "hunger" that has taken a creative turn in its desperation. Of the "overflowing energy" that expresses itself as "the desire for destruction, change and becoming," he does state: "my term for this is, as is known, 'Dionysian.'" But in this passage the (Apollinian) "desire for being" or "will to immortalize" is *also*, in its affirmative mode or form, linked to this same "super-abundance," by which the "gratitude and love" characteristic of it are "prompted" and made possible.

In short, the *healthy* forms of *both* of these "desires" are here suggested by Nietzsche to be alternative—different but each estimable—expressions of the same "over-fullness of life," and are the proper referents of the two denominations. "Art affirms" in both cases; both involve the "self-affirmation, self-glorification of life," to which he elsewhere maintains that "all of *great* art belongs" (CW Epilogue). Only they manifest it in different ways—one might say, in different moods. And the importance of this is not only that it enables one to understand Nietzsche's celebration of an "art of apotheosis," nor yet again simply that it shows that he accords "Apollinian" art a much higher status than one might think in view of his revision of the interpretive framework within which he initially identified and dealt with it. For it further serves to indicate that the idea of a fundamental diversity of forms of artistic expression carries over into his view of what art at its best is and would be.

The art forms to which Nietzsche here draws attention are those he somewhat earlier had characterized as "the genuine species of art, those of great repose and of great movement," *both* of which he contrasts with its "degenerate types—tired, blasé art and agitated art" (HH II:115). The first pair, he insists, should not be confused with the second; and he is particularly concerned that one should not stop after marking the difference between the latter two types. Of these, he is utterly disdainful of the first, and somewhat more appreciative of the second, referring to it as "that barbaric, if also still so charming, outpouring of hot and colorful things from an untamed chaotic soul, which is how we earlier understood art in our youth," and is what some perhaps continue to understand it to be. This is "an art of overstrain, of excitement, of aversion to the orderly," for which there may indeed be a need "which artists *must* meet," for the sake of those who suffer from it, and also for the sake of others who might otherwise suffer from *them.* But he contrasts it with "the true art," which represents "the overflow of a wise and harmonious manner of life" (HH II:173).

Art of *this* sort is characterized by the achievement of what Nietzsche calls "the grand style," of which he writes: "The grand style emerges when the beautiful is victorious over the monstrous" (WS 96). Much of what now passes for "great art" surpasses "petty art, the art of recreation, of delightful diversion" only in that it employs "the most powerful stimulants," by means of which it manages to "overwhelm the exhausted and bring them into a night's overanimation" (WS 170). But this, he contends, is merely "aping the high tide of the soul," and should by no means be confused with attaining it (GS 86). Such art is at the furthest remove from an art of the "grand style." And it also is anything but conducive to the emergence of an enhanced form of human existence to which this character could likewise be attributed. It is in these terms, however, that Nietzsche conceives of "the hardest and final task of the artist," even though he recognizes that the achievement of such style in art is difficult and rare, and observes that its extension to "the depiction of the *ultimate* man, that is, the simplest and yet the most complete, is something no artist up to now has achieved," with the possible exception of "the Greeks" (HH II:177).

The "grand style," as Nietzsche understands it, relates to a combination of elements, among which are the greatest strength, the strictest discipline, and the highest cultivation; and it answers to a type of spirituality that is "neither a Dionysian nor an Apollinian state," but rather transcends both, incorporating features of each even as it supersedes them. "The highest feeling of power and sureness finds expression in a grand style. The power which no longer needs any proof, which spurns pleasing, which does not answer lightly, which feels no witness near, which lives oblivious of all opposition to it, which reposes within itself, fatalistically, a law among laws—that speaks of itself as a grand style" (TI IX:11).

In passing, it may be noted that, through his reference here to obliviousness to any "witness," Nietzsche links his distinction between art in which the "grand style" is and is not attained to what he elsewhere terms "the first distinction to be made regarding works of art": namely, that between "monological art" and "art before witnesses." "I do not know of any more profound difference in the whole orientation of an artist than this," he writes, "whether he looks at his work in progress (at 'himself') from the point of view of the witness, or whether he has 'forgotten the world,'" and is concerned only with what he is doing (GS 367). Not all "monological art" is as such possessed of "grand style," of course; but it would appear that for Nietzsche all art in which this style is achieved is essentially "monological" in its creation. It should also be remarked, however, that he balances this point by disparaging "the modern mania for originality" and "abhorence of convention" (WS 122), and maintaining that an artist is one who not only "communicates" but "must communicate" (TI IX:24). It is only in the abstract that these points conflict; there is no real contradiction between them.

"Art as the will to overcome becoming" finds its highest expression in art of "grand style," which transcends the flux of becoming by introducing order into it. Thus it manifests what Nietzsche terms "the supreme will to power," which is "to impose upon becoming the character of being." In "the new desert" that has been made by "the destruction of ideals," it is to it above all that he looks in speaking of "new arts by means of which we can endure it, we amphibians" (WP 617). Much more is at stake here than mere "artistic formulas," according to Nietzsche. It will not be easy for us to be able to carry on in this altered landscape of human life; and such art is taken by him to prefigure a new manner of existence appropriate to it: "one should remodel life so that afterward it *has* to remodel itself" (WP 849). The great significance of art possessed of such style is that it foreshadows this development and awakens us to its possibility.

It is undoubtedly in no small measure for this reason that Nietzsche returns repeatedly to the idea of such art, and esteems it so highly. Thus the terms in which he characterizes it also point beyond it, and show him to be thinking beyond it as well. "The greatness of an artist," he writes, "cannot be measured by the 'beautiful feelings' he arouses," but rather only "according to the degree to which he approaches to the grand style, to which he is capable of the grand style." And here, he continues, one "disdains to please" and "forgets to persuade." Instead, one "commands" and "wills," in the following sense: "To become master of the chaos one is; to compel one's chaos to become form" is the fundamental nature of "the grand ambition here" (WP 842). This style is what he sees as the ultimate artistic issue of the "antagonism of [the] two natural artistic powers" he calls by the names "Apollinian" and "Dionysian," when they interact most felicitously. It incorporates "plenitude of power and moderation, the highest form of self-affirmation in a cool, noble, severe beauty," which "the further development of art" can do no more than amplify, and human life can do no better than to emulate (WP 1050).

But Nietzsche is acutely aware that art and artists for the most part fall far short of this sort of excellence and greatness; and to balance the picture it is well worth pausing to consider briefly what he regards as some of their typical limitations and shortcomings. Even when they transcend the mediocrity and avoid the decadence he discerns and laments, they are held often to exhibit certain "all-too-human" tendencies, owing to which he finds them wanting. In particular, he writes, they

> do not stand nearly independently enough in the world and *against* the world for their changing valuations to deserve attention *in themselves!* They have at all times been valets of some morality, philosophy, or religion: quite apart from the fact that they have unfortunately often been all-too-pliable courtiers of their own followers and patrons, and winning flatterers of ancient or newly arrived powers. They always need at the very least protection, a prop, and established authority: artists never stand apart; standing alone is contrary to their deepest instincts. . . . (GM III:5)

In the same work, Nietzsche goes on to observe that "nothing is more easily corrupted than an artist" — even though, in the very same section, he also presents art in a very favorable light, saying that it "is much more fundamentally opposed to the ascetic ideal than is science," and implying that it is the closest thing to a "natural antagonist of the ascetic ideal" to be found (GM III:25).

The artist is thus regarded as typically constituting a mixed case. On the one hand, if he is an artist at all, then at least to some extent Nietzsche's answer to the question "What does all art do?" applies to him: "Does it not praise? glorify? choose? prefer? With all this it strengthens certain valuations," and so enhances "the desirability of life" (TI IX:24). But, on the other hand, the direction his efforts take is suspect: "An artist cannot endure reality," and "seriously believes that the value of a thing lies in that shadowy residue one derives from colors, form, sound, ideas," in effect subscribing to the principle, "the less real, the more valuable" (WP 572). And while artists do "alter and transform," it is only "images" they produce; whereas "strength organizes what is close and closest," and reaches beyond images into the world and life themselves (WP 585A).

Nietzsche has much more to say with respect to what is "all-too-human" in art and artists generally, and much else to say on the different topic of the very "human" and indeed fundamentally physiological and biological factors with which the emergence and existence of the phenomenon of art are connected. These are ultimately only preliminary concerns for him, however, which I must pass over in order to be able to consider more fully his views on another matter that is in the final analysis of much greater importance to him. This is what might be called *our debt to art,* which he considers to be great indeed, even though different from what most of its admirers and philosophical interpreters have supposed it to be. And it should be noted that his mature assessment of it also differs from that which he initially gave of it in BT, where it was proclaimed to serve to "make life possible and worth living" (BT 1). One might put the latter difference in terms of a shift from an emphasis upon the life-*sustaining* function of art to an emphasis upon its contributions to the *enhancement* of life. These contributions, on his view, are several, and are of almost inestimable importance.

One of them relates to the metamorphosis of the "states of animal vigor" that Nietzsche considers to underlie and figure crucially in artistic activity and experience (WP 802), and of the basic phenomena of "sexuality, intoxication, [and] cruelty" that he takes to "preponderate in the early 'artist'" (WP 801). These proto-artistic forces not only are naturally transfiguring, he holds, providing the initial impetus to the emergence of art, but moreover themselves become increasingly transfigured as they learn artistic employment. Art manifests them and further stimulates them; but it also involves their sublimation and transforming redirection. In art they are not merely repressed, nor is their weakening and extirpation attempted. (Such cruder and more "stupid" tactics of dealing with the problems they pose in human life create other and no less dangerous problems of their own, as he so often observes.) Rather, they are humanized and "spiritualized" in the manner of their expression, and so are able to be enlisted in the service of the enhancement of life. Thus if (in the language of Zarathustra) man may be said to be a "bridge" between "beast" and *Übermensch,* art has played a major role in the construction of the bridge; and it can be taken as paradigmatic in exhibiting the nature of the crossing and as indicating what lies on the other side. It constitutes the best available illustration of what Nietzsche has in mind when he has Zarathustra say: "Once you had wild dogs in your cellar, but in the end they turned into birds and lovely singers" (Z I:5). It exemplifies his conception of "man's self-overcoming"—in a restricted sphere, to be sure, but in a way that points to a larger and more comprehensive human "self-overcoming."

Nietzsche also regards art as "the countermovement" to what he terms the various "decadent forms of man," among which he includes "our religion, morality, and philosophy" (WP 794). It is important to observe, however, that he does not accord this status to art because it might be supposed to contrast with such forms of human "decadence" by involving the removal of constraints upon basic impulses, which then are given free rein in spontaneous expression. This is not what he thinks occurs in artistic activity; and it is also the last thing he wishes to advocate in human life more generally. "Every artist knows how far from any feeling of letting himself go his 'most natural' state is—the free ordering, placing, disposing, giving form in the moment of 'inspiration'—and how strictly and subtly he obeys thousandfold laws precisely then" (BGE 188). Art involves no abandonment of the plane of "high spirituality." Essential to it is a self-mastery, discipline, and rigorous control exercised in relation to the "passions," which perhaps differ in kind from those associated with the devices of "civilization," but are not surpassed by them in rigor. And it is only because he considers art to constitute an advance, rather than to be regressive in this regard, that Nietzsche views it not merely as a "stimulus to life" but also as a phenomenon representing its qualitative enhancement, and exhibiting the character of such enhancement.

Art thus has served as a kind of special schooling of the spirit, in which capacities of expression other than those characteristic of merely vital existence have been cultivated, and a form of self-mastery contrasting with that taught in the obedience-school of society. The distinction Nietzsche draws between "training" and "breeding" here finds application, with art giving substance to the latter notion and standing as its best exemplification thus far. Both involve the transformation of the "human animal," but along importantly different lines and in very different ways. The sort of spiritual "breeding" involved in the emergence of the phenomenon of art in human life may leave much to be desired, as he suggests in remarking upon its merely "preliminary" status (WP 796). But as an initial great experiment along these lines, providing an indication of "what might yet be made of man" (BGE 203) and a sense of direction with respect to the attainment of a "higher humanity," he considers that we owe it very much indeed, quite apart from the immediate satisfactions and delights it may afford us.

We also are indebted to art, according to Nietzsche, for the "idealizing" manner of addressing ourselves to things that it cultivates, and that when well learned is of the greatest importance in enabling us to attain a fundamentally affirmative stance in relation to existence. This may be regarded as a development of one of the central ideas advanced in BT, to the effect that "it is only as an *aesthetic phenomenon* that existence and the world are eternally *justified*" (BT 5). At the same time, however, it also involves a significant departure from the general standpoint of his analysis in that early work. There the artistic generation of "illusion" of one sort or another is taken to be essential to the attainment of this result, and especially to the phenomenon of "idealizing," which he had associated with "Apollinian" art in particular. In later works such as *Twilight of the Idols,* on the other hand, it is in terms of the "perfecting transformation of things" that he conceives of art and its affirmation-inducing power (TI IX:9); and his understanding of "idealization" as it applies to art is altered accordingly.

"Let us get rid of a prejudice here," Nietzsche writes; "idealizing does not consist, as is commonly held, in discounting the petty and inconsequential." And neither, it may be added, does it consist in the substitution for the real of beautiful but unreal images. "What is decisive," he continues, "is rather a tremendous drive to bring out the main features so that the others disappear in the process." And what come to *be* the "main features" are themselves not merely *found* characteristics; for, as he observes in this connection, the "process" of "idealizing" is one in which "one lends to things, one forces them to accept from us, one violates them" (TI IX:8). So conceived, "idealizing" neither leaves everything as it is nor turns away from everything as it is, but rather involves imposing a construction upon what one encounters that alters its aspect and its character as well. Thus it serves and teaches how to "embellish life," not by diverting attention entirely away from "everything ugly" (which can be neither eliminated from it nor ignored for long), but rather by "allowing the *significant* to shine through unavoidable or insuperable ugliness" (HH II:174).

This is a recurrent theme in Nietzsche's discussions of art postdating BT, relatively early as well as quite late, as these two passages show. Another variation on this theme is sounded in a section in *The Gay Science,* which bears the heading "What should win our gratitude." Here he writes: "Only artists . . . have taught us the art of viewing ourselves as heroes—from a distance and, as it were, simplified and transfigured." And the significance of this is considerable: "Only in this way can we deal with some base details in ourselves. Without this art we would be nothing but foreground and live entirely in the spell of that perspective which makes what is closest at hand and most vulgar appear as if it were vast, and reality itself" (GS 78).

In this passage Nietzsche obviously has in mind "artists of the theater" in particular; but later in the same work, in a section on "What one should learn from artists," he puts the point in more general terms, which are meant to embrace other sorts of artists as well. Beginning by asking, "how can one make things beautiful, attractive, and desirable for us when they are not?" he suggests that we can "learn something . . . from artists who are continually trying to bring off such inventions and feats," through such devices as "moving away from things until there is a good deal that one no longer sees and there is much that our eye has to add if we are still to see them at all." While we owe much to art for the development of this capacity to "idealize," however, Nietzsche considers it a limitation of artists that "with them this subtle power usually comes to an end where art ends and life begins." For the real importance he attaches to it lies in its further extension: "we want to be the poets of our life — first of all in the smallest, most everyday matters" (GS 299).

This leads to a final point concerning our debt to art, which may be introduced by reference to another section in *The Gay Science*. Its subject is "Our ultimate gratitude to art." Here Nietzsche suggests that art consists in a "kind of cult of the untrue," which has served to cultivate a "*good* will to appearance" that now proves to be of the utmost importance by enabling us to live with "the realization that delusion and error are conditions of human knowledge and sensation." If art had not taught us to be well disposed to "appearance" notwithstanding its ultimate "untruth," he submits, and if instead "honesty" were our only concern, this realization would be "utterly unbearable." Without a sensibility enabling us to take satisfaction in that which we ourselves have created, we could not but be deeply dismayed upon recognizing the extent to which everything transpiring in our lives is and inescapably will continue to be a merely contingently established human affair, answering to nothing written into the fundamental nature of reality. It may be a mere prejudice we were better to dispense with (as Nietzsche elsewhere urges), to think of human reality and experience as mere "appearance" for this reason. Given certain of our deep-seated intellectual predilections, however, the grip of this prejudice upon us is not easily broken. The emergence of "art as the good will to appearance" constitutes an important step in that direction, and points the way to a reassessment of what we have made and might further make of ourselves. "As an aesthetic phenomenon existence is still *bearable* for us, and art furnishes us with eyes and hands and above all a good conscience to be *able* to turn ourselves into such a phenomenon" (GS 107).

This general point is made by Nietzsche in a variety of ways on a number of occasions, both earlier and later. Thus, for example, in considering "What remains of art" in *Human, All-Too-Human,* he writes: "Above all it has taught us over thousands of years to look upon life in every form with interest and enjoyment, and to carry our sensibility to the point that we finally exclaim, 'However life may be, it is good.'" And he goes on to observe that "this teaching has grown into us," to the point that "one could give art up, but would not thereby lose this ability learned from it" (HH I:222). The suggestion that this involves what might be called the cultivation of a "good will to appearance" is likewise echoed in his contention that art "is much more fundamentally opposed to the ascetic ideal than science," and so is much more closely aligned with "the *opposing ideal*" of a "value-creating" relation to existence, by virtue of the fact that in art "the *will to deception* has a good conscience" (GM III:25).

Here again the language Nietzsche uses is loaded and deliberately provocative; but his meaning should be clear enough. Artistic creativity transfigures, heedless of the way things may happen to be. "Unlike men of knowledge, who leave everything as it is," artists "are productive, to the extent that they actually alter and transform" (WP 585). What they produce are not so much representations as *re-presentations* of life, which depart from it, thereby in a sense "falsifying its image" (BGE 59). And they have no qualms about doing so, discovering and teaching us that there is no contradiction between relishing and embellishing life, and that more is gained than is lost by altering its aspect.

Thinking along similar lines, Nietzsche suggests that "one can get at the dangerous concept of the artist" best by reflecting on "the problem of the actor," in whom one is confronted with the phenomenon of "falseness with a good conscience; the delight in simulation exploding as a power that pushes aside one's so-called 'character,' flooding it and at the same time extinguishing it." And here one also encounters an "excess of the capacity for all kinds of adaptations that can no longer be satisfied in the service of the most immediate and narrowest utility." "All of this," he continues, "is perhaps not *only* peculiar to the actor" (GS 361), implying that this may be seen in the artist as well. And even greater significance attaches to this phenomenon owing to the possibility of its extension beyond the domain of art into human life more generally. It makes its initial appearance, however, and thereby gains a first foothold in human life, in this special domain. And we are indebted to art because the establishment of this foothold is an indispensable first step in the larger process of the transformation of human life in such a way that "all nature ceases and becomes art" (GS 356). It is with this transformation that "the destiny of the soul changes," and "a new goal" comes into view, along with the idea of a "new means" to it consisting in "a new health, stronger, more seasoned, tougher, more audacious, and gayer than any previous health." This "new goal" is the emergence of "a spirit who plays naively ... with all that was hitherto called holy, good, untouchable, divine," and for whom all truths are merely points of departure, and all knowledge only an instrument (GS 382). It is this figure, whose outlines embrace the distinguishing features of the higher humanity Nietzsche envisions, for whom he elsewhere selects the designation *Übermensch*.

In sum: beyond all it has been and has meant in peoples' lives and has done to sustain and stimulate life, and notwithstanding all that may be rudimentarily human in it and all-too-human about it, art has fostered and continues to promote the cultivation of human abilities and possibilities reaching beyond the confines of its established sphere of activity and experience. And in so doing it prepares the way for the emergence of this higher form of human life, which would be at once its supersession and its consummation. If artists are for Nietzsche but an "intermediate" type, and art but a "preliminary" state in relation to this "higher concept of art" (which is also a conception of a higher type of human being and state of human existence), that is not only their limitation; it is also their great significance and their glory.

In this light it is understandable that Nietzsche found a very warm reception in many artistic and literary circles around the turn of the century, and has to some extent continued to do so. Few philosophers have accorded art as much significance for human life, and have given it so much attention. Few also have known it so intimately, and written about it with such sensitivity. Nevertheless, most recent English-speaking philosophers of art have devoted little attention to what he has to say about it, beyond taking notice of certain of his views in BT and of his subsequent repudiation of the art of Wagner. I consider this to be unfortunate, in a number of respects.

In the first place, Nietzsche is surely right to insist upon the importance of thinking about art as much in terms of the activity of the artist as in terms of the experience of the observer. To be sure, it would be artificial to suppose that the former can be understood in isolation from the latter, both because art is a cultural phenomenon of which both are interdependent moments, and because they are interrelated in the case of artists themselves. But Nietzsche does not propose doing so, making much of these very points. He does, however, seek to counter the relatively widespread tendency among philosophers to develop their accounts of art from the perspective in which they most commonly encounter it, as observers rather than creators or performers. Even if it should be the case that art for most people is something on the order of a spectator sport, it does not and should not be taken to follow that it is to be construed as though this were its fundamental nature. On Nietzsche's view it must in the first instance be recognized as a form of activity in which engagement rather than observation is primary. And this means that it is above all upon the artist that attention should be centered, even if not exclusively.

Next, there is also much to be said for Nietzsche's contention that art should be considered "in the perspective of life," in several respects. First, he has in mind the importance of inquiring into what might be termed the sources and springs of artistic activity and experience in human nature. Whether or not his own specific reflections along these lines are sound, it would seem desirable to open up philosophical inquiry into art in this direction. He also suggests the importance of viewing art in the context of the larger social, cultural, and intellectual setting in which it exists at any particular historical juncture, and which can and often does have a significant influence upon the forms and direction it takes. His accounts of the character of art in earlier and modern times may admit of improvement; but here again he at least draws attention to certain sorts of questions that should be pursued.

Finally, Nietzsche proposes that art is fundamentally to be conceived and assessed with reference to the larger question of its significance for the preservation, flourishing, and "enhancement" of human life. To be sure, the merit of this proposal depends upon the cogency of these latter notions, and upon the possibility of elaborating them in such a way that sense may be made of the idea that art may be either conducive or detrimental to the attainment of these specified ends. These are matters that cannot be settled in the abstract, requiring rather that one extend one's investigations beyond art itself to the exploration of human life and its development, and to basic problems of value. Even if one finds what Nietzsche has to say along these lines to be questionable, however, it must be allowed that what he tried to do was something worth trying.

Postscript: On *The Case of Wagner*

"One pays heavily for being one of Wagner's disciples." This refrain, which Nietzsche repeats five times in his first postscript to *The Case of Wagner,* is one of the main themes of the entire essay. He meant it to apply primarily to those who, like him, had been "seduced" by Wagner, but who, unlike him, remained under Wagner's spell. Yet it applied to him as well. For he paid heavily for having been one of Wagner's disciples, remaining preoccupied almost obsessively with what might be called "the problem of Wagner" up to the very end of his productive life. And while the early Nietzsche had believed that Wagner was showing and leading the way to a cultural and spiritual renewal offering the best hope of surmounting the crisis of post-Christian modernity, the later Nietzsche (as in this essay) saw Wagner as the gravest symptom and most sinister temptation issuing from that very crisis, to be resisted at all costs.

So, from first to last, Wagner mattered more to Nietzsche than any artist probably ever has to any philosopher—but in radically differing ways. He mattered so greatly to Nietzsche because of the significance Nietzsche attached to the possibilities he associated with Wagner's kind of art for human life. He undoubtedly exaggerated its importance greatly, no less in his polemic against it in *The Case of Wagner* than in his early panegyrics to it. This polemic, however, is also without question one of the most provocative, interesting, and penetrating treatments of Wagner's art ever written.

In this short essay of twelve sections, a preface, two postscripts, and an epilogue, Nietzsche subjects Wagner to a devastating version of the kind of analysis and critique he elsewhere accords to various types of metaphysical, religious, and moral thought and thinkers. The great "redeemer," Nietzsche argues, was in fact the supreme "artist of decadence," who "corrupts our health—and music as well" (CW 5). He depicts Wagner as a kind of latter-day artistic successor to the ascetic priests whose pernicious influence he had discerned in his *Genealogy of Morals.* Wagner, he contends, panders to certain deplorable traits and tendencies of the modern soul, which he also shares, and drags all too many potential exceptions to the human rule down with him at the same time. He may not have been the source of the various developments Nietzsche takes to be the perverting, sickening, and weakening artistic, cultural, and spiritual life in his time and ours; for Nietzsche allows that he is more their product and symptom than their cause. However, he not only uses "the case of Wagner" to bring them to light, but also attacks Wagner for exploiting them, accelerating them, and giving their promoters and victims alike a good conscience with respect to them.

What does Nietzsche have in mind? Among other things, the threefold "corruption" of "taste," "concepts," and our psychological constitutions, together with art in general and music in particular. In Wagner's art, *"the emergence of the actor in music"* occurs (CW 11), and theatricality takes the place of style (CW 8). With the "change of art into histrionics" (CW 7), music becomes "a means to excite weary nerves" (CW 5), in which the production of strong "effects" is everything (CW 8). To this end, incessant use is made of the "three great *stimulantia* of the exhausted—the *brutal,*

the *artificial,* and the *innocent* (idiotic)" (CW 5), and full advantage is
taken of the responsiveness of the undiscerning to "the sublime, the
profound, the overwhelming" (CW 6). In place of real profundity, insight,
or understanding, however, what is supplied in Wagner's art is held to be
a mere pretense of deep meaningfulness, with a profusion of enigmatic
symbols dressing up ideas that would be banal or ridiculous if clearly
expressed (CW 9-10). And, on the other hand, this pseudoprofundity is
conjoined with a sinister form of irrationalism, encouraging the willing
suspension of one's critical faculties and cognitive powers—"excommuni-
cation of inquiry and questioning" (CW 3)—in favor of a surrender akin
to a leap of faith, which Nietzsche regards as a recipe for disaster.

It will no doubt seem odd to many readers today that Nietzsche should
make Wagner the focus of his attack, when most of the things he finds so
lamentable and objectionable in Wagner and his art pale in comparison
with what was to come. Wagner may have "won the crowd" in his day,
but he lost it long ago; and now Wagnerian opera has become almost a
paradigm in most people's eyes of a kind of esoteric music and art for
which a taste is hard to acquire. I do not think, however, that Nietzsche
would have found this very surprising. He would have been more likely to
suggest, rather, that Wagner was one of the chief sowers of the wind, and
that we are now reaping the whirlwind. Popular culture is that whirlwind;
and Wagner's spirit lives on in it much more than it does in the opera
houses and concert halls in which his art is preserved. Were Nietzsche
writing today, he would not be focusing his attention and critical fire
upon Wagner; for the "diagnosis of the modern soul" would now require
the selection of different phenomena as clues and symptoms and dangers.
He might consider Wagner deserving of mention in a genealogy of "the
modern soul"; but he would no longer accord him the significance he
does in *The Case of Wagner.*

That, however, does not deprive this essay of its significance, in a
number of respects. For one thing, it remains an extraordinarily insightful
examination of certain tendencies that are still very much at work—and
indeed, may be even more pronounced today than they were a century
ago—in our culture, our art and music, and ourselves. If Nietzsche's
charges of corruption, decadence, sickness, and impoverishment had any
validity in his day, they have even greater force in ours. The essay further
serves as a very useful introduction to some of Nietzsche's central concerns and views, and as an important corrective to impressions of his
thought based chiefly on a reading of *The Birth of Tragedy.*

But it is also of continuing value to anyone concerned with trying to
come to terms with Wagner—at least in the same sort of way in which
Nietzsche's *The Antichrist* should prove to be of value to anyone con-

cerned with coming to terms with Christianity. Even those who hold Wagner's work in high esteem, as well as those who do not know what to make of it, should undertake at least once to look at it through the eyes of the Nietzsche of *The Case of Wagner*. One may in the end decide that Nietzsche does not do justice to it, and that his analysis and assessment should be rejected. But one's right to one's own estimation will be much stronger after one has come to terms with Nietzsche's.

One also may well find, as I have, that Nietzsche's critique of Wagner is like a refiner's fire, burning away much that is best ignored or dismissed, but leaving more than a little music that is far better than Nietzsche is prepared to allow in this essay. The dangers with which he is concerned may still be great; but Wagner no longer represents them—and so this is something Nietzsche might now be able to concede. Undoubtedly, however, he would still fault Wagner for what he says (CW 10) he misses in him—and with good reason too: "*la gaya scienza,* light feet, wit, fire, grace; the great logic; the dance of the stars; the exuberant spirituality; the southern shivers of light; the *smooth* sea—perfection."

CHAPTER THIRTEEN

Nietzsche's Nietzsche: The Prefaces of 1885–88

Like so many authors, Nietzsche began by supposing that his books would speak for themselves, or at any rate would be understood by those kindred spirits he sought to reach. He knew that many would misunderstand him; but he persisted for more than a decade in the hope that his books would find discerning readers who would be able to comprehend and appreciate what he was seeking to say and do in them. Not surprisingly, however, this most unconventional of philosophical writers met with one disappointment after another on this score, culminating in the dismaying reception of his *Thus Spoke Zarathustra*.

His response was not merely to become increasingly critical of his contemporaries and ever more polemical in his style—although this was indeed a part of it. Another part of it was to write a "Prelude to a Philosophy of the Future"—as he subtitled *Beyond Good and Evil*—with a preface setting the stage for it. And yet another part of his response was to devote a good deal of the following year (1886) to writing a series of retrospective prefaces to all of his pre-*Zarathustra* books. In these remarkable prefaces he sought to provide the readers he hoped one day to have with guidance to the comprehension of these earlier works, while reflecting upon their concerns, significance, and places in his intellectual and philosophical development from the vantage point he had attained.

Nietzsche continued this new practice of providing his books with prefaces through the brief remainder of his productive life. These prefaces of 1885–88 may have been to little avail in his attempt to make himself understood at the time; but they are of considerable value to those who seek to make sense of him today. Indeed, I believe their collective worth to surpass that of *Ecce Homo* in this respect. For the period they span is that of his philosophical maturity, during much of which the Nietzsche who addresses us managed to be more calmly reflective than he was able to be during the final frenzied months preceding his collapse, when *Ecce Homo* was written.

There is much of interest in these prefaces on which I shall not comment here. Whole books could be written about them, and perhaps one day will be. I shall comment only briefly on each of them, to draw attention to points Nietzsche makes in them that I consider to be of particular significance in connection with the comprehension of his philosophical development and enterprise, as he came to understand them in these culminating years of his productive life. My remarks may provoke others to their own differing interpretations of the sense and significance of these prefaces as they bear upon Nietzsche's larger efforts; but as he would say — so much the better.

1

Consider first the preface to *Beyond Good and Evil,* written in the summer of 1885. It begins with the strange question "Suppose that truth is a woman — what then?" and goes on to reflect upon the point he apparently intends to make by means of it. This passage has occasioned a good deal of commentary, much of it critical of its seemingly sexist sentiments. Nietzsche's point here, however, may be appreciated even if the sexism embedded in his way of putting it is not.

What I believe Nietzsche means to suggest by this way of speaking, as his like remarks about "woman" elsewhere show, is the idea that "truth" — or at any rate the "truth" with respect to at least a good many things into which philosophers need to inquire — may be usefully likened more to the stereotyped figure of "woman" that Nietzsche could assume would be familiar to his contemporary readers, than to its stereotyped male counterpart. His point is that those who would pursue it will fare better if they adapt their pursuit more along the lines of the correspondingly stereotyped way to win the heart of such a "woman" than if they proceed as though they were playing a different sort of game, of a stereotypically male nature.

If one becomes preoccupied with the question of whether these stereotypes are to be accepted or rejected, one will miss the point of the remark, which neither stands nor falls with the answer to this question. For present purposes, the thing to do is simply to consider the upshot of Nietzsche's invocation of these stereotypes in order to say something about the nature of "truth" in matters of the sort with which he is concerned, and about the kind of philosophy that will have the best chance of getting somewhere with it. (One also should not fail to notice that in German the noun *Wahrheit* is feminine. It may well be that it was this circumstance that initially prompted Nietzsche to pose his opening question, as a fact of language suggesting the line of reflection he briefly pursues. This certainly would not be the only instance in which he plays with and capitalizes upon the lead offered by a linguistic point.)

The kind of philosopher Nietzsche is here concerned to ridicule—the "dogmatist"—is suggested to be rather like Henry Higgins in *My Fair Lady,* wanting truth to be "more like a man," to be dealt with in the direct manner of manly games in which the rules are simple and straightforward, and victories may be won in clear-cut fashion by frontal assault conducted with sufficient force. But this, for Nietzsche, is not how matters stand here; for philosophy as he conceives of it is a much trickier and more delicate business, in which such assaults are doomed to failure, and a sensitive mix of more indirect approaches is much more likely to be successful—even though success in achieving one's heart's desire here too is never complete and final, and one can never be certain of its attainment.

If the opening paragraphs of this preface are read in this way, good and important sense can be made of them, which accords very nicely with the "perspectival" strategy that is central to Nietzsche's kind of philosophy. There may be some domains of inquiry in which knowledge is to be differently conceived and differently won—logic, for example, or mathematics. Where most things human are concerned, however, and perhaps in dealing with the real world with which we are confronted in experience as well, it is Nietzsche's conviction that matters are not so simple. And his first order of business, at the outset of his "Prelude to a Philosophy of the Future," is to make this point by way of a vivid image guaranteed to get our attention. (Unfortunately, this image can all too easily divert attention away from its point—as so often happens when he avails himself of such borrowed imagery.)

Nietzsche goes on to insist that we must rid ourselves not only of dogmatic ways of thinking and proceeding, but also of the many old "superstitions" (such as the "soul superstition") that have long been articles of faith in one form or another among philosophers as among others; of unquestioning and naive reliance upon received meanings of words and upon grammar (as though they were touchstones of truth); and of the tendency to make hasty generalizations on the basis of "very narrow, very personal, very human, all too human facts." His kind of philosophy begins with the suspicion of all of these habits of thought, submitting them one and all to the refiner's fire before allowing any of the concepts and ideas associated with them to reappear and play roles in modified form in the reinterpretations and revaluations he goes on to propose.

To these critical injunctions Nietzsche then adds a positive one; and here the term "perspective" appears in a different guise and application. His heralded "philosophy of the future" is further to begin and proceed by recognizing and bearing in mind "perspective, the basic condition of all life." Here he hearkens back to a theme of his second *Untimely Meditation* on history and others of his early writings, which from *Beyond Good and Evil* onward is moved to the fore and continually stressed. Human life, like all life, is for Nietzsche a *relational* affair, in which particular creatures and types of creatures come to exist and preserve themselves—and can develop and flourish—only by way of the establishment of relations with their environing world. These relations give us the access to it needed for active engagement with it, while also simplifying our interactions with it sufficiently to make them manageable. Our constitutions are thus bound up with the world in which we find ourselves in ways that set up specific sorts of relationships, in and through which things that may make a difference to us can register, while those that do not are screened out.

"Perspectives" thus are engendered, on this fundamental functional level, corresponding to and varying with differing human constitutions and situations. The link between this conception of "perspective" and the perspectival strategy Nietzsche advocates is of great importance. The key to comprehending anything that is a function of its place in such a perspectival arrangement is to learn to appreciate the relationship involved—and the only way to do this is by acquiring the eyes needed to discern them in different cases (which adeptness is just what this strategy calls for).

Indeed, far from associating the idea of "perspective" with the dissolution of the very notion of "truth," Nietzsche here directly links the appreciation of this idea with "truth" positively conceived, suggesting that "when one spoke of spirit and the good as Plato did," this meant "standing truth on her head and denying perspective, the basic condition of all life." The suggestion obviously is that an appreciation of the ways in which "all life" involves the establishment of and operation within "perspectives" is a step in the direction of getting these matters right. And to underscore this point, Nietzsche remarks with emphasis that "we, *whose task is wakefulness itself,* are the heirs of all that strength which has been fostered by the fight against this error." Indeed, he goes on to suggest that this "fight"—against both Platonism and Christianity—"has created in Europe a magnificent tension of the spirit the like of which has never yet existed on earth." And he adds that "with so tense a bow we can now shoot for the most distant goals" (BGE P).

When one recalls that this is asserted in the preface to a book whose subtitle refers to a "philosophy of the future," it is evident that this is what Nietzsche has in mind here. So armed and prepared, and roused from the long dogmatic slumber induced by Platonism and Christianity (and determined not to lapse into it again), his kind of philosophers are to set their sights upon new tasks and goals. Venturing beyond old ways of thinking in terms of unquestioned notions of "good and evil," and likewise beyond attachment to metaphysical "realities" that are nothing of the kind, such philosophers may achieve a more truthful comprehension of the perspectivally conditioned phenomenon of life—and perhaps may thereby contribute to its enhancement as well. It is no "end of philosophy" that is here announced, but rather its renewal, or even its real advent.

2

In the spring of 1886, shortly after completing *Beyond Good and Evil*, Nietzsche supplied the first volume of *Human, All Too Human* with a preface. In it he begins by reflecting on the possibility that he may not have been ready yet, when he wrote this volume nearly a decade earlier, to be able to "permit" himself what he calls "*my* truthfulness" (HH I P:1). He confesses that at that time he still needed to take "shelter" in some errors, fictions, and enthusiasms that he subsequently was able to discern and dispense with—while at the same time playing with some extreme nihilistic ideas that he likewise later abandoned as exaggerated, ill-considered, and detrimental (HH I P:3). In both cases, he writes, they now appear to him as having been needful during his intellectual and spiritual "convalescence," but as needed no longer. Their only larger significance is that they served him as preparations for what he calls "the great liberation"—not only from traditional ways of thinking, but also from the paralysis and pessimism attending their rejection.

A long road had to be traversed, Nietzsche writes, on the way "to that *mature* freedom of spirit which is equally self-mastery and discipline of the heart and permits access to many and contradictory modes of thought" (HH I P:4). These are hallmarks of the kind of philosophy he at length had come to embrace, made possible by this "great liberation," and leaving pessimism too behind him. Among other things, it involves coming to have new eyes for "what is *close at hand*" (HH I P:5), drawing upon "many and contradictory modes of thought," each of which may reveal something about them that others miss.

Reference is made again in this preface to "perspectives" and their importance. But here too, Nietzsche's point is that they require to be *employed* and taken into account in dealing with "value judgments," and more generally, in the understanding of "life itself as *conditioned* by the sense of perspective and its injustice." This is an insight to which Nietzsche accords great importance in dealing with matters of this sort; but it is not taken to compromise or subvert the possibility of philosophical inquiry. So, anticipating what he would write a year later (in GM III:12), he says to those who would join him in his "free-spirited" kind of philosophy: "You shall get control over your For and Against and learn how to display first one and then the other in accordance with your higher goal" (HH I P:6).

Near the end of this preface, Nietzsche has more to say both about the goal he has in mind and about the development of the sort of thinking he believes to be both possible and needful in pursuing it:

> Given it is *the problem of order of rank* of which we may say that it is *our* problem, we free spirits: it is only now, at the midday of our life, that we understand what preparations, bypaths, experiments, temptations, disguises the problem had need of before it was *allowed* to rise up before us ... penetrating everywhere, almost without fear, disdaining nothing, losing nothing, asking everything, cleansing everything of what is chance and accident in it and as it were thoroughly sifting it—until at last we had the right to say, we free spirits: "Here—a *new* problem!" (HH I P:7)

In this connection, it may be observed that, in the above ellipsis, Nietzsche mentions specifically that these philosophers are to proceed above all "as adventurers and circumnavigators of that inner world called 'man,' as surveyors and gaugers of that 'higher' and 'one above the other' that is likewise called 'man'" (ibid.). This too is a task the aim of which is comprehension, and the complexity of which calls for the multiply perspectival and experimental approach that is the hallmark of Nietzsche's kind of philosophy.

A few months later Nietzsche wrote a preface to *The Birth of Tragedy,* notable for its sharp self-criticism, but also for what he exempts from that criticism: the large and fundamental tasks and questions he observes that he had gotten hold of with respect to art, science, morality, and life (BT P:2–4). In this preface he is more than candid about the book's many imperfections, describing it as "image-mad and image-confused, sentimental . . . , without the will to logical cleanliness, very convinced and therefore disdainful of proof, mistrustful even of the *propriety* of proof" (BT P:3), among other things. Nonetheless, he contends in its favor that it was grappling with a number of matters of great importance, and that it had the further merit of recognizing the necessity of addressing them by way of a variety of perspectival reflections.

These critical and appreciative remarks together suggest that what Nietzsche had come to deem both possible and needful is a form of inquiry dealing more explicitly and self-consciously with matters of this sort and in this way—but in a manner freed from these youthful failings: no longer "image-confused" and "sentimental," no longer "disdainful of proof" and of the propriety and need for it, and no longer dogmatic and lacking in "the will to logical cleanliness." Here as elsewhere in his writings of this final period, Nietzsche's conception and practice of philosophy are informed by these demands, and are anything but heedless or dismissive of them. They make up a considerable part of that "hardness" he so often insists upon in his injunctions to his kind of philosopher (cf. BGE 210).

A month after writing this preface, Nietzsche composed a preface to the several supplements to the first volume of *Human, All Too Human* that he then published as its second volume. Beginning with a review of his earlier writings, he observes that they "speak *only* of my overcomings." In them, he reflects, "so far as my own development was concerned," he was "already deep in the midst of moral skepticism and destructive analysis, *that is to say in the critique and likewise the intensifying of pessimism as understood hitherto.*" But he goes on to say that he now (in these supplements written in 1879 and 1880) began to disentangle himself from this predicament, attaining "something of the almost cheerful and inquisitive coldness of the psychologist who takes a host of painful things that lie *beneath* and *behind* him and identifies and as it were *impales* them with the point of a needle" (HH II P:1). He was still a pessimist at that time, he observes, as a kind of antidote to his romantic tendencies; but he was on the road to a recovery that would lead some years later to an emancipation from both (HH II P:2). "Thus I again found my way to that courageous pessimism that is the antithesis of all romantic mendacity, and also, as it seems to me today, the way to 'myself,' to *my* task" (HH II P:4).

Here his "task" is not stated explicitly; but it is suggested to be associated with coming "to know the way to a *new* health" to be attained and enjoyed by "you overcomers of your age," who to this end "have to be the *conscience* of the modern soul and as such have to possess its *knowledge*" (HH II P:6). And here again we encounter the idea of "perspective" employed in this connection, in what I am suggesting to be its most basic application. Nietzsche refers to what he calls "my pessimistic perspective . . . a novel perspective . . . a perspective that even today is still weird and strange" (HH II P:7). But he then goes on to speak of the experiment he made in the writings brought together in this volume: "it was then that I turned my perspective *around,*" and experimented with a kind of "optimism," in "a patient and tedious campaign against the unscientific basic tendency of that romantic pessimism to interpret and inflate individual personal experiences . . . with condemnations of the world" (HH II P:5).

Here too Nietzsche's talk of "perspective" clearly has to do with the possibility of looking at things in a number of different ways, which one may cultivate successively and learn to *play off against each other,* "in the service of knowledge" (as he would put it a year later in GM III:12). This is held to be a way—and perhaps the best and even only way—of escaping confinement within one or another of them, and of arriving at an understanding that both draws upon and transcends each of them.

3

In the fall of 1886 Nietzsche wrote two more prefaces, to *Daybreak* and to *The Gay Science*—his last two pre-*Zarathustra* works. They completed this series of retrospective reflections. The first of these two prefaces, to *Daybreak* (which he had published in 1881), is for the most part a reflection on the kind of *philosophical conscience* he takes himself to have been developing during the time of recovery in which he wrote this book.

In a sense, Nietzsche's recovery—without which he never could have gone on to write *Zarathustra* and all that followed—is the underlying theme of all of these prefaces of 1886. And this recovery, of his philosophical as well as (he thought) his psychosomatic health, was of the greatest significance to him. For it meant nothing less than the rebirth of his conviction and confidence that there is after all important constructive philosophical work to be done—and that there are humanly possible ways of getting on with it, and of getting somewhere with it. The things he went on to write, along with these prefaces, provide ample indications of what he had in mind.

This constructive task has its deconstructive preliminaries, with which his preface to *Daybreak* suggests he saw himself as still having been preoccupied when he wrote that book. Its immediate concerns, he observes, were to "undermine our faith in morality" (D P:2), and our "faith in logical evaluation" (D P:3) and "faith in reason" (D P:4) as well. But another and more basic concern was to sharpen the insistence upon "honesty" in all such matters, so that it becomes unthinkable to accept anything that proves to be "outlived and decayed," and so "unworthy of belief" (ibid.). Moreover, Nietzsche remarks, the kind of philosopher he sees himself as becoming here is one who is able to "read"—and also to think and write—in the manner of a good philologist: "Slowly, deeply, looking constantly before and aft, with reservations, with doors left open, with delicate eyes and fingers" (D P:5).

Nietzsche tells a part of the story (though only a part of it) when he observes that "we immoralists, we godless men of today" are undertaking and accomplishing what he calls "the *self-supersession of morality.*" His immediate point here is that "we too are still *men of conscience,*" impelled by that "last moral law" commanding an honesty that will not tolerate "anything 'unworthy of belief' " and "any bridges-of-lies to ancient ideals" (D P:4). This is a point of no little significance; for it suggests that an initially all-too-human way of thinking, originating in nothing like an innate "will to knowledge," may nonetheless issue in an *attained* impulse to the pursuit of knowledge. It also points to one of the kinds of strategies that may be employed in the deconstructive phase of this pursuit: namely, that of immanent or internal critique.

But as Nietzsche shows, in his critical remarks about philosophers like Kant, he also is appreciative of the importance of looking at them in another perspective as well: that of a psychological reflection upon them, which renders their thinking problematic in yet another respect, by bringing to light its ulterior motivation. So, for example, in the case of Kant's "critique of pure reason," he suggests that Kant "would not have had need of it if one thing had not been more vital to him than anything else: to render the 'moral realm' unassailable, even better incomprehensible to reason" (D P:3).

Here again, therefore, Nietzsche is at least implicitly commending a multiperspectival approach to the consideration of what is to be made of a phenomenon like that of "our faith in morality." In this preface too, he thus at once gives expression to his advocacy of such an approach, and also makes it clear that he conceives of this approach as furthering the attainment both of comprehension and of an enhanced form of human life.

In the nearly simultaneously written preface Nietzsche supplied (along with a new fifth book) to *The Gay Science,* which he had published four years earlier (in 1882), he lays these cards even more clearly on the table. He again reflects on the "relation of health and philosophy," and on his recovery of constructive philosophical aspirations, which enables him to speak of goals that are "permitted again, believed again" (GS P:1). In philosophy previously, he observes, the "psychological needs" of philosophers whose "health" is suspect have predominated. "What was at stake in all philosophizing hitherto was not at all 'truth' but something else" (GS P:2).

Now, however, a different sort of philosophizing has become possible, as the pain and distress of those like Nietzsche himself "makes us more *profound,*" and impels such new philosophers to question "more deeply, severely, harshly, evilly and quietly than one had questioned before" (GS P:3). To this end, "new arts and wiles" are needed, and a different "sense of truth" as well; for "We no longer believe that truth remains truth when the veils are drawn." Truthfulness demands that the veils previously allowed to remain closed be recognized as such—even though the human need for them is to be grasped as well. Indeed, returning to his metaphorical association of "truth" with "woman," Nietzsche remarks: "Perhaps truth is a woman who has reasons for not letting us see her reasons" (GS P:4).

His point here, as his following discussion shows, is that where life—and especially human life—is concerned, "truth" is a matter not so much of what it is beyond all "appearance," but rather of processes engendering relations and forms in which the reality of which we are a part manifests itself. In this respect life may also be likened (as Nietzsche likens it) to *art,* which has the same basic character—as he suggests the Greeks grasped, in making more of surfaces and appearances than of what might underlie them (ibid.). This renders all the more important the ability to be light on one's philosophical feet, the better to shift perspectives nimbly. It also places a premium upon the acquisition of the different eyes associated with shifting perspectives—and along with them, the development of the philosophical "common sense" that makes it possible to make comprehensive sense of what they enable one to discern.

This distinguishes Nietzsche's kind of philosophy from "all philosophizing hitherto," in which "what was at stake . . . was not at all 'truth' but something else"—namely, the prompting of various "psychological needs" that dictated particular narrow and often distorting ways of looking at things, precluding others without which justice to them cannot be done. It further allows him to stress the "relations between health and philosophy" without abandoning the idea that philosophizing can amount to more than mere symptoms of and responses to the differing pathologies of philosophers. That sort of thinking may hitherto have been the rule, to the detriment of the interpretations and evaluations that have been born of such pathologies. Nietzsche has higher hopes, however, for those more fortunate types whose thinking reflects and draws upon "their riches and strengths," which free and equip them for a more daring and comprehensive reckoning with all that does or should concern us (cf. BGE 39).

The health and strength Nietzsche associates with his kind of philosophy and "will to knowledge" are not of the merely robustly natural variety. Rather, they are those that may be attained on the far side of despair, and of pain and sickness endured and overcome. His kind of philosophy may indeed be both an expression of a kind of health and a product of a kind of sickness (and may owe much to both). The whole point of this discussion, however, is that such inquiry *also* is a kind of thinking that neither is to be equated with the expression of mere healthy vitality, nor is to be reduced to the contrasting afflictions of body and spirit that sap it. It transcends both—and it may lead to a comprehension of things "more *profound*" than either of them can yield (GS P:3). Here Nietzsche anticipates one of his underlying topics in his next book (*On the Genealogy of Morals*): the "genealogy" of that exceptional type of human being—that "higher type" among whom his "philosophers of the future" may be reckoned—whose emergence has been made possible by the prior emergence of the various other human and philosophical types he considers.

Nietzsche here would have us make new sense of the idea of "truth" rather than abandon it. He would have us learn to look at and think about things differently, with greater sensitivity, subtlety, and appreciation. He would have us learn also to question "more deeply, severely . . . than one had questioned before." And he would also have us recognize that for the genuine philosopher, tasks and goals are "permitted again." Nietzsche's kind of philosophy involves all of these things. His concluding gestures toward art and the Greeks (with their attunement to "surfaces" and "appearances") are instructive in this connection. Art and life are both affairs in which realities are constituted whose significant features are *relational* phenomena, which escape us if we do not avail ourselves of the perspectives within which these features are discernable. These perspectives are multiple, contingent, and conditional; but they are no more purely subjective than they are purely objective. Moreover, we are implicated in them; and through our relations to them, we may acquire a sensibility enabling us to grasp as much of their constituted and emergent reality as may have any relevance to us and for our lives. Through the discovery of new ways of relating to them, they may take on further significant features, which then are also to be reckoned with. Neither art nor our world nor we ourselves remain ever the same. But that only makes the task of Nietzsche's kind of philosopher more interesting.

With this preface to *The Gay Science,* Nietzsche's series of retrospective prefaces was concluded. In a sense, even this preface was not merely retrospective, since it was accompanied by a new fifth book that he also added to *The Gay Science* at the same time. In this fifth book he shows what the practice of the kind of philosophy he preaches in the preface involves, when pursued more self-consciously and maturely than he had done in the first four books, written some five years earlier. He continued to supply his books with such prefaces thereafter, the most important of which was to *On the Genealogy of Morals,* published in the same year (1887). I shall return to his preface to it after commenting briefly on his prefaces to his subsequent and final works of 1888.

4

Prior to 1888, Nietzsche's decade-long pace of something like one major project for publication per year had been notable enough for one whose health was as miserable as his was so much of the time. It was positively leisurely, however, compared to his frantic pace during that final year of his productive life, in which no less than four such projects were rushed to completion. It is small wonder, therefore, that the prefaces with which he hastily supplied them are much shorter and far less calmly reflective than those that preceded them. They are of no little interest, however, precisely because his very haste underscores the significance of what he saw fit to comment upon in them.

First from Nietzsche's hand, in May of that year, came *The Case of Wagner* and his short preface to it. Here again his theme is the importance of his "recovery" from debilitating ways of thinking of manifold origins. Among them he numbers those owing to the influence of Schopenhauer as well as of Wagner, and of the larger "decadence" of "modernity" more generally, of which Schopenhauer and Wagner are seen as mere but notable symptoms. This decadence in turn is suggested to derive ultimately from the sway of that "life-denying" moral and religious outlook against which Nietzsche had long been waging war. What he adds here is his recognition that this war must be waged at once within and without by his kind of philosopher, who begins like everyone else as "the child of his time." "What does a philosopher demand of himself first and last? To overcome his time in himself, to become 'timeless.'" The kind of philosopher he attempts to be "has to be the bad conscience of his time"—and to this Nietzsche immediately adds: "for that he needs to understand it best" (CW P). Comprehension is required, if one is to place oneself in a position to assess and move beyond anything in or about one's time; for there can be no meaningful reckoning with what one does not comprehend.

To this end, Nietzsche further observes, one must learn to take advantage of such salient symptoms as Wagner, his art, and his reception, and this requires new "eyes" for them, or perspectives upon them, differing from those through which they are commonly viewed. Thus someone like Wagner is said to be "indispensable for the philosopher," as a "guide" to "the labyrinth of the modern soul," through it and beyond it. "Once one has developed a keen eye for the symptoms of decline, one understands morality too." This, Nietzsche asserts, requires "a special self-discipline": "A profound estrangement, cold, sobering up—against everything that is of this time, everything timely—and most desirable of all, the eye of Zarathustra, an eye that beholds the whole fact of man at a tremendous distance—below" (CW P).

This same line of thought is taken up again in the short preface to *The Antichrist,* written a few months later. Here Nietzsche casts the greater part of his remarks in terms of a description of the kind of reader for whom he is writing; but it serves equally well as a description of the kind of fellow philosopher he seeks and calls for. His topic in this book is Christianity — another such phenomenon he considers it to be of the utmost importance to comprehend and reckon with, in his envisioned larger project of a "Revaluation of All Values" of which he calls this the "First Book." But he nowhere provides a better or more succinct general portrait of this kind — his kind — of philosopher.

> The conditions under which I am understood, and then of *necessity* — I know them only too well. One must be honest in matters of the spirit to the point of hardness before one can even endure my seriousness and my passion. One must be skilled in living on mountains — seeing the wretched ephemeral babble of politics and national self-seeking *beneath oneself.* One must have become indifferent; one must never ask if the truth is useful or if it may prove our undoing. The predilection of strength for questions for which no one today has the courage; the courage for the *forbidden;* the predestination to the labyrinth. An experience of seven solitudes. New ears for new music. New eyes for what is most distant. A new conscience for truths that have so far remained mute. *And* the will to the economy of the great style: keeping our strength, our *enthusiasm* in harness. (A P)

There are two last prefaces of which account must be taken as well, written within a few months of this one. Indeed, the first of them — to *Twilight of the Idols* — is dated "September 30, 1888, on the day when the first book of the *Revaluation of All Values* [i.e., *The Antichrist*] was completed." Equally brief, it complements the previous one by leaving no doubt about the nature of that "destiny of a task" in which Nietzsche conceived himself to be engaged, and also by gesturing again to his perspectival strategy for proceeding with it. This task, "fraught with unmeasurable responsibility" that carries with it the danger of "a heavy, all-too-heavy seriousness," is this very *"revaluation of all values"* (TI P). And this revaluation is held to require all of the wiles and unconventional eyes and ears of the "psychologist and pied piper before whom just that which would remain silent must become outspoken." Only such sharp and shifting eyes can discern their true colors; and the hollowness of these hallowed idols can be detected only by the sensitive fingers and ears of one who knows how to touch them "with a hammer as with a tuning fork," and how to listen to their sounds.

Nietzsche could hardly give clearer expression to his commitment to a conception of his enterprise as both an interpretive and an evaluative affair, intended to arrive at a better comprehension and assessment of the matters into which he proposes to inquire than received ways of thinking about them represent. And it is precisely to this end that he stresses the need for approaching these matters with all of the artful strategies—and for viewing them from all of the unconventional perspectives—that he associates with the idea of a sophisticated and versatile psychological experimenter and inquirer.

In his last preface, to *Ecce Homo*, Nietzsche again takes up the same theme. He makes it clear at the outset that while "overthrowing idols" is "part of my craft," it is not the whole of his kind of philosophy—even though it is not his intention merely to replace those overthrown by "new idols" of the same sort, wedded to some equally fictitious vision of the ideal. So he writes: "One has deprived reality of its value, its meaning, its truthfulness, to precisely the extent to which one has mendaciously invented an ideal world." His larger concern, beyond his war against all such "idols" and his "revaluation of all values" associated with them, is to recover what has thus been "deprived" and obscured, and so to achieve a comprehension of that upon which mankind's "health, its future, the lofty *right* to its future" depends (EH P:2).

In one of the most significant and remarkable passages in this preface, Nietzsche describes his kind of philosophy very vividly:

> Philosophy, as I have so far understood and lived it, means . . . seeking out everything strange and questionable in existence, everything so far placed under the ban of morality. . . .
>
> How much truth does a spirit *endure,* how much truth does it *dare?* More and more that became for me the real measure of value. . . .
>
> Every attainment, every step forward in knowledge, *follows* from courage, from hardness against oneself, from cleanliness in relation to oneself. . . .
>
> *Nimitur in vetitum* [We strive for the forbidden]: in this sign my philosophy will triumph one day, for what one has forbidden so far as a matter of principle has always been—truth alone. (EH P:3)

This passage leaves no doubt about Nietzsche's fundamental commitment to a conception of philosophy wedded to the task of comprehension, which he does not hesitate to characterize in terms of "truth" and "knowledge." He then goes on, in the final section of this preface, to invoke his *Zarathustra*—and to insist that even in the case of Zarathustra's speeches, "no *faith* is demanded," but rather only the willingness and

ability to look and see as Zarathustra bids. For the great significance
Nietzsche claims for this work is held to be owing to its being "the
deepest, born out of the innermost wealth of truth" (EH P:4). Whether
or not one agrees with the assessment and claim, the fact that he
concludes this last preface in this manner lends further credence to the
conception of his kind of philosophy I am advancing.

5

I have deferred consideration of Nietzsche's preface to the *On the Genealogy of Morals,* written a year earlier (in the summer of 1887), because it
is the richest of those he supplied to the works of his last few years, and
the last he wrote in which he was able to reflect in an unhasty manner
upon the sort of inquiry that had become his kind of philosophy.

The *Genealogy* and its preface of 1887 occupy a very special place in
the last years of Nietzsche's productive life. In it Nietzsche speaks to us at
the height of his powers, following the stock-taking previous year, and
prior to the frantic rush of the next and last year remaining to him. This
preface is dated "July 1887" (and from Sils Maria at that), and so was
written in the summer that might be considered his final "great noon," at
the summit of his philosophical ascent, and before the sun of his life
began its accelerating downward journey into night. What he has to say
about his kind of philosophy in this preface is of particular importance
and authority. If one reads and rereads it, and really *listens* to what he is
saying and how he talks about his concerns and efforts in it, one will find
all the confirmation of the interpretation I am advancing that I could
wish.

"We are unknown to ourselves, we men of knowledge" (GM P:1).
With these opening words, Nietzsche lets us know that this is something
with which he is concerned, and upon which he intends to shed some
light through his "genealogy of morals." The book itself does indeed deal
first and foremost with "morals" and their genealogy; but it deals with a
host of other matters as well, to which he considers "the genealogy of
morals" to be relevant. They include our own attained human nature and
its prospects, and also the nature and prospects of those who are not only
human beings but human "knowers" as well.

Nietzsche's "genealogical" inquiries are often taken to have a kind of
reductionist interest, as though he believed that the manner in which
something originated *settled* the questions of its nature and what is to be
made of it. In fact, however, while he does believe (and here tells us) that
one does well to begin by considering how something may have originated,
he is equally insistent that this settles nothing on either point, and that

what is of decisive importance in both respects is what thereby has emerged and become possible. It is by what becomes of them—and not merely by their origins—that he would have us assess them, whether it is "morals" or "the type 'man'" or ourselves as "men of knowledge" that is at issue. And to this end, he suggests that a variety of kinds of questions must be posed and investigated, from a variety of different perspectives.

In this preface, Nietzsche makes this point—which is fundamental to the understanding of his kind of philosophy—by way of yet another retrospective reflection, on the development of his own thinking about morality, beginning in the second section. Observing that he had long been interested in "the *origin* of our moral prejudices" (GM P:2), and earlier still in "the question of where our good and evil really originated," he then remarks that this interest eventually gave rise and gave way to other questions, both interpretive and evaluative: " . . . *what value do they themselves possess?* Have they hitherto hindered or furthered human prosperity? Are they a sign of distress, of impoverishment, of the degeneration of life? Or is there revealed in them, on the contrary, the plenitude, force, and will of life, its courage, certainly, future?" (GM P:3).

Nietzsche recognizes that his early efforts left a good deal to be desired, as he proceeded "ineptly" but nonetheless with a determination, "as becomes a positive spirit, to replace the improbable with the more probable"—even if this may often have been only to replace "one error with another," while "still lacking my own language for my own things" (GM P:4). Quite clearly, however, the picture he is painting of the kind of philosopher he was becoming is the picture of such a "positive spirit," engaging in this task of "replacing the less probable with the more probable" to the best of his ability.

As Nietzsche immediately goes on to observe, his concerns further extended to evaluation as well as interpretation. He makes this point by remarking: "Even then my real concern was something much more important than hypothesis-mongering . . . on the origin of morality. . . . What was at stake was the *value* of morality," and especially of "the 'unegoistic,' the instincts of pity, self-abnegation, self-sacrifice" (GM P:5). An understanding of the former was needful, but only served to help set the stage for the interpretation and evaluation of these phenomena, both as "symptoms" of a culture on the wane, and also as a "great danger to mankind" (ibid.). Nietzsche summarizes the relation between these sorts of inquiry—all encompassed within and characterizing his kind of philosophy—as follows: "Let us articulate this *new demand:* we need a *critique* of moral values, *the value of these values themselves must first be called in question* —and for that there is needed a knowledge of the conditions and circumstances under which they grew, under which they evolved and changed . . . a knowledge of a kind that has never yet existed or even been desired" (GM P:6).

It is this kind of preparatory "knowledge" that his genealogical inquiries are intended to provide; and it is this further "demand" that his larger philosophical enterprise is (among other things) intended to meet. I say "among other things," because this "revaluation of values" is not the whole of it. This larger enterprise is a response to other such "demands" that he elsewhere articulates as well, extending to a reckoning with the nature and significance of phenomena as diverse as the varieties of art, religion, social organization, science, and humanity itself—all of which Nietzsche touches upon in this book. It also is an attempt to come to terms with questions pertaining to the character, scope, pursuit, and value of the varieties of humanly attained and attainable knowledge, as Nietzsche's opening remarks suggest.

Looking at these matters in the light of their relation to "morals" and their development is not the only way to look at them, and is not by itself decisive with respect to their nature or their significance. Yet this does afford a perspective upon them that is illuminating of them. Looking at them in other perspectives illuminates them in other ways; just as looking at moral phenomena in a variety of perspectives likewise is necessary to enable one to do anything approaching justice to them. And this is the very point Nietzsche makes next, availing himself yet again of the image of "new eyes" he so often employs in characterizing the perspectival manner of engaging in his kind of philosophy. Having recognized how profoundly problematic morality is, he writes:

> Let it suffice that, after this prospect had opened up before me, I had reasons to look about me for scholarly, bold, and industrious comrades (I am still looking). The project is to traverse with quite novel questions, and as though with new eyes, the enormous, distant, and so well hidden land of morality—of morality that has actually existed, actually been lived; and does this not mean virtually to *discover* this land for the first time? (GM P:7)

I do not see how anyone can read this preface, and take the Nietzsche one encounters in it seriously, without recognizing that the kind of philosophy to which he is committed is a kind of philosophy that aspires to *comprehension* in a strong sense of the term, and will settle for nothing less. Some may find this unwelcome, or hard to understand; but as Nietzsche observes in its final section, anticipating that there will be those for whom this book is "incomprehensible" or uncongenial, "the fault, it seems to me, is not necessarily mine" (GM P:8). And he concludes with another equally apt remark, withr espect to the "art of exegisis" that he insists must be mastered and practiced if one is to be able to read him properly: "To be sure, one thing is necessary above all . . . something that has been unlearned most thoroughly nowadays— and therefore it will be some time before my writings are 'readable' —something for which one has almost to be a cow and in any case *not* a 'modern man': *rumination*" (GM P:8).

The interest and significance of these prefaces for the understanding of Nietzsche's kind of philosophy should be clear. He would not have supplied them if he did not believe that they would be helpful to readers trying to figure out what he is up to—as indeed they are. His post-*Zarathustra* works themselves—from *Beyond Good and Evil* and the fifth book of *The Gay Science* onward—show us this kind of philosophy in practice. If they are read with these prefaces in mind, they reveal a kind of philosopher and a kind of philosophical activity rather different from the portraits often given of them by both his admirers and his detractors. And I would suggest that the tasks and ways of going about them that Nietzsche sets forth in these prefaces and pursues are well worth taking seriously by philosophers today—for what they are, and also for the examples they set. I know of no more promising "prelude to a philosophy of the future."

Unscientific Postscript:
A Fable

In the horizon of the infinite —We have left the land and have embarked. We have burned our bridges behind us—indeed, we have gone farther and destroyed the land behind us. Now, little ship, look out! Beside you is the ocean: to be sure, it does not always roar, and at times it lies spread out like silk and gold and reveries of graciousness. But hours will come when you will realize that it is infinite and that there is nothing more awesome than infinity. Oh, the poor bird that felt free and now strikes the walls of this cage! Woe, when you feel homesick for the land as if it had offered more *freedom* —and there is no longer any "land." (GS 124)

We are like sailors who must rebuild their ship on the open sea, without ever being able to break it down in drydock and reconstruct it using the best materials.
—Otto Neurath

There once was a people living on a group of islands in a vast sea. Each island was different from the others, though they resembled each other in various ways. At first the inhabitants of each island were unaware of the existence of islands other than their own, and thought theirs to be the only one there was. Eventually, the existence of the other islands became known to them; but the inhabitants of each one remained convinced that even though their island was not the only one, it was at any rate the best one, most truly exhibiting the natural order of things. At length, however, certain sages among them began to perceive that each of the islands— their own included—was really far from perfect; and that when one considered both the order and the disorder that each displayed, they in point of fact came out quite even. The order interested them more than the disorder. They sought to explain it; and it seemed to them most reasonable to suppose that each island, in its own way, must (in spite of its evident untidiness) reflect the general outline of the natural order of things. After all, it was observed, each was solid ground on which their ancestors had lived since time immemorial, presumably emanating from the same firm foundation as the others; and anything as stable and enduring as their islands must have its roots in the very nature of things.

Rejoicing in their newfound understanding, the sages on one of the islands decided to build a tower reaching to the heavens, from which vantage point they would be able to see and survey all of the islands and, rising above the turmoil and confusion of their immediate surroundings, to discern more clearly the basic features of their world. They realized that such a tower could only be erected on a deeper foundation than had been laid for any of their existing structures—a foundation that rested on the very bedrock of their island; and so they began to dig, determined not to stop digging until bedrock was reached. Their first excavation was near the coast; and it was with some surprise that, after digging for some time, they struck not bedrock but water. However, they attributed this to the fact that they had chosen a spot too near the sea and, moving further inland, they began a new excavation. Again, however, they met with the same result; and finally, after repeated attempts at the very center of the island ended in the same way, it slowly began to dawn on them that their island did not rest on bedrock at all, but was floating on the sea itself! Expeditions to other islands were hurriedly organized; and it was soon found that they too were simply floating on the sea.

This discovery distressed the sages greatly; but even more disturbing to them were certain other things they learned about their islands, as they reflected on what they found while digging down toward the sea. Their first inclination had been to think that, even though their islands were not anchored in bedrock, they still might be supposed to reflect the natural order of things; for, as the logicians among them were quick to point out, the mere fact that the islands were floating did not entail the contrary conclusion. What they found, however, as they examined what there was between them and the sea, was nothing more than the sort of stuff that washed up on their shores, crudely lashed together by clearly human and evidently very primitive hands. The surfaces of their islands, untidy though they were, were very orderly by comparison.

The sages gradually came to the shattering realization that their dwelling places were not really floating islands reflecting the natural order of things at all, but rather great rafts fashioned by their remote ancestors out of whatever materials had been at hand that had floated up from the depths. At length they understood that their ancestors originally had been creatures of the sea, who at some point in the distant past had escaped from it, in order to afford themselves a more secure and stable abode than the sea itself, by constructing their raft-islands for themselves, thereby beginning a new life quite different from that which their fellow sea creatures continued to live. With the passage of time others had added to the bulk of what must have originally been small and very precarious rafts, until finally the rafts reached something like their present dimensions. The descendants of their early ancestors, unaware of their own and their islands' origins, took themselves for land creatures, and their great raft island for fixed land, in spite of the nearness of the sea and the occasional tempests that from time to time threatened to engulf them.

And so, the sages realized, far from occupying a fixed and permanent dwelling place, their race had been drifting on the surface of the sea for countless generations, carried here and there by currents to whose very existence it had been oblivious, and developing in ways determined by the conditions of life on their floating islands. They know now that what they had taken to be their knowledge of the natural order of things was only a knowledge of their particular circumstances, which had been quite fortuitously arranged. And they saw that the order they had perceived to exist on their raft-islands was but the result of the efforts of generations of their race to render their dwelling places as habitable as possible. Now pandemonium ensued among the sages, so unsettled were they by their discoveries. Their most fundamental assumptions had been undermined, and what had passed for wisdom among them had been revealed as error and folly. Some among them despaired, and with cries of anguish leapt from high places to their deaths. Others, exclaiming that they were really creatures of the sea, threw themselves into it; these drowned.

The majority of their fellow islanders however, simply paid no attention to their cries and exclamations, or even to their reports of their discoveries, which seemed to them too far-fetched and contrary to common sense to take seriously. They simply went about their business as they always had. Some of the sages followed their example, and took up trades, forsaking the pursuit of knowledge entirely. But most of them did not react in any of these ways. They recovered from their initial shock and disillusionment, upon reflecting that their astonishing discoveries did not really change anything at all. They were still there, on their islands; they were the same people, and the islands were the same islands as they had been before. They now saw themselves and their island differently than they had before; but it seemed to them that the only reasonable thing to do was to acknowledge their situation and to make the best of it. They knew now that their islands did not have the sort of place in the scheme of things that they once had thought them to have, but they were all they had — and while the islands weren't much, they were *their own,* God bless them! Moreover, there was plenty of work to be done on them, by way of tidying them up and reshaping them here and there, in order to make them more liveable and agreeable to look upon; and these sages saw that their knowledge of the features of their islands, and their cultivated ability to discern places where improvement might be made, placed them in a good position to guide the undertaking of such projects. Putting aside all thought of the sea, and confining themselves to thinking in terms of what was possible and desirable given the general and particular characteristics of the islands on which they found themselves, they devoted themselves to such projects; and eventually the people of the islands came to esteem them for their contributions to the common weal.

But a few of the sages took a very different course. They did not despair as a result of the discoveries that had been made; but neither could they bring themselves to embrace their islands as their world, now that they knew them for what they were. Their thoughts were drawn in other, quite different directions: to the sea, and to the possibility of dwelling places on the sea other than the island-worlds in which they found themselves. They longed to explore the sea, in order both to come to know that larger, deeper world on which their little artificial island-worlds floated, and also to enhance their understanding of themselves and their potentialities. And, while they knew better than to think they could survive other than on something like their islands, they could see no reason to suppose that the raft-islands created by their struggling, primitive ancestors were better than any that might be more self-consciously devised.

Observing how aimlessly their islands drifted about the sea, how unmaneuverable they were, how poorly suited to exploration, how cluttered with remains of countless generations' undertakings, and how crudely fashioned from such shoddy stuff, these sages conceived a strong desire to leave them. Their race had needed the islands, and the islands had served their race well; but that, they felt, was no reason for them at least to continue to live out their lives upon them. They resolved to fashion a vessel on which they could escape the islands, large enough to live on (for they did not suppose that they would anywhere find fixed land), yet maneuverable and well suited for the exploration of the sea. The only material at hand was that to be found on the islands themselves; and this placed limits on the sort of vessel they could construct. But they found much that they could use, once it was refined, reworked, and tempered; and they felt sure that out upon the sea, as they came to know it better, they would find further material with which to improve their craft.

Their fellow islanders and the other sages thought them fools, to abandon the security of their ancient homes for the open sea. This, however, did not deter them. They were quite content to leave undisturbed those who wished to live out their lives within the narrow confines of the islands; but they themselves did not wish to do so. They knew that they would never be able to come to know the sea as long as they lived upon the islands; for the islands were distractions and obstructions, and were too much with them. They felt blinkered and shackled by the islands. Out upon the sea, they recognized, they risked madness and also destruction at the hands of the elements; for their race had never attempted anything like what they contemplated, and they could not be sure that their vessel would prove seaworthy. But they resolved to take the risk.

And so, one day, they quietly sailed away. It was some time before they were even missed. None who remained lamented their departure; and soon they were forgotten. They never returned. On the islands, life went on much as before. Small improvements were continually made; sea walls were erected, roads were straightened, old buildings were replaced, and more efficient use was made of available areas and resources. The islanders were quite content. But in the market places, in later generations, small children listened in wonderment to old fishermen, who told tall tales of sightings of strange, great, graceful craft in the distance far out at sea, moving swiftly as the wind, manned by godlike beings in almost human form.

Bibliography

Editions and Translations of Nietzsche's Writings

Kritische Gesamtausgabe: Werke (KGW), ed. Giorgio Colli and Mazzino Montinari, 30 vols. (Berlin: de Gruyter, 1967-78).

Kritische Gesamtausgabe: Briefwechsel (KGBW or BW), ed. Giorgio Colli and Mazzino Montinari, 24 vols. (Berlin: de Gruyter, 1975-84).

Sämtliche Werke. Kritische Studienausgabe (KSA), ed. Giorgio Colli and Mazzino Montinari, 15 vols. (Berlin: de Gruyter, 1980).

Werke in drei Bänden, ed. Karl Schlechta, 3 vols. (Munich: Carl Hanser, 1954-56), with an index in a fourth volume (1965).

The Birth of Tragedy (*Die Geburt der Tragödie,* 1872)
   Trans. Walter Kaufmann, with *The Case of Wagner* (New York: Vintage, 1966);
   Trans. Frances Golffing, with *The Genealogy of Morals* (Garden City, N.Y.: Doubleday, 1956).

Philosophy in the Tragic Age of the Greeks (*Die Philosophie im tragischen Zeitalter der Griechen,* 1870-73)
   Trans. Marianne Cowan (South Bend, Ind.: Gateway, 1962).

"On Truth and Lies in a Nonmoral Sense" ("*Über Wahrheit und Lüge im aussermoralischen Sinne,*" 1873)
   Trans. Daniel Breazeale, in *Nietzsche, Philosophy and Truth,* ed. Breazeale (Atlantic Highlands, N.J.: Humanities Press, 1979);
   Trans. Walter Kaufmann, in *The Portable Nietzsche,* ed. Kaufmann (New York: Viking, 1954).

Untimely Meditations (*Unzeitgemässe Betrachtungen,* 1873-76)
   Trans. R. J. Hollingdale, as *Untimely Meditations* (Cambridge: Cambridge University Press, 1983);
   Ed. William Arrowsmith, as *Unmodern Observations* (New Haven: Yale University Press, 1990).

David Strauss, the Confessor and the Writer (*David Strauss der Bekenner und der Schriftsteller,* 1873)
   Trans. R. J. Hollingdale, in *Untimely Meditations;* intro. by J. P. Stern;
   Trans. and intro. Herbert Golder, in *Unmodern Observations,* ed. Arrowsmith.

On the Uses and Disadvantages of History for Life (*Von Nutzen und Nachteil der Historie für das Leben,* 1874)
   Trans. R. J. Hollingdale, in *Untimely Meditations;*

Trans. Gary Brown, as *History in the Service and Disservice of Life*, in *Unmodern Observations;* intro. by Werner Dannhauser;

Trans. Adrian Collins, as *The Use and Abuse of History* (Indianapolis: Liberal Arts Press, 1957);

Trans. Peter Preuss, as *On the Advantage and Disadvantage of History for Life* (Indianapolis: Hackett, 1980).

Schopenhauer as Educator (*Schopenhauer als Erzieher,* 1874)

Trans. R. J. Hollingdale, in *Untimely Meditations;*

Trans. William Arrowsmith, in *Unmodern Observations;* intro. by Richard Schacht;

Trans. James W. Hillesheim and Malcolm R. Simpson; intro. by Eliseo Vivas (South Bend, Ind.: Gateway, 1965).

Richard Wagner in Bayreuth (*Richard Wagner in Bayreuth,* 1876)

Trans. R. J. Hollingdale, in *Untimely Meditations;*

Trans. and intro. Gary Brown, in *Unmodern Observations.*

We Classicists (*Wir Philologen,* 1875)

Trans. and intro. William Arrowsmith, in *Unmodern Observations.*

Human, All Too Human (*Menschliches, Allzumenschliches,* first vol., 1878; first part of second vol., *Assorted Opinions and Maxims,* 1879; second part of second vol., *The Wanderer and His Shadow,* 1880); intro. by Erich Heller

Trans. R. J. Hollingdale (Cambridge: Cambridge University Press, 1986);

Trans. Marion Faber, with Stephen Lehmann (Lincoln: University of Nebraska Press, 1984, first vol. only).

Daybreak: Thoughts on the Prejudices of Morality (*Morganröthe,* 1881)

Trans. R. J. Hollingdale, intro. Michael Tanner (Cambridge: Cambridge University Press, 1982).

The Gay Science or *Joyful Wisdom* (*Die fröhliche Wissenschaft,* books I–IV, 1882; second edition with Preface and Book V, 1887)

Trans. Walter Kaufmann, as *The Gay Science* (New York: Vintage, 1974);

Trans. Thomas Common, as *Joyful Wisdom* (New York: Frederick Ungar, 1960).

Thus Spoke Zarathustra (*Also Sprach Zarathustra,* Parts I and II, 1883; Part III, 1884; Part IV, 1885)

Trans. Walter Kaufmann, in *The Portable Nietzsche;*

Trans. R. J. Hollingdale (Harmondsworth: Penguin, 1961);

Trans. Marianne Cowan (Chicago: Gateway, 1957).

Beyond Good and Evil (*Jenseits von Gut und Böse,* 1886)

Trans. Walter Kaufmann (New York: Vintage, 1966);

Trans. R. J. Hollingdale (Harmondsworth: Penguin, 1973);

Trans. Marianne Cowan (Chicago: Gateway, 1955).

On the Genealogy of Morals (*Zur Genealogie der Moral,* 1887)

Trans. Walter Kaufmann and R. J. Hollingdale, with *Ecce Homo* (New York: Vintage, 1967);

Trans. Francis Golffing, with *The Birth of Tragedy* (Garden City, N.Y.: Doubleday, 1956).

The Case of Wagner (*Der Fall Wagner,* 1888)

Trans. Walter Kaufmann, with *The Birth of Tragedy* (New York: Vintage, 1966).

Twilight of the Idols (*Götzen-Dämmerung*, completed 1888, first published 1889)
Trans. Walter Kaufmann, in *The Portable Nietzsche;*
Trans. R. J. Hollingdale, with *The Anti-Christ* (Harmondsworth: Penguin, 1968).
The Antichrist (*Der Antichrist*, completed 1888, first published 1895)
Trans. Walter Kaufmann, in *The Portable Nietzsche;*
Trans. R. J. Hollingdale, with *Twilight of the Idols.*
Nietzsche contra Wagner (*Nietzsche contra Wagner*, completed 1888, first published 1895)
Trans. Walter Kaufmann, in *The Portable Nietzsche.*
Ecce Homo (*Ecce Homo*, completed 1888, first published 1908)
Trans. Walter Kaufmann, with *On the Genealogy of Morals* (New York: Vintage, 1967);
Trans. R. J. Hollingdale (Harmondsworth: Penguin, 1979)

Selections and Collections

The Will to Power (*Der Wille zur Macht*, a selection of notes from Nietzsche's notebooks of 1883–88 made and arranged by his sister and others, published in several editions of increasing size in 1901, 1904, and 1910–11)
Trans. Walter Kaufmann and R. J. Hollingdale (New York: Vintage, 1967).
Basic Writings of Nietzsche, ed. and trans. Walter Kaufmann (New York: Modern Library, 1968).
The Portable Nietzsche, ed. and trans. Walter Kaufmann (New York: Viking, 1954).
Nietzsche Selections, ed. Richard Schacht (New York: Macmillan, 1993).
A Nietzsche Reader, ed. and trans. R. J. Hollingdale (Harmondsworth: Penguin, 1977).
Philosophy and Truth: Selections from Nietzsche's Notebooks of the Early 1870's, ed. and trans. Daniel Breazeale (Atlantic Highlands, N.J.: Humanities Press, 1979).
The Poetry of Friedrich Nietzsche, ed. and trans. Philip Grundlehner (New York: Oxford University Press, 1986).
Nietzsche: A Self-Portrait from His Letters, ed. and trans. Peter Fuss and Henry Shapiro (Cambridge: Harvard University Press, 1971).
Nietzsche: Unpublished Letters, ed. and trans. Kurt F. Leidecker (New York: Philosophical Library, 1959).
Selected Letters of Friedrich Nietzsche, ed. and trans. Christopher Middleton (Chicago: University of Chicago Press, 1969).

Selected Studies in English or English Translation

Ackerman, Robert. *Nietzsche: A Frenzied Look.* Amherst, Mass.: University of Massachusetts Press, 1990.

Alderman, Harold. *Nietzsche's Gift.* Athens: Ohio University Press, 1977.

Allison, David B., ed. *The New Nietzsche: Contemporary Styles of Interpretation.* New York: Dell, 1977.

Behler, Ernst. *Confrontations.* Trans. Steven Taubeneck. Stanford: Stanford University Press, 1991.

Bergmann, Peter. *Nietzsche: The Last Antipolitical German.* Bloomington: Indiana University Press, 1987.

Blondel, Eric. *Nietzsche, the Body and Culture: Philosophy as a Philological Genealogy.* Trans. Sean Hand. Stanford: Stanford University Press, 1991.

Clark, Maudemarie. *Nietzsche on Truth and Philosophy.* Cambridge: Cambridge University Press, 1990.

Cooper, David. *Authenticity and Learning: Nietzsche's Educational Philosophy.* London: Routledge & Kegan Paul, 1983.

Copleston, Frederich. *Friedrich Nietzsche: Philosopher of Culture.* New York: Barnes and Noble, 1975.

Crawford, Claudia. *The Beginnings of Nietzsche's Theory of Language.* Berlin: Walter de Gruyter, 1988.

Danto, Arthur C. *Nietzsche as Philosopher.* New York: Columbia University Press, 1980.

Darby, Tom et al., eds. *Nietzsche and the Rhetoric of Nihilism.* Ottawa: Carleton University Press, 1989.

Del Caro, Adrian. *Nietzsche Contra Nietzsche: Creativity and the Anti-Romantic.* Baton Rouge: Louisiana State University Press, 1989.

Deleuze, Giles. *Nietzsche and Philosophy.* Trans. Hugh Tomlinson. New York: Columbia University Press, 1983.

Derrida, Jacques. *Spurs: Nietzsche's Styles.* Trans. Barbara Harlow. Chicago: University of Chicago Press, 1979.

Detwiler, Bruce. *Nietzsche and the Politics of Aristocratic Radicalism.* Chicago: University of Chicago Press, 1990.

Gilman, Sander L. *Conversations with Nietzsche.* Trans. David Parent. New York: Oxford University Press, 1989.

Graybeal, Jean. *Language and "the Feminine" in Nietzsche and Heidegger.* Bloomington: Indiana University Press, 1990.

Grimm, Ruediger Hermann. *Nietzsche's Theory of Knowledge.* Berlin: Walter de Gruyter, 1977.

Haymann, Ronald. *Nietzsche: A Critical Life.* New York: Oxford University Press, 1980.

Heidegger, Martin. *Nietzsche,* four vols. Trans. David Farrell Krell. New York: Harper and Row, 1979–84.

Heller, Erich. *The Importance of Nietzsche.* Chicago: University of Chicago Press, 1988.

Heller, Peter. *Studies in Nietzsche.* Bonn: Bouvier, 1980.

Higgins, Kathleen Marie. *Nietzsche's Zarathustra.* Philadelphia: Temple University Press, 1987.

Hollingdale, R. J. *Nietzsche.* London: Routledge & Kegan Paul, 1965.

———. *Nietzsche: The Man and His Philosophy.* Baton Rouge: Louisiana State University Press, 1965.

Houlgate, Stephen. *Hegel, Nietzsche, and the Criticism of Metaphysics.* Cambridge: Cambridge University Press, 1986.

Hunt, Lester H. *Nietzsche and the Origin of Virtue.* London: Routledge, 1991.

Jaspers, Karl. *Nietzsche: An Introduction to the Understanding of His Philosophical Activity.* Trans. Charles Walraff and Frederick J. Schmitz. Tucson: University of Arizona Press, 1965.

———. *Nietzsche and Christianity.* Trans. E. B. Ashton. Chicago: Regnery, 1961.

Jung, C. G. *Nietzsche's Zarathustra.* Ed. James L. Jarrett. Princeton: Princeton University Press, 1988.

Kaufmann, Walter. *Nietzsche: Philosopher, Psychologist, Antichrist.* Fourth ed. Princeton: Princeton University Press, 1974.

Koelb, Clayton, ed. *Nietzsche as Postmodernist: Essays Pro and Con.* Albany: State University of New York Press, 1990.

Krell, David F., and David Woods, eds. *Exceedingly Nietzsche: Aspects of Contemporary Nietzsche Interpretation.* London: Routledge, 1988.

Lampert, Laurence. *Nietzsche's Teaching: An Interpretation of Thus Spoke Zarathustra.* New Haven: Yale University Press, 1987.

Love, Frederick. *The Young Nietzsche and the Wagnerian Experience.* Chapel Hill: University of North Carolina Press, 1963.

Magnus, Bernd. *Nietzsche's Existential Imperative.* Bloomington: Indiana University Press, 1978.

———, Jean-Pierre Mileur, and Stanley Stewart. *Nietzsche's Case: Philosophy as/and Literature.* New York: Routledge, 1993.

Martin, Glen D. *From Nietzsche to Wittgenstein: The Problem of Truth and Nihilism in the Modern World.* New York: Peter Lang, 1989.

May, Keith M. *Nietzsche and Modern Literature.* New York: St. Martin's Press, 1988.

———. *Nietzsche and the Spirit of Tragedy.* New York: St. Martin's Press, 1990.

Moles, Alistair. *Nietzsche's Philosophy of Nature and Cosmology.* New York: Peter Lang, 1990.

Morgan, George A. *What Nietzsche Means.* Westport, Conn.: Greenwood, 1975.

Nehamas, Alexander. *Nietzsche: Life as Literature.* Cambridge, Mass.: Harvard University Press, 1985.

O'Hara, Daniel, ed. *Why Nietzsche Now?* Bloomington: Indiana University Press, 1985.

Parkes, Graham, ed. *Nietzsche and Asian Thought.* Chicago: University of Chicago Press, 1991.

Pasley, Malcolm, ed. *Nietzsche: Imagery and Thought.* Berkeley: University of California Press, 1978.

Pettey, John Caron. *Nietzsche's Philosophical and Narrative Styles.* New York: Peter Lang, 1991.

Pfeffer, Rose. *Nietzsche: Disciple of Dionysus.* Louisburg, Penn.: Bucknell University Press, 1972.

Pletsch, Carl. *Young Nietzsche: Becoming a Genius.* New York: Free Press, 1991.

Podach, E. F. *The Madness of Nietzsche.* Trans. F. A. Voigt. New York: Gordon, 1974.

Rickels, Laurence A., ed. *Looking After Nietzsche.* Albany: State University of New York Press, 1990.

Sallis, John. *Crossings: Nietzsche and the Space of Tragedy.* Chicago: University of Chicago Press, 1991.

Sautet, Marc. *Nietzsche for Beginners.* New York: Writers and Readers Publishing, 1990.

Schacht, Richard. *Nietzsche.* London: Routledge & Kegan Paul, 1983.

Schacht, Richard, ed. *Nietzsche, Genealogy, Morality: Essays on Nietzsche's* On the Genealogy of Morals. Berkeley: University of California Press, 1994.

Schrift, Alan. *Nietzsche and the Question of Interpretation.* New York: Routledge, 1990.

Schutte, Ofelia. *Beyond Nihilism: Nietzsche without Masks.* Chicago: University of Chicago Press, 1984.

Scott, Charles E. *The Question of Ethics: Nietzsche, Foucault, Heidegger.* Bloomington: Indiana University Press, 1990.

Shapiro, Gary. *Alcyone: Nietzsche on Gifts, Noise, and Women.* Albany: State University of New York Press, 1991.

Shapiro, Gary. *Nietzschean Narratives.* Bloomington: Indiana University Press, 1989.

Silk, M. S., and J. P. Stern. *Nietzsche on Tragedy.* Cambridge: Cambridge University Press, 1981.

Sloterdijk, Peter. *Thinker on Stage: Nietzsche's Materialism.* Trans. Jamie Owen Daniel. Minneapolis: University of Minnesota Press, 1989.

Solomon, Robert C., ed. *Nietzsche: A Collection of Critical Essays.* Notre Dame: University of Notre Dame Press; originally published by Doubleday, 1973.

Solomon, Robert C., and Kathleen M. Higgins, eds. *Reading Nietzsche.* New York: Oxford University Press, 1988.

Stack, George J. *Lange and Nietzsche.* Berlin: Walter de Gruyter, 1983.

——. *Nietzsche and Emerson: An Elective Affinity.* Columbus: Ohio State University Press, 1992.

——. *Nietzsche: Man, Knowledge and Will to Power.* Wolfeboro, N.H.: Hollowbrook Publishers, 1991.

Stambaugh, Joan. *Nietzsche's Thought of Eternal Return.* Baltimore: Johns Hopkins University Press, 1972.

——. *The Problem of Time in Nietzsche.* Philadelphia: Bucknell University Press, 1987.

Staten, Henry. *Nietzsche's Voice.* Ithaca: Cornell University Press, 1990.

Stern, J. P. *Friedrich Nietzsche.* New York: Penguin, 1978.

——. *A Study of Nietzsche.* Cambridge: Cambridge University Press, 1979.

Strong, Tracy B. *Friedrich Nietzsche and the Politics of Transfiguration.* Berkeley: University of California Press, 1975.

————, and Michael Gillespie, eds. *Toward New Seas: Philosophy, Aesthetics, and Politics in Nietzsche.* Chicago: University of Chicago Press, 1988.

Thiele, Leslie Paul. *Friedrich Nietzsche and the Politics of the Soul: A Study of Heroic Individualism.* Princeton: Princeton University Press, 1990.

Warren, Mark T. *Nietzsche and Political Thought.* Cambridge, Mass.: MIT Press, 1988.

White, Alan. *Within Nietzsche's Labyrinth.* New York: Routledge, 1991.

Whitlock, Greg. *Returning to Sils-Maria: A Commentary to "Also Sprach Zarathustra."* New York: Peter Lang, 1990.

Wilcox, John T. *Truth and Value in Nietzsche: A Study of His Metaethics and Epistemology.* Ann Arbor: University of Michigan Press, 1974.

Young, Julian. *Nietzsche's Philosophy of Art.* Cambridge: Cambridge University Press, 1992.

Yovel, Yirmiyahu, ed. *Nietzsche as Affirmative Thinker.* Dordrecht: Martinus Nijhoff, 1986.

Index

RICHARD SCHACHT is professor of philosophy and Jubilee Professor of Liberal Arts and Sciences at the University of Illinois at Urbana-Champaign, where he has taught since 1967. His books include *Alienation* (1970), *Hegel and After* (1975), *Nietzsche* (1983), *Classical Modern Philosophers: Descartes to Kant* (1984), and *The Future of Alienation* (1994).

Books in the series International Nietzsche Studies

Schopenhauer and Nietzsche
Georg Simmel; translated by Helmut Loiskandl,
Deena Weinstein, and Michael Weinstein

Nietzsche's Revaluation of Values: A Study in Strategies
E. E. Sleinis

Making Sense of Nietzsche: Reflections Timely and Untimely
Richard Schacht